A CAPITALIST MANIFESTO

'William Davis's spirited defence of the capitalist system is a useful reminder that there is nothing immoral, or even reprehensible, in attempting, within the law, to mitigate some of the worst effects of living in a country which has the highest taxation rate in the Western world' – *The Times Literary Supplement*

'Written with characteristic wit' – *The Bookseller*

'William Davis puts up a spirited and timely defence of capitalism in his usual lively and readable style' – *Manchester Evening News*

It's No Sin To Be Rich

WILLIAM DAVIS

SPHERE BOOKS LIMITED
30/32 Gray's Inn Road, London WC1X 8JL

First published in Great Britain by Osprey Publishing Ltd. 1976
Copyright © William Davis 1976
First Sphere Books edition 1978

TRADE
MARK

Set in Intertype Times

Printed in Great Britain by
Hazell Watson & Viney Ltd
Aylesbury, Bucks

Contents

Introduction

This is a biased book. Biased because it seeks to make a case for private enterprise, biased because it is based on the belief that a free society – that is, liberal capitalism – is the only system that can uphold and protect individual rights. 'Rights' is a moral concept and it is proper, indeed essential, that a book of this kind should deal with moral as well as economic issues. It is written for laymen rather than experts, practical people rather than academic theorists, individuals rather than 'the masses'. I have tried to be objective but I do not pretend to be detached. It would be patently absurd to claim detachment when none exists.

Capitalism has been under persistent attack throughout my lifetime and yours. Some of the criticism has been well deserved. But there has also been a great deal of ill-informed comment and deliberate distortion. Historians have focused on the misery caused by the industrial revolution and ignored its benefits. Economists, fascinated by the brilliant theorizing of Marx and his disciples, have condemned free enterprise without bothering to acknowledge the repression which exists in alternative societies. (Like Marx, they are concerned chiefly with material forces. All else in society – law, art, social relations – is 'super-structure'.) Authors have written about the ruthlessness of the Morgans, the Vanderbilts, and the Rockefellers, but have chosen to forget the contribution made to human progress, and the alleviation of suffering, by the experiments and failures of countless small enterprises. Students have proclaimed their rejection of the 'system' but continue to quarrel bitterly about what, if anything, should take its place (while, of course, happily accepting whatever financial assistance the system has to offer). And teachers, journalists, high-minded civil servants and others who fancy themselves as intellectuals have adopted an attitude of moral superiority to the businessman, the money-maker. Their sympathy lies with institutions which run at a loss. Scholars and writers who see merit in the profit motive and support the principle of private enterprise are branded as 'apologists' for the capitalist system and, more often than not, described as fascists.

The hostility is expressed in other ways. Environmentalists behave as if pollution was a capitalist device; in fact, of course, it is a problem for all industrialized countries. Socialist smoke pollutes as much as capitalist smoke. Sociologists cry, with Marx, that people who work for big companies feel alienated from the product of their labour and, inevitably, grow bored and increasingly militant. In fact, alienation is just as likely to take place if one works for a large state-owned industry (it helps to account for the appalling shoddiness of so many goods made in the communist world) and anyone who has ever visited a Soviet factory, as I have, soon realizes that boredom is not a result of capitalism but of industrialization itself. (In most managed economies, needless to say, militancy is kept strictly in check: a strike by workers is a crime against the state.) Not least, there is strong antagonism towards America as the chief symbol of capitalism, not only in the Third World but also in many European countries. For years now politicians have tried to frighten us with horror stories of America's financial might. Europe, we have been given to understand, has been overrun by ruthless, grasping Yankee businessmen out to ravish our plucky little countries and, worse, to change our precious habits and customs.

When Jean-Jacques Servan-Schreiber published his *Le Défi Americain* it outsold all other books – fiction or non-fiction – published in France since the Second World War. Billed as 'a timely and alarming exposé of the American industrial and intellectual invasion of Europe', it tried to make American investment look both sinister and terrifying. Europe, M. Servan-Schreiber declared, was sinking into decadence. In fifteen years' time the third most powerful industrial force in the world, after the United States and the Soviet Union, would be not Europe, but American industry based in Europe. Statements of this kind were bound to arouse emotions. Fear, pride, prejudice and plain envy all played (and still do) a much bigger part in people's reactions than logic. And because they thrive on controversy, newspapers were all too ready to spread the word. In Britain, the press was certainly delighted when, in October 1966, Vauxhall's car factory workers attacked their American masters. They were pictured outside the plant, during a dispute, shouting, 'Yankees go home! Bloody Americans! String 'em up!' One shop steward was quoted as saying: 'The best thing that could happen to Vauxhall's is for all the Yanks to go home.' Some American corporations have begun to do just that. Several have pulled out of Europe, or drastically reduced their involvement, and more are likely to follow. It's not just that they have grown tired of the abuse – they can handle it – or even that political and bureaucratic interference has reached an intolerable level. The main reason is, quite simply, that for many corporations *le Défi Americain* has come badly unstuck. Their European operations, far from being a ruthless exercise in capitalist exploitation, have either been losing money or making very little. Predictably they are now under fire for refusing to throw good money after bad and 'heartlessly abandoning' the poor, downtrodden European workers.

But the real venom is reserved for those who still have the audacity to be rich. No one is immune. In Britain, where incomes policies have introduced an extra element of envy and bitterness, the Queen has become a favourite target for self-appointed levellers who believe, or claim to believe, that everyone should be reduced to the lowest common denominator. We remain largely indifferent when it's a matter of how much to spend on fighter planes, foreign aid, and grants and subsidies, even if the amounts involved run to hundreds of millions of pounds. Public money is a concept which, to most people, has little meaning. But let an individual, or a group of individuals, try to procure a little extra and we all feel qualified, indeed compelled, to pass instant judgment. The immediate, emotional response to news of a successful commercial venture, a profitable deal, or even a pay increase is that, in some unsavoury way, the people involved have managed to get away with something they shouldn't. There is, today, a basic shabbiness about all our arguments about money: a joyless, suspicious, resentful mood which makes Britain look disturbingly petty. From time to time the powers of Government are used to single out individual businessmen and pillory them for giving themselves a rise. Banker Jocelyn Hambro was one of the more prominent victims of this witch-hunt, and there was no mystery about the motive. Hambro had attacked the Labour Prime Minister in vigorous terms; this was the Government's way of hitting back. Hambro was publicly condemned for the heinous crime of getting his company to pay him a little more from its earnings.

Somewhere in the middle are the people who have neither wealth nor the trade unions' bargaining power. They are the teachers, doctors, parsons and judges who resent the fact that status should be judged by a yardstick which seems to put them into second or third place. Unable to keep up, they condemn 'materialism' and attack 'excessive' ambition. 'Money doesn't buy happiness,' they intone. And, of course, 'Money is the root of all evil.' All sections seem agreed on at least one thing: even worse than trying to make money is to enjoy spending it. To enjoy money is considered vulgar and depraved; to enjoy it publicly is a sin. If you want the approval of the trendy rebels you must profess to be disgusted by symbols of wealth like the Rolls, the yacht, expensive restaurants, high fashion, and winter cruises in the sun. (One trade union leader once told me it made him furious to see well-dressed men drink brandy.) The Treasury is swamped with suggestions from people who feel compelled to make moral judgments about the way others should live. Elderly couples who choose to spend some of their savings on a long cruise are attacked with a ferocity which would be amusing if it were not so nasty. We lecture other countries on the importance of freedom but seek to deny fellow citizens the right to spend their money as they see fit. We claim to be a nation of individuals but help Governments to stamp out individualism.

Andrei Sakharov, the Nobel prize winner and architect of the Russian H-bomb, has warned the West against 'the thoughtless, frivolous pursuit of leftish-liberal faddishness'. It is a timely warning from an unusual quarter. 'Left-wing faddishness,' he says, 'is now dominant in the West and has achieved that position through the complex interplay of various factors. Two of these are the eternal hankering of youth after radical change and the fear of the more experienced and cautious representatives of the older generation that they may lag behind their own children. In the West, as everywhere else, there exist complex social problems that cannot be solved immediately, within the framework of the existing system. But radical solutions, with their persuasive, surface simplicity, create the illusion that those problems can be quickly solved. Another factor is the fact that for decades the Western world of free competition among ideas has been constantly fed by a small stream of pro-Soviet or pro-Chinese propaganda in which basically sound socialist ideas are tendentiously mixed with half-truths and out-and out lies.... The leftists usually accept too trustingly the dogma of the advantages of the socialist system, and avoid listening to anything that contradicts it.... I hope that in the final analysis the Western intellectual won't let the rest of us down.'

Much the same warning has come from Alexander Solzhenitsyn, who spent eight years in a Siberian concentration camp and something like twenty years doing battle with a totalitarian state. 'The decline of contemporary thought,' he told a BBC interviewer early in 1976, 'has been hastened by the misty phantom of socialism. Socialism has created the illusion of quenching people's thirst for justice: socialism has lulled their conscience into thinking that the steamroller which is about to flatten them is a blessing in disguise, a salvation. And socialism, more than anything else, has caused public hypocrisy to thrive; it has enabled Europe to ignore the annihilation of 66 million people on its very borders. There is a myth that socialism represents a sort of ultra-modern structure, an alternative to dying capitalism. And yet it existed ages and ages before any sort of capitalism. My friend, Academician Igor Shafarevich, has shown, in his extensive study of socialism, that socialist *systems* – systems, that is, which are being used today to lure us to some halcyon future – made up the greatest portion of the previous history of mankind: in the ancient East, in China; and were to be repeated, later, in the bloody experiments of the Reformation. As for socialist *doctrines*, he has shown that they emerged far later, but have still been with us for over 2,000 years; and that they originated, not in an eruption of progressive thought, as people think nowadays, but as a reaction – Plato's reaction against Athenian democracy, the Gnostics' reaction against Christianity – a reaction against the dynamic world of individualism and a return to the impersonal stagnant system of antiquity. And if we follow the explosive sequence of socialist doctrines and socialist utopias preached in Europe – by Thomas More, Campanella, Winstanley, Morelli, Deschamps, Babeuf, Fourier, Marx, and dozens of others – we cannot help shuddering as they openly proclaim certain features of that terrible form of society.'

Most of us take freedom, and the rights of the individual, so much for granted that we tend to be complacent about possible threats. The United States has a Bill of Rights and a Supreme Court with a constitutional duty to defend individuals against infringement by legislation and administrative action. We in Britain have never considered such precautions necessary. We show little interest when press freedom is threatened by arbitrary Government action or when bodies like the Inland Revenue, or the Police, are given greater power to intrude on our private lives. We condemn 'permissiveness' and applaud censorship. And, increasingly, we not only allow Governments to limit freedom because 'there's a crisis', or because some

Minister invokes 'the national interest' (a vague enough phrase to permit whatever interpretation he chooses to put upon it) but actually insist on having a go ourselves. Everywhere in today's Britain there are people who want to plan the lives of others – who claim the right to decide what people should be allowed to read or see, where and under what circumstances they should be permitted to work, what they should be allowed to earn, how they should spend their money, and what opinions they should be free to express. Everywhere, it seems, there are people to be smashed, powers to be overthrown, whole classes to be attacked, citizens (both rich and poor) whose possessions are to be seized. We cheer Ministers who tell us that they mean to 'make the rich howl with anguish' and we nod approvingly when workers, in a modern version of the Tolpuddle martyrs, find themselves deprived of jobs and livelihood by the unyielding insistence of trade union officials (supported by employers who, nowadays, dare not do otherwise) that the closed shop must be enforced regardless of personal principles or considerations.

Much of this is done in the name of equality, the thing itself as distinct from equality of opportunity. We are all to be equal except ideologues in power, which is where they want to be. The cry has never come from the British people in general, whose watchword has been *liberty*, not *equality*. It is the socialist politicians, supported by left-wing intellectuals, who want the state to impose equality by coercion and force. To some extent, one goes along with them. There are real (as well as phoney) injustices in our society which conscientious young people very properly will not tolerate. No one, today, would seriously quarrel with the contention that people are or should be equal before the law, that they should have equal voting rights, and that they should have equal opportunities in education and employment. Much has been done to end discrimination on the grounds of sex and race, and there is more to do. But there is a difference between opportunity and flat equality, between fairness and the dogmatic insistence on equality of *result*.

The most obvious defence and explanation of inequality is

that it exists. People are different from each other, in physical and mental endowment and achievements. Attempts to create an abstract equality leads to unhappiness because people have to be untrue to themselves, and to a loss of liberty because the force of law has to be used to suppress natural differences. They also make for a dull society. Look at China, with its dreary standardization of thought, dress, and behaviour. Ask a Chinese what would happen to a Leonardo da Vinci in today's Peking, as a TV interviewer did not long ago, and he will tell you that, of course, Peking has no time for that kind of individuality. It's true that not everyone can afford to own a beautiful villa, but does that mean it shouldn't be built? Of course yachts are for the few, but does that mean boat builders should stop whatever they are doing and get themselves jobs on a collective farm? The aim, surely, should be to level up rather than down, to encourage people to create wealth – and enjoy the benefits – rather than enforce drab conformity. The diversity of a civilized society is its richness.

We shall return to all these arguments, and examine them more fully, in the course of this book. We shall also look at the case put forward by the Marxists, who for the past hundred years have posed the chief political alternative for capitalist societies. It is a pity, as John Kenneth Galbraith has pointed out, that Marx was so long forbidden to honest thought because honesty and courage have now become associated with the full acceptance of his system. Marxism and the kind of societies it has produced obviously merit close consideration. The hysterical reaction of the McCarthy era, with its juvenile 'better-dead-than-red' sloganizing, did much more harm to the cause of free enterprise than is generally acknowledged. It showed an appalling lack of confidence in a system which has produced enormous benefits. (The mood has changed with *détente*, but US officialdom still takes a firm line: if you have ever 'advocated, taught, believed in, or knowingly supported or furthered the interests of communism' you'd better forget about applying for citizenship of the Land of the Free. It leaves an awful lot of scope for interpretation. What *are* the interests of communism?

Did Henry Kissinger – to pick one name at random – 'support or further the interests of communism' by fixing trade deals with Moscow, pulling out of Vietnam, and eating chow mein in Peking?

At the same time, the case for private enterprise is sometimes put so stridently that it comes across as an unqualified defence of the rather crude values of early capitalism. Politicians like Edward Heath, a former British Prime Minister, have justly criticized businessmen who advocate a full-scale return to the days of Adam Smith. 'What characterized early capitalism,' he told a Rome conference in 1975, 'was the ruthlessness of its acquisitive instinct. In the stampede to make sudden and vast fortunes other values were trampled underfoot ... this concept of capitalism is hardly likely to have a wide popular appeal with a mass and mature electorate.'

Adam Smith, the Scottish philosophy professor who is generally credited with being the 'father' of free enterprise, wrote his classic *The Wealth of Nations* 200 years ago. Its basic point was that Man works best in his own self-interest; therefore he should be allowed to do just that. Out of each of us doing what is best for us individually, common good will flow. As he put it: 'It is not from the benevolence of the butcher, the brewer or the baker that we expect our dinner, but from their regard to their own interest.' Self-interest expresses itself as the drive for profit and produces that great marvel, the self-regulating market. If consumers are free to spend their money any way they wish, and businessmen can compete uninhibitedly for their favour, then capital and labour will flow 'naturally' (a favourite Smithian word) into the uses where they are most needed. If consumers want, say, more bread than is being produced, they will pay high prices and bakers will earn high profits. Those profits will lure investors to build more bakeries. If they wind up turning out more bread than consumers want to buy, prices and profits will fall and capital will shift into making something that consumers need and desire more – shoes, perhaps. Thus the businessman seeking only his own profit is 'led by an invisible hand to promote an end which was no part of his intention' – the common good. Moreover, the process is not only circular but dynamic. Competition keeps wiping out the inefficient businessmen, rewarding those who can turn out the most goods at the lowest prices and forcing even them to keep re-investing their profits in new products or better operating methods if they want to stay ahead of their rivals. As a result, production keeps rising, pulling up wages ('the liberal reward of labour ... is the natural symptom of increasing national wealth') and distributing to everyone more of 'the necessaries, conveniences and amusements of human life'.

Smith's system was designed to enthrone not the businessman, but the consumer. Far from admiring merchants, he looked upon them as a greedy lot who were for ever trying to bypass the market by conspiring to fix prices and hold down wages. But he thought that such monopolistic schemes could prosper only with the active aid of Government – which, in his day, they often got. So he advocated complete *laissez-faire* (literally, 'let go', a French phrase used by economists to sum up the doctrine that the market always knows best). Government, he said, should stop trying to regulate trade, cease all intervention in the market and let free competition work its wonders.

'The statesman who should attempt to direct private people in what manner they ought to employ their capital,' he wrote, 'would not only load himself with a most unnecessary attention, but assume an authority which could safely be trusted to no council whatever, and which would nowhere be so dangerous as in the hands of a man who had the folly and presumption to fancy himself fit to exercise it.'

These ideas were well to the left of the eighteenth century's mercantilist doctrine, which held that trade should be strictly regulated in order to pile up gold and silver in national treasuries. They also ran counter to the strong feelings among upper-level society that 'opulence' for the 'lower ranks' would be very dangerous. The privileged wanted to retain their privileges; they had no time for interlopers. But the industrial revolution was just beginning and the new bourgeoisie had no time for feudalism; Smith's theory that self-interest served the common good was ideally suited to their ambitions. Here was the perfect prescription for a ruthless businessman out to make a quick fortune. There was no reason to be troubled by his conscience; by looking towards his own profit he was helping the state as well. What could be better? For years afterwards it was held to justify excesses which no fair-minded person could defend today. Industrialists selected from Smith whatever justified their actions and overlooked the rest – a practice which later gave Marx much useful backing for his efforts to discredit, and ultimately to destroy, the whole system.

There are echoes of this in some of the comments made in the 1970s. There are businessmen, on both sides of the Atlantic, who consider any sort of concern for one's fellow man as a foolish weakness. Compromise is anathema, and trade union leaders are upstarts who must be treated with contempt. Some of the loudest protests against the alleged sinfulness of trying to acquire money come from those who already have more than an adequate amount of it. They are bitterly opposed on what they claim are moral grounds to pay claims, strikes, betting, welfare benefits, and other ways of making what appears to them as a wholly unjustified attempt to encroach on their territory. The moral grounds, invariably, consist of the assertion that 'the country is in a mess' – which, in one form or another, it always is. (If it isn't the balance of payments, it's inflation; and if it isn't inflation, it's unemployment.) Trade unions who want more money are 'letting the country down'. It never occurs to these die-hards that trade union leaders are simply behaving like old-style capitalists. They seek to maximize profits only for the benefit of members with the power to hire and fire. The profit ethic, as seen by dogmatic businessmen, is meant to apply to one side only. Workers are not supposed to copy their masters. So there are passionate protests against the earnings of car workers and disc jockeys and angry demands, by people who profess to believe in the principles laid down by Adam Smith, for curbs on the 'greed' of working-class people who use capitalist methods to better their lot. It is, you will agree, an odd way of trying to make converts. (Another

17

ironic development is that the same businessmen show an increasing readiness to ditch the doctrine of free enterprise when the going gets rough. They want freedom, but insist on Government protection as soon as 'the market' goes against them. They agree that free enterprise means 'standing on your own two feet', but readily accept Government grants and subsidies.)

Capitalist societies simply no longer function in the nineteenth-century way. Adam Smith maxims were never truly applied anywhere and the world today is further than ever from adopting his doctrines *in toto*. Capitalism, as visualized by him, died a long time ago. In its place we have what is known as a 'mixed economy', with the mixture varying from one country to another. There are several different types of twentieth-century capitalism; the American and/or German version differs in many respects from the British or Italian, while the Scandinavian and Japanese mixtures are different still. But all have this in common: they accept the need for, and importance of, some form of private ownership and they are trying to adapt themselves to the growing complexities of modern industrial and political life. What we are talking about, then, is not so much the survival of capitalism as the future of private enterprise – and with it the future of liberties we have long taken for granted.

Chapter One
For the Record

The very ink with which all history
is written is merely fluid prejudice.
MARK TWAIN

A good deal of the hostility to private enterprise, on both sides
of the Atlantic, is based not so much on personal observation
and experience as on impressions gained from history books,
novels, and the voluminous writings of Socialist intellectuals.
Academics and writers have never had much time for big business, and this is reflected in their interpretation of, and
comments on, economic history. The businessman has rarely
been depicted as a hero by those most influential in forming
public opinion. Novelists, poets, playwrights, and historians
have consistently presented a one-sided picture of private enterprise and invented emotive labels to go with it: the jungle, the
robber barons, the Hungry Forties, the money lords, the Great
Crash. This is as true today as it was a hundred years ago; perhaps more so. If you want to win the approval of fellow academics, or write a best-seller, you must attack some aspect
of capitalism – or, better still, denounce some prominent
millionaire. The capitalists are the exploiters. The rest of us are
the exploited. Period.

Ironically, one of the few people who has had a good word
to say for private enterprise is the man who opposed it so fiercely
for most of his life: Karl Marx. 'The bourgeoisie,' he wrote early
in his career (see Chapter Five), 'has been the first to show what
man's activity can bring about. It has accomplished wonders
far surpassing Egyptian pyramids, Roman aqueducts and
Gothic cathedrals ... the bourgeoisie ... draws all nations ...
into civilization ... it has created enormous cities ... and thus

rescued a considerable part of the population from the idiocy of rural life ... the bourgeoisie, during its rule of scarce one hundred years, has created more massive and more colossal productive forces than have all the preceding generations together.' But this is not how most historians see it. The general tendency has been to romanticize the pre-industrial world – to paint a vague, rosy picture of a lost golden age of the working classes which, allegedly, was destroyed by the industrial revolution. Dark satanic mills replaced the charming weaver's cottage; grim town life took over from a peaceful, happy rural existence. Friedrich Engels, Marx's collaborator, claimed that before the arrival of machinery 'the workers vegetated throughout a passably comfortable existence, leading a righteous and peaceful life in all piety and probity; and their material condition was far better than that of their successors'.

This was written of an age characterized by staggeringly high mortality rates, especially among children; crowded towns and villages untouched by sanitation; notoriously high gin consumption; a drab and meagre diet consisting mostly of oatmeal, milk, cheese and beer; and a system of domestic industry in which families lived and worked together in badly lit, improperly ventilated, and poorly constructed cottages. In short, an age in which the economy was barely able to support the population, and in which death from starvation and exposure was commonplace.

A more honest view has come from Professor T. S. Ashton, who took the trouble to go through the reports of a long series of Royal Commissions and Committees of Inquiry, beginning in the eighteenth century but reaching full steam in the 1830s, 1840s and 1850s. 'A careful reading of the reports,' he says, 'would have brought home to the mind that it was not among the factory employees but among the domestic workers, whose traditions and methods were those of the eighteenth century, that earnings were at their lowest. It would have provided evidence that it was not in the large establishments making use of steam power but in the garret or cellar workshops that conditions of employment were at their worst. It would have led to the conclusion that it was not in the growing manufacturing towns or the developing coalfields but in remote villages and the countryside that restrictions on personal freedoms and the evils of truck were most marked. But few had the patience to go carefully through these massive volumes. It was so much easier to pick out the more sensational evidences of distress and work them into a dramatic story of exploitation.'

It would clearly be absurd to suggest that the Industrial Revolution was an unqualified blessing and that every nineteenth-century businessman was an architect of progress. But it is equally absurd to suggest that misery only began when wicked capitalists introduced machinery. 'Historians,' says Bertrand de Jouvenel, 'have done their obvious duty in describing the miserable social conditions of which they found ample evidence. They have, however, proved exceptionally incautious in their interpretation of the facts. First, they seem to have taken for granted that a sharp increase in the extent of social awareness of and indignation about misery is a true index of increased misery; they seem to have given little thought to the possibility that such an increase might also be a function of new facilities of expression (due partly to a concentration of workers, partly to greater freedom of speech), of a growing philanthropic sensitivity (as evidenced by the fight for penal reforms), and of the new sense of human power to change things, mooted by the Industrial Revolution itself. Second, they do not seem to have distinguished sufficiently between the sufferings attendant upon any great migration (and there was a migration to the towns) and those inflicted by the factory system. Third, they do not seem to have attached enough importance to the Demographic Revolution. Had they used the comparative method, they might have found that a massive influx into the towns, with the resultant squalor and pauperism, occurred as well in countries untouched by the Industrial Revolution, where they produced waves of beggars instead of underpaid workers.'

People like Ashton and Jouvenel are very much in a minority, but they are not alone. Professor F. A. Hayek is another academic who maintains that 'the historical beliefs

21

which guide us in the present are not always in accord with the facts'. While, he says, 'there is every evidence that great misery existed, there is none that it was greater than – or even as great as – it had been before ... we must not, long after the event, allow a distortion of the facts, even if committed out of humanitarian zeal, to affect the view of what we owe to a system which for the first time made people feel that this misery might be avoidable'.

American accounts of the nineteenth century show, for the most part, the same anti-capitalist bias as those of their European colleagues. It is invariably portrayed as a period in which unprincipled men – the 'robber barons' – seized control of vital areas of the economy and exacted tribute from the entire nation. Most, if not all, of the social evils of the day are attributed to the machinations of ruthless, greedy, utterly corrupt millionaires whose sole concern was to grow richer still at the expense of their fellow men. A handful of people made fraudulent fortunes by looting the country's natural resources; it wasn't until the Government intervened on a large scale that the economy began to serve the many rather than the few. This is history as taught in American schools. It's no wonder that names like Rockefeller, Carnegie, Vanderbilt, Hill, Morgan, and even Ford still attract the most extraordinary amount of abuse and that, in the eyes of many young Americans, capitalism is a system which merits nothing but contempt.

There is no doubt that most of these 'robber barons' conducted their business in a way which would not be tolerated today. But they were not living in the 1970s. Theirs was a very different era: a period when Americans were tackling the enormous task of developing their huge, half-empty continent, spanning it with a railway network, settling new lands, opening new resources, planning new towns, and developing the steamship and the magnetic telegraph – all within a remarkably short spell of time.

They were ruthless, to be sure, but that was nothing new. The *conquistadores* of the sixteenth century, and the Elizabethan adventurers who are such romantic folk heroes in Britain today, were no less ruthless and, for that matter, no less eager to plunder America. The 'robber barons' broke rules which we regard as elementary, but which did not actually exist in their day. George Washington was one of the greatest land speculators of the time; today his activities would no doubt deprive him of all chance to become President. I make no apology for their conduct but I do think that it should be seen in context – and that their achievements should be acknowledged. They were – in the words of their contemporary, Karl Marx – 'agents of progress'. There *were* other ways in which the country could have been developed: communism would have done the job in time. The price, though, would have been a good deal higher than that exacted by the 'robber barons' – a permanent loss of the freedom which generations of Americans have come to take for granted.

Many of those who made their fortunes in that era were immigrants who had grown up in poverty and who were, inevitably, driven on by the memory of their harsh early days. They could never quite shake off a deep-rooted feeling of insecurity. It was this, rather than pure greed, which often accounted for their acquisitiveness, and for the thriftiness which so many writers have mocked. 'If you've ever really been poor,' wrote Arnold Bennett, 'you remain poor at heart all your life.' Vanderbilt, Carnegie, Rockefeller, Guggenheim, Astor, and Gould would no doubt have agreed with him. America was the land of opportunity – the opportunity to bury the past. *Anyone* could become rich if he tried hard enough; you didn't have to come from an aristocratic European landowning family or from a wealthy merchant's home.

Cornelius Vanderbilt was born of poor Dutch peasants in 1794 and started work as a ferry-boy in New York harbour. He had no formal education – indeed, he never really learned to spell – but he possessed other useful assets: great vitality, courage, and a peasant's cunning. He was proud, and fiercely independent. In short, the kind of man immortalized, later, in a thousand Westerns. The Commodore, as he was known for most of his life, was the first of the great shipping millionaires but, like Onassis many years later, never really found accept-ance in society drawing rooms. (He had his revenge, in a way, when one of his offspring became Duchess of Marlborough.) The Establishment dismissed him as one of the *nouveaux riches*, a term of abuse invented by snobbish aristocrats (or, more likely, people who liked to think themselves aristocrats) to keep self-made men in their place. Vanderbilt didn't give a damn for any of them. He made a fortune in shipping and, at the age of 68, earned millions more in the railroad business. As a young man he struggled against established shipping interests, working sixteen hours a day in conditions which would appall and terrify his twentieth-century critics. As an old man he was tough, aggressive, and increasingly eccentric. He was also parsi-monious: his wife and nine children led a comparatively frugal existence. There are several famous anecdotes which are said to sum up his character. When associates tried to exploit his absence on a European journey by seizing control of one of his properties, Vanderbilt wrote a short letter: 'Gentlemen,' it said, 'You have undertaken to cheat me. I will not sue you, for law takes too long. I will ruin you. Sincerely yours, Cornelius Van-derbilt.' He did just that. On another occasion he came up with a comment which has been used, by countless commentators, to illustrate the arrogance of his kind. 'What do I care about the law? Hain't I got the power?' He was neither likeable nor, for that matter, particularly enviable. But one doesn't have to like a man in order to recognize his contribution to the world in which he lived. Vanderbilt helped to open up America and, in the process, gave employment and prosperity to countless fellow citizens.

Andrew Carnegie, who dominated the US steel industry and, like Vanderbilt, became one of the world's richest men, also came from a humble background. He was born in Scot-land, the child of poor Scottish weavers. At 14 he was set to work as a bobbin-boy in a cloth mill. At 16 he came with his parents to Allegheny, near Pittsburgh, and was delighted by the vigour and optimism of his new country. He became a telegraph clerk and, later, telegraphist and secretary to Thomas Scott, the general superintendent of the Pennsylvania Railroad. Scott rose rapidly in the railroad, then still in its infancy, and took Carnegie with him. He was made assistant secretary of war in 1861, and helped Carnegie to get the post of superintendent of eastern military and telegraph lines during the Civil War. In 1862, while working for the Government, Carnegie helped reorganize a bridge construction company. He realized that iron bridges would be needed in the war effort, and that such a company would have no trouble making a financial success of it. So he put in some of his own money. At the same time he and his brother Thomas got involved with a German named Kloman, who was making iron axles for railroad rolling stock and owned a modern mill. Kloman needed more cash for expansion and Carnegie found it for him, in return for a junior partnership. Within a few years Carnegie and his brother had acquired half, then a majority interest. The two companies were merged and Carnegie resigned from the railroad to become a full-time entrepreneur. He thought of himself as a businessman rather than a manufacturer, a salesman and projector rather than an ironmaster. By 1868, he had an income of $50,000 a year – and he was still only 33. His dream, at that time, was to arrange his affairs in such a way that the $50,000 would be assured for life, and to 'cast off business for ever'. He wanted to 'settle in Oxford and get a thorough education, making the acquaintance of literary men – this will take three years' active work – pay especial attention to speaking in public. Settle then in London and purchase a controlling interest in some newspaper or live review and give the general management of it attention, taking a part in public matters, especially those connected with education and improvement of the poorer classes. . . .'

Alas, he was much too involved in his business to let go. It is a familiar story even today: brilliant self-made men are frequently imprisoned by the company they have created. In 1872 Carnegie visited England and learned more of steel-making. He returned to America convinced that steel was the key to an industrial economy, and that the Bessemer process was the key to steel. He formed a new company, and a year later began construction of one of the biggest and most modern steel mills of the time, the Edgar Thomson Steel Works. His interests prospered and he was able to buy out others; in 1881 he restructured and consolidated his holdings, forming Carnegie Brothers and Co., which was capitalized at $5 million with Carnegie owning $2·7 million of the stock. Other take-overs and mergers followed, and when Carnegie finally decided to sell out to Pierpont Morgan, at 63, the business was valued at a staggering $492 million – with Carnegie himself receiving over $300 million in bonds and preferred stock. (There is a splendid story about a meeting between the two men, a year or two afterwards, on the deck of an ocean steamship. Carnegie said: 'I made one mistake, Pierpont, when I sold out to you. I should have asked you $100 million more than I did.' Morgan, according to legend, replied: 'If you had, I should have paid it – if only to be rid of you.')

Carnegie had a large number of protégés who, if they showed promise, were given both quick promotion and shares in the company as a bonus. 'We cannot,' he said, 'have too many of the right sort of men interested in the profits.' Many of them became millionaires in their own right. They are all, of course, forgotten men. No one ever writes about them. But their careers do underline a point that is rarely made: a great many Americans besides the 'robber barons' did well for themselves and their families during this extraordinary period.

John D. Rockefeller grew up in western New York and later near Cleveland. His father was a salesman – a purveyor of quack medicine – who spent much of his time away from home and seldom supported his wife and five children. John's childhood, by all accounts, was marked by continuous struggle. He had very little schooling and worked for neighbouring farmers in all his spare time, saving every penny he could. When the family moved to Cleveland he went to the Central High School and studied book-keeping, a subject which he liked and for which he appeared to have a natural aptitude. He spent little on himself, regularly attended church, and generally seems to have missed most of the normal childhood pleasures. In 1858, at the age of 19, he opened his own business in partnership with a young Englishman called Clark. The firm – a commission house – did half a million dollars worth of business in its first year. He might have stayed with it, and become one of thousands of well-off but not particularly outstanding merchants, if it had not been for the chance discovery of oil in Pennsylvania during the following year. Rockefeller visited the oilfield, liked what he saw, and decided to invest in a local refinery. In 1865 he abandoned the commission business in order to take personal charge of his refining interests, which were united under a new firm, Rockefeller & Andrews. During the next few years he established new companies, constructed additional facilities and generally expanded the business. In 1870 he consolidated his various interests into a single firm – Standard Oil of Ohio, destined to become the biggest name in the American oil business.

Like Vanderbilt and others, Rockefeller was careful with his money – a direct reflection of his puritanical upbringing. His taste in clothes was simple, he ate sparingly, and was a dedicated teetotaller. But he could also be remarkably generous: he gave away several fortunes during his lifetime, to a variety of worthy causes. Starting with $2·77 in 1855, his various gifts reached half a million in 1891 and by 1909 totalled over $71,000,000. In 1919 it was $138,000,000. 'I believe,' he once said, 'the power of money is a gift of God ... to be developed and used to the best of our ability for the good of mankind. Having been endowed with the gift I possess, I believe it is my duty to make money and still more money, and to use the money I make for the good of my fellow man according to the dictates of my conscience.' Humbug? Some people certainly think so. Rockefeller, they maintain, was a grasping 'money maniac' whose blind attachment to the stuff was sickening to behold and who tried to redeem himself by buying goodwill as a kind of insurance against the wrath of the Lord. Rockefeller himself, of course, was well aware of the hostility aroused by his success and, like most rich men, realized that helping others is often the quickest way to make life-long enemies. But he seems to have been quite content to follow the 'dictates of his own conscience'. What God made of it we do not know.

There are, as I have said, countless other rags-to-riches stories of the era. They match, and often surpass, anything a fiction writer like Harold Robbins or Irving Wallace could hope to invent. Think of John Jacob Astor, a German butcher's son who arrived in New York in 1783, apprenticed himself to a furrier, traded with the Indians, and eventually built up a family fortune to rival that of the Rothschilds in Europe. Or Jay Cooke, son of a temperance leader in a frontier village menaced by Indian tribes, who became a bank clerk at 18 and, by the time he was 40, not only had his own bank – financing all kinds of business ventures and buying up those who seemed about to fail – but also became Washington's chief supplier of funds for the Civil War. Or Frank Woolworth, born in 1852 on a farm in the town of Rodman, Jefferson County, New York, who left school at 16, worked five years on the farm, got himself an unpaid job with a dry-goods store, married a seamstress, borrowed some money from his employers to start his first Great Five Cent Store (it was a failure) and by 1912 was head of a company with sixty-six stores and sales of over 60 million a year. Or Richard Warren Sears, the founder of the giant Sears Roebuck. Born in 1863, the son of a farmer-blacksmith who lost all his money in a stock farm and died when Richard was 14, he became an agent for a railroad at $6 a week and, in his spare time, started to sell watches. He did so well that he left the railroad, started his own company, met a watchmaker called Roebuck, and laid the foundations for what is now the world's largest retailing group. (Retailers hardly ever seem to get a mention in critical studies of American business history, presumably because it is so much more difficult to brand them as evil men.) Or Isaac Merrit Singer, the son of poor German immigrants who left his New York home at the age of 12, tried his luck (without success) as a farmer and as an actor in a Shakespearean troupe, and at 39 borrowed forty dollars to make his first sewing machine in Boston. From this modest beginning grew America's first multi-national corporation, with sales in more than 200 countries. Mahatma Gandhi, who learned to sew on a Singer sewing machine while in jail, called it 'one of the few useful things ever invented'.

Robber barons or captains of industry? Exploiters or agents of progress? Self-reliant, hard-working individuals or wicked capitalists? There ought to be room for more than one opinion and I have, for once, taken the charitable view. No one could possibly describe them as angels and I certainly do not seek to do so. But I do think the abuse has been overdone: too often self-made men are condemned merely because their efforts have made them rich.

Chapter Two
The Rich Today

It requires a great deal of boldness and a great deal
of caution to make a great fortune, and when you
have got it, it requires ten times as much wit to
keep it.
EMERSON

Of all the names associated with that rumbustious era, the one
which still comes most readily to mind whenever 'money' is
mentioned is that of Rockefeller. Yet only one of John D.'s five
grandsons – David, the youngest – has followed him whole-
heartedly into a business career. David Rockefeller is president
of New York's Chase Manhattan Bank, America's second
largest, and has been called 'the most influential banker in the
world'. The label alone is enough to attract hostility; the Rockefeller millions guarantee it. 'Mr David', as he is known to
employees, is attacked for exercising influence, for 'working too
hard' when he doesn't have to, for being careful with money,
and for just being rich. Like his brothers, he even finds himself
criticized for being involved in philanthropic programmes. He
bears it all with remarkable equanimity.

David Rockefeller is six feet tall, unpretentious, mild-
mannered, soft-spoken, polite. No one outside the family knows
exactly how much he is worth personally, but it is certainly not
less than $100 million and probably close to $200 million. Rockefeller himself is not fussed by it. 'If things are right inside,'
he told me during one of several interviews, 'wealth can be a
great asset. I am, fortunately, an emotionally balanced and
stable kind of person.' The Rockefellers were taught that work,
hard work, was to be valued rather than despised, and they
were thoroughly indoctrinated with an appreciation of the
worth of a dollar. David's allowance in his first years of grade
school was 25 cents a week, and he had to spend eight hours

raking leaves to get that. He could earn extra money pulling weeds, one cent for each weed pulled, but was required to keep track of every expenditure he made. 'Father taught us,' he says, 'that excess of any kind was intolerable for a Rockefeller. His strict rule was that we should save ten per cent of our money and give away ten per cent.' The message came across, loud and clear, in a Ph.D. thesis David delivered to the University of Chicago at the age of 25. Entitled 'Unused Resources and Economic Waste', it included this statement:

'From our earliest days we are told not to leave food on our plates, not to allow electric lights to remain burning when we are not using them, and not to squander our money thoughtlessly, because these things are wasteful ... of all forms of waste, however, that which is most abhorrent is idleness. There is a moral stigma attached to unnecessary and involuntary idleness which is deeply embedded in our conscience.'

Chicago gave him his degree, but of course he did not need it to find employment. It is not generally known today that he could, if he wished, insist on being called 'Dr Rockefeller'. The thesis did, however, prove to himself – and to his family – that he had brains enough to make his own way, if necessary, in a highly competitive world. He was not, at this stage, automatically drawn to banking. Trying to get the feel of public service, he took a job as an unpaid assistant to New York's Mayor LaGuardia. 'I got involved in all sorts of decisions,' he recalls, 'and I learned a great deal.' LaGuardia gave him a number of special assignments, and many people expected David to embark on a political career. Flatterers assured him that, with his money and obvious ability, he had an excellent chance of eventually becoming President. The war, however, postponed the need for a firm commitment. He left LaGuardia's office late in 1941, when he was 26, to work for Mrs Anna Rosenberg who was running the New York office of the Office of Defence, Health and Welfare Services. He was given the imposing title of assistant regional director. Soon afterwards, however, he enlisted in the army with the more modest rank of private. The next year or so found him doing various jobs hardly appropriate to a doctor of philosophy, let alone a multi-millionaire: he worked as a filing clerk on Governor's Island, and looked after a colonel's horse on Miami beach. Eventually he went to an Officer Candidate school, and in 1943 he was sent to Algiers as an intelligence officer. He stayed there for eighteen months, and ended the war as a captain in France. The French gave him the Legion of Honour and, more importantly, taught him to appreciate good food as well as hard work and the worth of a dollar. (The appreciation has remained; as a host he ranks well above his brothers.)

In 1946 he joined the Chase National Bank (as it then was) as an assistant manager in the foreign department. It was a lowly job, but everyone knew that he wouldn't be in it for very long. A Rockefeller isn't expected to be an assistant manager all his life. But the old cartoon *cliché* about the millionaire's son—beginner one day, managing director the next—did not apply either. It was three years before he joined the ranks of vice-presidents (which were larger than the title may suggest) and another three before he was named a senior vice-president. He became president and chairman of the executive committee of the board of directors in 1961.

I once asked him why, after getting a ringside view of politics, he chose to devote himself to banking rather than moving in an arena which, he admits, has always held a curious fascination. 'I can't imagine a more interesting job than mine,' he said. But there is more to it than that. A much stronger reason, I believe, is simply that one politically prominent Rockefeller has always seemed enough. A lesser reason may be that David is not really the kind of personality who catches the imagination. People listen to him because he is a bank president and a Rockefeller, but he does not prompt an instant, enthusiastic response—unless, perhaps, his audience happens to be made up of cheerleaders planted by the PR Department.

David Rockefeller is an enthusiastic traveller, and he has probably seen more of the world than any of his brothers—or, for that matter, any other prominent American banker. His name, of course, opens doors everywhere. E. J. Kahn, in an excellent *New Yorker* profile published some years ago, told what happened when Rockefeller went to the Soviet Union for a conference and was invited to meet Khrushchev. Rockefeller, who has six children (two boys and four girls) took his second eldest daughter, Neva, with him to the Kremlin, and Khrushchev readily acceded to his request that she should be permitted to take notes. According to Kahn, Rockefeller subsequently called the two-and-a-half-hour confrontation 'the most intensive conversation I have ever had with anyone'. It was a far-ranging, if inconclusive, colloquy covering, among other subjects, the capricious attitude of the Russians towards international copyright law, the failure of the Soviet Union to repay its wartime lend-lease obligations, and the possibility of increased trade between the two men's nations. At one point, Rockefeller said that his mother had visited Russia in tsarist days – back in 1896, the year before she married John D. Rockefeller Jr. She had been travelling with her father, Senator Nelson Aldrich, of Rhode Island. That got Khrushchev going on what he called the inevitable evolutionary progress of the entire world towards communism. Waving a hand towards the scribbling, 20-year-old Neva, the Soviet leader told her father that sooner or later people everywhere would spontaneously embrace communism. 'Some day your daughter Neva will think as I do,' the Russian said amiably. Neither Neva nor her father replied.

Friends who have accompanied him on business trips call him 'the cruise director' because he is, as a rule, a relentless organizer, eager to meet everybody and everything. His calm and easy-going manner is certainly deceptive, but Rockefeller insists that 'I don't kill myself with work.' The secret, he says, is (1) never to do something you can get somebody else to do for you, (2) always leave everything behind when you go off for weekends and vacations'. Does he ever lose his temper? 'Oh yes. But it doesn't happen very often. And I don't keep a list of the occasions when it does.' He doesn't keep lists of his mistakes either. 'I am not a worrier,' he says. 'I find it easy to make decisions; I don't spend hours agonizing over it. I'm an optimist by nature; one probably needs to be in the banking business.'

Rockefeller's favourite sport is sailing – he's very good at it – but America's leading business game is golf, and out-of-town customers of consequence occasionally insist that the president of their bank accompanies them to the nearest golf course. Rockefeller calls it 'customer golf' and his readiness to play it is acknowledged to be a formidable Chase asset.

But perhaps the most interesting thing about him is his involvement with modern art. The bank's executive offices, and many of its branches abroad, are dominated by huge, vivid abstract paintings chosen by a committee which, in turn, was chosen by Rockefeller and is chaired by him.

'When we began our art programme in 1959,' he says, 'our objectives were limited to the decoration of certain key offices and areas. But the response of customers and staff was so enthusiastic that we felt it could profitably be enlarged to include all our places of business.' The result, he believes, has been to 'humanise the image of what was once considered a cold and impersonal business'.

His mother was one of the founders of the Museum of Modern Art, and his brother Nelson was a keen collector long before him. At the time of his marriage, David Rockefeller and his wife both leaned towards Chinese porcelain and eighteenth-century furniture. Their interest in modern art began when an associate recommended a Renoir which happened to be for sale – one of the painter's portraits of his maid, Gabrielle. They bought it and afterwards built up a fine collection of French impressionists. From there they went on to artists like Victor Vasarely, Bridget Riley, Adolph Gottlieb, Chryssa, and Ludwig Sander.

Rockefeller puts in his typical day in an elegant office on the seventeenth floor of the bank's lower Manhattan skyscraper. There he is surrounded by works of art, including a Picasso, a Chagall, a Utrillo, a Vasarely, and an abstract oil by Kenzo Okada. He also has some Greek vases of the fifth century B.C., a wooden Buddha, a Chinese lacquered chest, an early Mogul incense burner, and various objets d'art and artefacts.

Given his inbred concern with value for money, I asked him

how he felt about art as an investment. 'For any serious collector', he replied, 'it has to be a subordinate aspect. You have to buy things which are beautiful and which you like. If they increase in value, it's a bonus.'

One of the things he likes is a sculpture by Jean Dubuffet, entitled 'Group of Four Trees'. Rockefeller chose it himself – after spending a total of forty-five minutes in Dubuffet's workshop at Perigny-sur-Yerres, near Paris. It now stands, forty-two feet high, in the Plaza surrounding the massive Chase building.

Like most millionaires, he is very much on his guard against people who assume that, because he is enormously wealthy, anything goes. 'I won't be taken in,' he says. He tries to slip off to galleries between business meetings abroad, and if he likes something he will buy it either for the bank or for one of his four homes. Dealers frequently have no idea that they are bargaining with a Rockefeller: he prefers it that way.

Rockefeller is rich enough to buy a thousand beautiful objects, and to devote the rest of his life to them. He can indulge in whims (like his collection of 30,000 beetles, a hobby started as a boy) without worrying about cost or lack of storage space. But he clearly wants other things too – prestige, power, respect. He is conscious of what money can do, and tough enough to use it to effect. Even so, there are limits. Brother Nelson cannot buy the White House, and brother David cannot buy the genuine admiration of people he admires himself. It has to be worked for. Not least, money cannot guarantee the greatest asset of all – good health.

Rockefeller admits, ruefully, that he has 'a constant struggle to keep my weight down'. I don't know about you – but I find it comforting, somehow, to know that a multi-millionaire, a banker's banker, a Rockefeller, a man who seems to have absolutely everything the world can offer, has to keep his fingers crossed when he steps on the bathroom scales.

Few, if any, British millionaires can match the Rockefeller name – or even want to. The super-rich prefer to keep their heads well down. The great land-owning families, like the Dukes of Portland and of Westminster, take care to keep their affairs out of the headlines, and so do people like Lord Cowdray, who inherited a large and successful business empire. From time to time the press gleefully reports the money problems of some aristocrat or other, and the Royal Family's financial troubles always make news, but there is no one today whose wealth attracts international attention. For many years until his death in 1976 the richest man in Britain was not British at all but American: J. Paul Getty. Even the *nouveaux riches*, the people who have built up large post-war estates, no longer welcome publicity. In part, of course, this simply reflects the fact that wealth is out of fashion.

'In some ways,' said Getty, 'a millionaire just can't win. If he spends too freely, he is criticized for being extravagant and ostentatious. If, on the other hand, he lives quietly and thriftily, the same people who would have criticized him for being profligate will call him a miser. If he goes to parties and night clubs, he is labelled a wastrel and doubts are raised about his maturity and sense of responsibility. Let him shun the salons and saloons, and he is promptly tagged as a recluse or misanthrope.'

But there is another very good reason why millionaires prefer to keep away from the limelight: the risk that they or their relatives may be kidnapped. Kidnapping threats are far more common than the rich care to admit and, of course, some turn into ugly fact. A few years ago, Getty's grandson was grabbed in Rome and only returned, minus one ear, after the old man had handed over a large ransom. As in Italy and elsewhere, wealthy people who once employed public relations men to get their pictures into the newspapers nowadays pay them to make sure that they stay out. Just about the only Britons who still advertise their wealth are pop stars – and they are not wealthy at all. Driving around in a yellow Rolls Royce doesn't make you rich; nor does eating at the Ritz. According to Getty, no one is really rich if he can count his money. It is a definition which, I dare say, would be applauded by David Rockefeller. It would certainly be accepted by most of the other millionaires I have met in twenty-five years as a financial journalist. The truly rich don't even *bother* to count. The bulk of their money is locked up in business enterprises (I have yet to meet one who actually *has* a million) and like Rockefeller they devote most of their lives to work.

There is a widespread tendency to mix up incomes with the real basis of wealth – capital. It is hard for a £50-a-week man to accept that his chairman, earning £400 a week before tax, is not 'rich'. It suits both politicians and journalists to go along with the pretence. There are snide articles about the 'Bollinger Brigade' and bitter attacks on company chairmen who choose to spend their holidays in the south of France instead of Clacton or Blackpool. Much of this carping is unfair, because there is such a marked difference between gross and net earnings. The British chief executive of a large company has, for some years now, paid the highest rate of marginal tax of any Western company chief. His position has grown rapidly worse: a recent Royal Commission found that the real after-tax earnings of men on £10,000 a year had dropped by 17 per cent between July 1969 and July 1975, while those of men on £20,000 a year had fallen by a staggering 25 per cent over the same period. The managerial class which nowadays runs most of Britain's largest companies is far from 'rich'.

This, you may feel, is how it should be, but let me offer this thought: only capital buys true independence. A manager who is totally dependent on his salary is unlikely to risk a showdown with the people who control the purse-strings. Middle-aged, and accustomed to a fairly high standard of living, he is understandably reluctant to risk his job and his family's future. It tends to make him excessively cautious in his approach to new ideas, and reluctant to take any sort of decision. A man who has been able to build up reasonable assets is much more likely to show courage. This simple and obvious fact is much more readily accepted in America than it is in Britain, and helps to explain why American businessmen tend to be more positive. Americans also acknowledge one other obvious fact: it is irrational to argue, as so many of us tend to do, that you cannot give an industrialist a few thousands more a year while the country has a million unemployed. It may be more sensible to do just the opposite. When decisions involving millions are made, it is important to have the right man making them. If he costs a little more than a less suitable type, no matter. The wrong fellow can lose his organization more than that in a day – which, in turn, may mean still more unemployment.

We shall return to the subject, but let me make my own position clear. I am not, in case you are wondering, super rich (or even rich) myself. I am not even sure whether I want to be. Yes, dammit, I do. It would be hypocritical to pretend that I wouldn't enjoy the extra comfort, the leisure, and the freedom which (for the moment at least) money can buy. I have never been able to see any great merit in austerity. I am not prepared to make the personal sacrifices needed, these days, to make a million: there is no point in ruining one's health to acquire luxury which, once you have it, can't be enjoyed. Too many tycoons build themselves a prison and can't break out of it. But I am not envious of the rich. They are a luxury which a country like Britain should be able to afford. The rich are our main safeguard against the relentless push towards boring collectivism, our chief defence against Whitehall planners and big corporations, with their passion for standardization and slide-rule approach to everything from architecture and design to publishing and travel. The whims and enthusiasms of rich individuals have given Britain much of its character. Abolish the rich and who would build country houses, breed racehorses, publish *The Times*? Who would finance plays and concerts rejected by committees, back festivals, save lost causes? Who would bother to restore fine buildings and antique furniture? Who would keep boatbuilders, great chefs, and gossip columnists in employment? And where, if you please, would charities be without them? I don't know about you, but it has always been a comforting thought, to me, that we still have wealthy people who are willing and able to finance dotty ideas. The Arts Council does a splendid job, to be sure, but the angel provides much-needed patronage. And there is no doubt that, in the business world, the rich individual supplies the courage and imagination which most corporations, with their concern for profit, conspicuously lack.

Not, mind you, that concern with profit necessarily rules out the rest. Look at the careers of four businessmen who have made large personal fortunes in the last twenty years—Lew Grade, Roy Thomson, Charles Forte, and Nigel Broackes.

Lew Grade's story reads very much like a classical Hollywood soap opera. He was born Lewis Winogradsky in Tokmak, southern Crimea, the son of a poor tailor's assistant. His family came to England to escape religious persecution in 1913, and lived in poverty in the East End of London. Lew left school at 14 to help his father sew button-holes. His parents were amateur opera singers, and he and his brother Bernard, sharing their only good suit, followed the family's vague show business tradition into Charleston competitions. Prizes were sold to pay the rent. He went on tour in Britain and Europe as 'The World's Champion Charleston Dancer' but, he says, came to realize that as a dancing star he had his limitations. 'I really had no talent as a performer. I was just a dancer, and you can't go through life just dancing.' So he became an agent, and by 1947 was handling the European representation of celebrated American stars like Frankie Laine, Bob Hope, Johnnie Ray, Lena Horne, Jack Benny, Phil Harris, Dorothy Lamour, and many others. In the fifties he was part of the group that formed ATV, and Lew Grade was in television.

Today the ATV group takes in more than a dozen subsidiaries in various fields, from TV and feature films to music publishing, records, theatres, and bowling alleys. Journalists have dubbed him 'the world's most powerful television tycoon' and they are probably not far off the mark. He heads Britain's largest independent television company but he is very much an international figure. His company's programmes have been screened in 100 countries, have collected scores of international awards, including numerous 'Emmys'–America's top TV honours. His salesmanship got him a knighthood: he became Sir Lew in 1969 after selling £23 million worth of programmes in America during the previous year. In 1975 that country added its own accolade: the National Academy of Television Arts and Sciences gave a gala dinner in his honour at the New York Hilton, and presented him with a commemorative plaque inscribed 'A salute to Sir Lew Grade whose genius for showmanship has bridged the continents.' Prince Philip used the occasion for a different kind of tribute. 'I wonder,' he wrote, 'how many realise the extent to which your commercial and business enterprise is tempered by a warm-hearted response to charitable, voluntary, and sporting efforts of all kinds. The list of organisations, big and small, which have benefited directly or indirectly from your sympathy and support is a very long one, but even that is no measure for the sum of human happiness and relief the list represents.' In 1976 he became a peer.

Among recent partnership ventures are several ambitious – and costly – series produced by Grade's company and Radio Televisione Italiana. They include *Moses the Lawgiver*, the *Life and Times of William Shakespeare*, and the *Life of Jesus*. Another development is his enthusiastic involvement in feature films, at a time when many people are highly sceptical about the future of the cinema. 'My aim,' he says, 'is to make twenty films a year. We're going to be the biggest producers in the world.' Money, he claims, has never been a problem. 'I've proved to my bankers in the US that we know what we are talking about. They keep asking me if I need more.'

Lew Grade works at a furious pace. His working day begins at six ('The moment I get up,' he says; 'I can't wait to get to the office') and ends just before midnight. There are three telephones in every room of his London penthouse, including the sauna, and his evenings are spent making calls to people in different time zones. He crosses the Atlantic fourteen or fifteen times a year, mostly to see business contacts over the weekend, and during the past couple of years has made an equal number of trips to Rome and Milan. He takes no holidays – 'I don't need them' – and says his only form of exercise is walking from one office to another. What drives him on? 'I'm having fun,' he says. He reads all the scripts himself, and he insists, 'As I read I visualise the situation. I can see the actors and actresses who would be ideal for the parts. And I go after them.' Critics say this reliance on instinct, this penchant for snap judgments, is bound to trip him up one day. There have been flops, and some productions fall well short of his optimistic expectations. But, he says, 'none of my mistakes have a disastrous effect'. And the company's profit record is ample proof that, so far, they have been more than outweighed by his triumphs.

Like most successful men, Lew Grade has his share of enemies, including actors and producers he has turned down and, of course, people who resent his wealth. He accepts, too, that not everyone envies his life-style. But there is no denying that a great many talented people have benefited from his generosity and enthusiasm and that, in his own way, he is having fun.

Roy Thomson did not arrive in Britain until he was 59 – an age at which most people's thoughts turn to retirement. His career is a classic example of private enterprise at its ebullient best. Born in Canada, the son of a Toronto barber, Thomson left school at 14, went to work in a coal yard, and later sold spark plugs and other motor parts. His ambition, even then, was to become a millionaire by the time he was 30. He told me, in a long interview on his eightieth birthday in 1974, that his bad eyesight had a lot to do with it. 'I couldn't compete on the sports field, so I got interested in balance sheets instead.' But he didn't make it; indeed he was virtually penniless when he acquired his first newspaper at the age of 40. 'I haven't got cash,' he told the owners frankly. 'Tell you what I'll do, though.

41

I'll give you two hundred dollars down, and twenty-eight promissory notes of two hundred dollars each, repayable over twenty-eight months'. Today the Thomson Organisation owns hundreds of newspapers all over the world: in Britain alone they include *The Times*, the *Sunday Times*, and the *Scotsman*. It runs TV and radio stations, book publishing firms, and a travel agency. It also has interests in insurance, banking, transport, hotels, property, and oil. And the Thomson family has various enterprises in Canada. Altogether the business built up by the barber's son is reckoned to be worth $600 million.

To outsiders Thomson has frequently seemed daring to the point of recklessness. He has bought newspapers at a time when no one gave them a chance of survival, with money he had to borrow from banks, and he has marched boldly into situations which appeared to terrify everyone else. His venture into commercial television is perhaps the best example: when he went after the Scottish TV station (destined to become his famous 'licence to print money') almost no one shared his confidence sufficiently to support him with even a modest amount of cash. And yet he has never seen himself as a gambler. 'I don't like gambling,' he told me. 'When I had a villa in the south of France we occasionally went to the casino, but I never bet more than a couple of dollars. It would hurt me too much to lose. But business is different: I don't gamble, I take calculated risks.'

There are countless stories about his careful ways with money. Thomson cheerfully admitted that most of them were true. There was, for example, the time he was driving to the office with his son, Ken.

'What's that?' Thomson demanded as Ken unfolded his morning paper.

'*The Times*.'

'And where did you get it?'

'At the shop round the corner.'

'Well, Ken,' the old man said anxiously, 'you take it right back and let someone else buy it. You can have mine when I've finished.'

This from a man who, for some years, had readily borne a financial loss on that same paper's operations which, in recent years, had sometimes run as high as a million pounds. Russell Braddon, one of his biographers, also tells of the time when Thomson's doctor advised him to shed forty pounds. Thomson went on a crash diet and, right on schedule, went back to his doctor. 'How much,' he said, 'do I owe you?'

'Forty dollars,' said the doctor. 'That's a dollar for each pound you lost.' Thomson sat down and wrote a cheque for forty dollars; but as he handed it across the desk he laughed.

'What are you laughing at?'

'You robbed yourself,' Thomson told him. 'I lost forty-two pounds.'

There is an element of gamesmanship in that, of course. Like all self-made men, he has always loved to get the better of someone in a deal, however trivial. But another, more simple, reason is that Thomson has never had much money in his pocket. 'I've always owed plenty,' he told me. 'I believe in it.' How much did he have on him right now? 'Well, let's see. One, two, three, four, five, six, seven pounds.' But he added quickly, 'I've also got a few credit cards.'

Thomson got his first British paper, the *Scotsman*, because it was losing heavily. The Board didn't think much of the intruder at first, but he persisted. The Scottish TV licence seemed a natural after that, but his biggest *coup* was the acquisition of Kemsley Newspapers (owners of the *Sunday Times*, among others) in 1959. It was a complex deal and there were moments when it seemed highly improbable that he could pull it off. But he still found time – and credit – to buy five more newspapers in North America during that eventful year. 'Success,' according to Thomson, 'is a combination of lucky breaks, the ability to seize them as they arise, and a great deal of hard work and determination.'

His next objective was a peerage. To get it he had to give up his Canadian citizenship; Ottawa wouldn't hear of a Canadian accepting a British title. Harold Macmillan duly obliged in 1964, and two years later Thomson returned the compliment by taking over the ailing *Times*. Owning so many papers made him, potentially, a powerful figure. But Thomson insisted that he was no Beaverbrook. 'I never tell our editors what to write. I could have more power if I wanted it but I sometimes think that if one started to use this power there'd be more restrictions placed on you. If I were to run all my newspapers on one policy of abolish liquor or abolish something else, it wouldn't be long before I'd be abolished.'

His main regret in life, at 80, was that 'I haven't bought more papers.' He also took a dim view of radio and TV. 'You see,' he said, 'anything where the government has got you by the balls, I think your chance of getting rich out of it is very bad. As soon as you start to make more money, collectively, than they think is good for you they'll put in more restrictions. And I don't like that kind of business. It isn't free enterprise any more.'

As we parted, I asked him how he felt about his enemies. 'Nobody,' he said, 'has any sympathy for a rich man except somebody that's richer again.' Perhaps – but it is certainly possible to *respect* someone, who, throughout his life, has undeniably done his own thing.

The same is certainly true of Sir Charles Forte, who built up Europe's largest hotel and catering business from a most unlikely base – a milk bar. As recently as 1945 he only had nine milk bars; today his company operates more than 550 hotels and catering establishments. Forte was born in Italy in 1908. His father went to Scotland when he was five and Charles grew up there. He speaks with a Scottish accent but strikes most people as unmistakably Italian – spontaneous, voluble, gregarious. He is a *Cavaliere Gran Croce della Republica Italiana* and it comes as no surprise to learn that he adores spaghetti. ('But,' he says wistfully, 'I only eat pasta every two or three weeks. I have to watch my waistline.') He is president of the Italian Chamber of Commerce in Britain and – a very Latin touch this – Consul-General in London for San Marino in the Appenine mountains of Italy, which he says is the oldest and smallest republic in the world – 'which suits me because I am one of the oldest and smallest men around'.

When he started, at 26, his father and other relatives already had several shops around the coast. 'This,' says Forte, 'gave me the idea of a milk bar chain. I had a general knowledge of the business, from its roots. And I was just sufficiently educated in controls, accounting and general learning: I knew just enough to provide the basis of business management.' He had worked out a system, based on a strict analysis of the business – of turnover, gross profit, wages and other expenses and the resultant net profit – having decided what the minimum must be to make it a viable proposition. He applied this yardstick to compare one operation with another by the use of percentages or ratios. 'They are still the basics of the business,' he says. 'The system has been refined into more statistics, into graphs and so on, which are helping us to do better still. But if that simple system had not been there from the beginning, I would have stayed in two shops, turning up morning, noon and night and asking: "How are you doing, have you taken any money today, can I pay the rent tomorrow?"'

At first he did almost everything himself – 'I learned my catering the hard way' – but as the business prospered he began to look around for other premises and select associates. Some are with him today. The real expansionary phase began after the end of the Second World War, with the purchase of a place called Rainbow Corner off London's Piccadilly Circus. He bought it from what was then Britain's biggest catering group, J. Lyons. To Lyons, Rainbow Corner was a small unit in a very large organization. To Forte, it was his biggest venture by far and, he says, 'we put in everything we had and everything we then knew. We were emotionally involved in its success, and that was the beginning of our growth.' It was also a good example of how that growth has been financed. The basis of Forte's financing is still a) a certain cash flow, b) 'a bank that has always been good to us', c) financing the business through property purchases. Rainbow Corner cost £30,000, but Forte had only a few thousand pounds. 'We went to the Prudential Assurance Company and said: Here are our accounts, we are making good profits for a small company; and here are our references. If we take a tenancy at so much a year, would you advance us £30,000 on the property on a lease-back arrangement?' They did. 'I have never lost a deal yet because of lack of money,' Forte told the magazine *Management Today* in 1969. 'I have always managed to find money, although sometimes it has been extremely difficult. I have been thrown out of the back door of several insurance companies and one or two banks. But the proposition always held water, and my own bank – the Clydesdale Bank – has never said No.' The great financial advantage in the catering business, Forte added, 'is that we have credit on one side – facilities of at least four weeks, and sometimes six weeks, from suppliers: on the other side we have an immediate cash flow in payment for goods on the spot. Very considerable stocks have to be carried, but we try to keep them at the lowest possible level. We try and extend credit subject to the availability of discounts. If by paying four weeks sooner we can get $2\frac{1}{2}$ per cent discount, we take it. But with the small supplier we pay, if necessary, daily or weekly. If you keep anybody waiting, keep I C I or Lever Brothers waiting, but never the small man: he needs the money.'

With Rainbow Corner doing well, Forte's next step was to buy a much more substantial establishment, the Criterion. 'That was a big deal for us,' he says. 'We had to have courage. I am not sure that I would have had the same courage if I had been on my own. But with four or five other people you can get together and say, "Look, why do you think we can use this? Where are we going to get a chap to run it?" Then somebody says, "Maybe so-and-so can do it." Gradually you find that the operation is quite simple.' Soon afterwards he made a successful take-over bid for a company called Slater and Bodega, which owned a number of restaurants. 'We did that partially with the help of brewers who are still our suppliers. That is a policy I believe in: if somebody helps you, help them back as much as you can.' The company had become run down, with very valuable properties but little business. 'The part of the finance not arranged with the brewers was provided by the bank. Since banks can only give bridging finance, I had to arrange, first, that the money would be provided in due course by the brewers, who guaranteed the transaction up to a point on the security of the properties. The bank then let me have £2¼ million and I made the bid – but only after dealing with the chairman and making sure that he would recommend the deal to shareholders.'

Forte also acquired the Café Royal, one of London's most prestigious restaurants, and in 1962 his company 'went public'. This is always a milestone for self-made men, partly because it allows them to turn some of their assets into cash (by selling shares on the Stock Market) and partly because it brings in outside partners – investors – for the first time. Many entrepreneurs find it hard to cope with the transition; after a while, they take their money and run. Others see it as a useful (and logical) base for further expansion: a public company finds it easier to raise money for big deals than a privately owned concern. Forte belonged to the latter; he had no intention of pulling out and devoting the rest of his life to the pursuit of pleasure in the Italian sun. The shares did well enough at first but fell sharply afterwards. Forte, an emotional man, at first saw it as a personal affront but told himself that it was simply a market reaction and nothing to do with the basic health of the business. 'I knew we had a solid and safe business, based on assets. We deal in nothing which is not based on solid assets.'

This approach – music to banks and insurance companies – helped him with his next big move. A property developer came to Forte and asked how much he wanted for his lease on Rainbow Corner and adjacent sites. He sold it to him for £460,000 and bought his first hotel, The Waldorf, with the money. 'We didn't know much about hotels then,' he admits, 'but we knew about controls and we knew about catering, and it was the Waldorf's success which led us into hotels.' Various other deals followed – deals which took Forte into entertainment, airline and motorway catering, and the manufacture of chocolate and candy as well as the hotel business. In 1970 the company merged with an old-established hotel group, Trust Houses Limited, and within a year he was involved in two major battles: the first a dispute about policy with the head of Trust Houses, and the second a massive take-over bid by Allied Breweries. Forte won both, at considerable personal expense.

But the episode which, for me, says most about the man is his acquisition of three of the best hotels in Paris—the Plaza-Athénée, the George V, and La Tremoille. They belonged to Madame Dupré, a very charming but elusive widow who had always refused to meet anybody; she left it to her solicitors and accountants. A rival British hotelier, Max Joseph, was trying to buy the hotels from her but couldn't agree on the price. When he dropped out, Forte moved in. 'We looked at the figures and at the hotels and stayed there for several days—I had known them well already as a customer, with no intention of buying. We concluded that this was a worthwhile deal. But how to do it? Although we had no experience of finding money abroad we actually raised $22 million. I then approached Madame Dupré and eventually met her one evening in her house in Paris. I convinced her that we were serious, and I was also able to prove that we had the money in hand. Of course, when this came to the knowledge of the staff, they started agitating. Their leader, the head porter of the Plaza-Athénée, claimed that British control would debase the standards of the hotels. But we managed to persuade them that they had no need to worry.' The negotiations lasted about a year and he frequently thought of giving up. But he persisted. 'The turning point came when Madame Dupré said to me, "My solicitors will see you this evening at six o'clock. My accountants will be there and so on." She was never there. So I said, "Madame Dupré, at six o'clock this evening, either you are in my solicitor's office with me to discuss this matter or I am going back on the first plane I can get, and the deal is off." That persuaded her to turn up. We had the usual backwards and forwards argument for three or four hours: it didn't finish there. We had to meet again next morning. She said: "I am not going to come tomorrow," and

I said, "Well, neither am I." She got the deal off the table immediately.' One of Forte's first actions, after that, was to call in the Plaza-Athénée's head porter and appoint him manager.

Today the group has hotels in places as far apart as Majorca, Nassau, Barbados, Jamaica, Bermuda, Ceylon, and South Africa. In 1972 it joined a consortium to take over and operate the internationally renowned travel firm of Thomas Cook. A year later Forte acquired the American-owned Travelodge International operation, adding a further 460 hotels and motels (in USA, Canada, and Mexico) to his chain. He also bought the world-famous Pierre Hotel in New York. All this activity has, inevitably, brought its share of problems – the hotel business is neither as easy nor as glamorous as it seems – and there are persistent rumours that Forte will, before long, lose the proprietorial control he has maintained ever since his milk bar days. Forte himself often talks about taking life easier (though not about retirement) and in the last few years has devoted more time to his hobbies – fishing, shooting, golf, and music. He admits that he is 'not a one hundred per cent relaxed person', but reckons that any business executive who prides himself on never taking time off is a fool. He detests hanging around airports but enjoys travel. 'I like going to see new places and staying there for a while.'

He and his wife have six children (the eldest, Rocco, works for the company and speaks fluent French and Italian) and summer holidays are usually spent on a boat – he refuses to call it a yacht – in the Mediterranean. The boat/yacht has a crew of five and sleeps twelve: it's his home for six weeks every year. He likes to get up early, around seven, and to have a leisurely breakfast on deck. He'll go through all the English newspapers he can get and a few Italian papers too. There is a radio telephone to keep him in touch with the office, which he does on most days 'out of curiosity'. He likes to swim, water-ski, and read historical biographies. He has also been known to invade the galley. 'I'm not a cook,' he says, 'but I *can* cook. There are one or two recipes I am quite good at. What are they? Well, there's a nice spaghetti sauce. Take some good quality olive oil, some butter, and some finely chopped onions. Let that simmer until it starts to get brown, season it with salt, pepper and pepperoncini, add fresh tomatoes and tinned tomatoes, and let it bubble. Then put in a bit of parsley. *Magnifico!*'

He has an occasional Scotch and water, but greatly prefers wine to cocktails. He is careful with his health; his day starts with a dozen pressups and he has a whole range of keep-fit gadgets. (He once talked me into buying a rowing machine and almost succeeded in persuading me to add a few dumb-bells as well. Alas, I lack his discipline. The machine is, at best, used once a week.) Money? 'I am anything but frugal in my private life,' he says. 'But I seldom carry much cash and I don't like shopping.' His wife—they were married in 1943—buys nearly all his clothes. He doesn't care for 'terribly vivacious colours' but generally accepts her choice without complaint. He owns a London house filled with lovely things, and estates in Surrey, but he has a puritanical streak that the story of a painting by Lowry illustrates. The painting was a favourite of his (Forte was one of the first to collect Lowry's work) and when a very close friend did him a good turn he decided to give it to him. The friend said he could not possibly accept it. Could he not have one of the Lowry drawings instead? Forte said no, it had to be a painting. Well, said the friend, could he not buy him one when another came up for auction? 'No,' Forte said firmly, 'you must take this one; otherwise it wouldn't hurt me enough.'

Forte can be tough and, at times, maddeningly impatient. 'But,' he says, 'I never raise my voice.' Chefs, kitchen-hands and doormen respect him as a professional who has worked his way up, and find him easy to talk to. Walking through a kitchen with him, as I have done on several occasions, is an enlightening experience: there is nothing, but nothing, which escapes his practised eye. Critics say he is too demanding; Forte counters that in a service industry like catering you have to do your best. He is old-fashioned in his attitude to trade unions ('Why,' he asks in despair whenever the industry is threatened with a strike or go-slow, 'can't we all work together as one big, happy team?') but on the whole labour relations in the company have been very much better than in many other industries. 'The human aspect in business,' he says, 'is vital: you can keep drawing squares and lines, but in these squares you must have people, and the people must be the right people, and they must be deeply involved with the business. If this doesn't happen, then the lines and squares in the diagram mean nothing.'

'I hope,' Nigel Broackes told an interviewer recently, 'that when you write this you will not refer to me as a whiz-kid.' The interviewer, David Brewerton of the London *Daily Telegraph*, said that nothing was further from his mind. The temptation is, nonetheless, considerable because few businessmen have a better claim to that over-used label. Son of a country solicitor and an artist mother from the Wakefield district of Yorkshire, he started work as a four-guinea-a-week insurance clerk and was managing his first public company by the time he was 28. Today, at 41, he is the millionaire chairman of a massive company with 27,000 direct employees and assets of £400 million. He is eminently respectable and holds a number of important jobs in public service.

I first met Broackes many years ago, and wrote about him in my book *Merger Mania*. He has come a long way since then – proof that, despite the alleged death of capitalism, an able young man from a middle-class background can still do remarkably well. Broackes hated life as an insurance clerk ('I felt fearfully cramped and restricted and had a sense of claustrophobia') and unlike so many others in the same position decided to do something about it. His father had died during the war and Nigel had few friends who could lend a helping hand. But he did have one useful asset: his grandfather had left £25,000 in trust for him. The field which attracted him was property: the post-war successes of Jack Cotton, Harry Hyams, Max Rayne and many others showed there was plenty of scope. His first move was to visit the Government's Stationery Office, where he bought all Acts of Parliament affecting property, a manual on company secretarial practice, and sundry other papers that seemed likely to be useful. He used £7,600 to buy two old houses in Chelsea, confidently expecting a quick killing. 'Everything conceivable went wrong,' he recalls. 'It took much longer than I expected and I spent more than I had bargained for.' In the end he was lucky to make a profit of £100. He then tried the hire-purchase business, which was fashionable at the time. Everything went well until one bad debt wiped out the firm's profits and most of his investment. He put another £15,000 into a plastics firm, but this too was proving a disaster. He was just 22, on the point of getting married, and no one would have blamed him if he had gone back to insurance. Instead he joined a West End estate agency to learn thoroughly about property. 'I realised,' he says, 'that I had to stop being an amateur and doing things I understood virtually nothing about. A spell in an estate agency is the best training you can get. It gets you into contact with all sorts of useful people, and shows you how to avoid costly mistakes.' While there, he teamed up with a family friend who was running an investment company in the City. Together they decided to convert a property which Broackes had found in Piccadilly. They formed a company to handle it and, when the project proved to be a great success, Broackes left the agency to become a full-time entrepreneur. Sir Geoffrey Crowther, ex-editor of the *Economist*, joined the board and through him he established a link with Commercial Union Assurance. Crowther, a shrewd judge of men, replied to comments about his lively young associate's age by quoting Pitt the Younger: 'If it's a defect, it is one that time will cure.'

Commercial Union acquired 28 per cent of the company's shares, and agreed to lend up to £500,000 on a debenture. When Broackes went to its offices to collect the cheque, he got talking to the Commercial Union's company secretary. The upshot of their conversation was his first take-over bid. Commercial Union, he discovered, owned a company called Westminster and Kensington Freeholds, which it seemed to regard as something of a nuisance. Broackes, then 27, thought it had considerable potential and asked if it was for sale. Commercial Union said it was but that it would prefer to invite tenders from several other parties to see what price it would get. Broackes offered £3,345,000, a sum which everyone knew he hadn't got, and was accepted. He raised the money by persuading the seller to put up almost 100 per cent of the purchase price! The company was renamed Trafalgar House and was publicly floated in July 1963 – as a prelude to no less than three simultaneous take-overs. The first he went after were under the same management, and Broackes got a frosty reception. Undeterred, he began to buy shares in the market and arranged to borrow up to £8 million from Barclays Bank on the guarantee of his merchant bankers, Kleinwort Benson, who fully shared the Commercial Union's faith in his judgment. The subsequent battle naturally attracted a good deal of attention. It ended with Broackes getting his hands on only one of the three, but he was able to meet the £4·6 million cost partly by selling the shares he had bought in the other two at a handsome profit.

Not long after that I spent several hours interviewing him for a series called 'The First £100,000 and How to Make it', which I was writing for the London *Evening Standard*. He came out with a lot of useful advice. 'If you have to start from scratch,' he said, 'join a good agency, as I did, and get to know its bank manager. Get him to acquire respect for your judgement but don't let him know your aspirations at once. Do one thing at a time. After a year or two, go and have a talk with him. If he's formed a good impression, and you have an attractive project, he will probably take a chance. Pick a suitable site for your first venture, and make sure you build the kind of place that will sell quickly. Never get stuck with something that won't move – it affects your reputation. I can't stress this too much. Your reputation, at this stage, is all-important and you can't afford to make a mistake. Once you do well, you get plenty of offers – but you must never risk spoiling your credit rating. Don't go to small builders or unknown architects. And don't get greedy: it wasn't until I stopped concentrating on making money that I really started to make it.' Broackes went on to say that he possessed considerable self-confidence, but that it had needed a lot of topping up at first. He didn't find it easy to make friends. 'I tend,' he told me, 'to be autocratic, impatient, and very wrapped up in business.'

In 1967, Broackes made a successful bid for one of Britain's oldest and most successful construction companies, Trollope and Colls. Founded in 1778, Trollope was the kind of firm to whom the whole business of bids and mergers was anathema. Lord Mais, the chairman, loftily declared that under the youthful Broackes 'our image and client relationship would never be the same'. But the company had been doing poorly and a loss was expected in 1967; shareholders decided to take the offer. Broackes was less fortunate when, a year later, he decided to have a go at a still bigger outfit – the giant City of London Real Property Group. This time he came up against a shrewd and powerful rival, Sir Harold Samuel, then the world's biggest property developer and one of the most successful of the post-war take-over tycoons. Samuel's bid for C L R P was more than £160 million and won the day.

More recently, Broackes has branched out into various other fields, with his most notable deal the acquisition, a few years ago, of the famous Cunard liner fleet and freight line. Cunard was in a bad way when he appeared on the scene but it had formidable assets and, with its history of losses, had built up tax credits with the Inland Revenue. 'We have never sought to acquire something by purchase or by take-over just for a quick turn,' Broackes insists. 'In fact we never took anything which we did not think we could provide with continuing management and improve. That is a point of philosophy and intellectual approach to the whole business. I like to think we have an integrity here which really does coincide with the national interest. We have not been short-term opportunists.' This, he believes, is the most important reason why Trafalgar has prospered where so many others have failed. Another is that, when it was decided to diversify into more management situations, he recognized that while he was 'the thinker, the entrepreneur'. he wasn't cut out to be the manager of large numbers of people. 'I never wanted to have a one-man band which would have been vulnerable to investment assessment, to my being run over by a bus, or to pride. I wanted to be the person who really had caused an important development in the corporate sense to have happened. This called for other people.'

Broackes became full-time chairman and an able associate, Victor Mathews, was made sole managing director. Mathews and another associate, Eric Parker, now look after day-to-day running of the company. It enables Broackes to be more relaxed, to take more time off for holidays and the like. He has a villa in the south of France, which he likes 'for a month or two a year', and a country house at Wargrave complete with swimming pool. (He also owned a farm once but, he says, 'it did not grip me at all'.) He and his ex-model wife Joyce have three children and he maintains that his devotion to business ('I used to work like a fiend') has helped rather than marred his domestic life. 'If I had a less active business life I might have been in my private life more bad-tempered, more errant. A busy commercial life has kept me very happy – and consequently my family.'

At 41, Broackes has no urge to start again and build another business. This is partly because having done once what he set out to do, he doubts that he could do it again. 'This is partly a reflection on me, partly a reflection on how things have changed in twenty years.' But retirement is far from his mind. 'I would not,' he told the *Telegraph*'s David Brewerton, 'expect ever to retire. But I suppose most people say that. I certainly have no plans to go off and live in the Bahamas or the south of France or anything like that – ever.' Brewerton asked him if he wanted to take on more public work and he said he wouldn't rule it out. 'But,' he added, 'a lot of public jobs are totally thankless. It is the way to break your heart. I am not interested in that and am under no pressure to do it.'

Chapter Three
One-Track Minds

Like it or not, there is such a thing as a Millionaire
Mentality.
PAUL GETTY

All these men have certain things in common – self-confidence,
enthusiasm, and a tremendous capacity for hard work. But, of
course, that alone doesn't constitute a success formula. A great
many people have the same qualities and still can't manage
to reach the millionaire class. If I had to add just one other
factor I would say 'concentration'. Most of us spend a great
deal of energy – nervous and physical – on quite unconnected
things. We worry about train timetables, blocked drainpipes,
unpaid bills, shopping lists, and the weather. We spend hours
watching television, doing the crossword, or reading books. We
fret about the telephone service, newspaper articles, and stupid
people on the road. By the end of the day we sink exhaustedly
into bed. Our batteries have run down. We've had a busy day.
The really successful tycoon is different. He worries too – but,
by and large, he is more single-minded. His business is all. And
faced with a problem, he will tackle it with a dogged concentration that leaves room for little else. Few could tell you, honestly,
why they are like that. In some cases, it probably goes back
to a deep-seated inferiority complex. A fierce determination
burns within them to prove a point – and they know, from hours
of quiet self-appraisal, that they must pool all they've got, and
channel it into one direction, if they want to score with sufficiently impressive force.

One comes across this single-mindedness, this ability to concentrate, in self-made men all over the world. In Japan a few
years ago I went to see Soichiro Honda, head of the motor com-

pany that bears his name. An American-educated PR man collected me in a Mercedes, and explained that the boss rarely appeared at his head office. 'The presidential suite is always empty,' he said. 'Mr Honda says it's a most uncomfortable place. Everyone is wearing a suit and tie, and the atmosphere is very formal. He much prefers putting on a white overall and cap, working among the 800 technicians employed on basic research. The actual running of the business is left to bankers and accountants: Mr Honda feels every man should concentrate on the things he can do best.'

When we got there, I was surprised to see the entrance draped with a Union Jack and a large message, in gold letters, over the door: 'Welcome, Mr Davis', it said. The PR man said this was one of Mr Honda's favourite gimmicks. 'He keeps flags of every nation, except of course Red China and the Iron Curtain countries.' I was shown into a small room and given a moment to study a large notice on the wall. It was headed 'Management Policy' and listed five points: proceed always with ambition and youthfulness; respect sound theory, develop fresh ideas and make the most effective use of time; enjoy your work and always brighten your working atmosphere; strive constantly for a harmonious flow of work; be ever mindful of the value of research and endeavour. There was a polite knock at the door, and Honda came in, dressed in overalls – a small man with rosy cheeks, a healthy tan and a mouthful of gold teeth. We settled down to discussing some of his unorthodox views on Japanese attitudes – the general worship of educational qualifications, for example. 'I am not impressed by diplomas,' he said. 'They don't do the work. I went to a technical high school, but was dismissed. I was 28 when I joined, and I had already held down a job. I attended only the classes I wanted to go to. Other students memorized the lessons, but I compared them with my practical experience. My marks were not as good as those of others, and I did not take the final examination. The principal called me in and said I had to leave. I told him I didn't want a diploma. They had less value than a cinema ticket. A ticket at least guaranteed that you would get in. A diploma guaranteed nothing.' Education, said Honda, was important. But he disliked people who had 'a sense of *élite*' because they went to college. I asked him how he felt about the Japanese seniority system, under which promotion is governed by length of service rather than merit. He said he hated it. 'I promote by ability. Many people take pride in saying, at their retirement ceremony, that they got through their working lives without making mistakes. I prefer them to say they made many errors, but always tried to advance. People who never made mistakes simply did what their boss told them to do. They are not the kind I want.' What qualities did he look for? 'First,' he said, 'I try to find out what a man is good at, and whether he has ideas of his own. Then I assess whether he can get along with others. A man must have self-confidence, but he must be modest enough to learn from others.' And the secrets of his own success? 'Imagination, resourcefulness, fresh ideas, sound theories, and economy of time. Life is based on seeing, listening and experimenting. But experimenting is the most important. This company has grown to today's dimensions because it had no traditions.'

Japan, he went on, had done well out of losing the war. 'We'd never have had the freedom we have now. I'd never have been allowed to get where I have got. With everything flattened, we could start from scratch, plan from the word go and think big. You can see it in Tokyo to this day: the blitzed areas are now booming, but those which escaped are backward. I love this new freedom. It allows me to go down to the shop floor. I couldn't bear sitting in my presidential suite, as I should have had to do in an old-fashioned firm, supposing I had risen to the top.'

Despite Honda's liberal views on education, today's candidates for employment with the firm have to take a competitive examination. They spend one morning on an essay, and another on a stiff oral exam. 'If I had to go through that,' said Honda, 'I wouldn't pass.' The PR man claimed that workers were well looked after, and pointed out that they could buy shares in the company. Honda himself said several times that, in his view, profits must be shared between employees and management. One had to strive for higher profits 'so that both the company and its workers can progress'. He thought expense account living – very much a feature of the Japanese scene – was all right provided it helped the company, but it wasn't fair for bosses to throw around money earned collectively. He did not believe in long business lunches himself, and his night life was 'under the control of Mrs Honda'. But he did go to geisha parties. 'Now that I have met you,' he said, 'you will be my excuse.' He laughed uproariously at these cracks, but became serious again when I asked him whether he believed in firing inefficient people. 'Some people,' he replied, 'are efficient, others less so. Firing a man creates a serious social problem. If someone proves inefficient, I give him an assignment where he can use his limited capacity to the maximum. Dismissal is possible only when someone causes serious damage and loss to the company, or in the case of a serious moral wrong.'

We turned to his own attitude towards money. Wealth, he said, gave him the freedom to do what he wanted to do – which, in his case, meant experimenting with new ideas. He didn't get much time for leisure ('The fellows here are such slave drivers') and he didn't have a yacht or anything like that. 'I have three cars – a Lotus Élite, a Fiat and a Honda sports car. But I drive them myself. My house? Yes, it's large and luxurious. When I go abroad I get invited to a lot of big houses, and I have to have somewhere to entertain people who come to Tokyo.'

I asked him if he thought it difficult for a brilliant young man to repeat his success story – given that in Japan, as in Britain, the trend was towards giant industrial groups. He said it would be very difficult. 'When I started, a knowledge of machinery was enough. Today everything is so terribly complicated, and the competition is tremendous.' What advice would he give to his sons? 'Simply to do what they would like to do. One must be happy at work. That's the most important thing of all.'

A day or two after seeing Honda, I interviewed another prominent Japanese – Masaru Ibuka, the founder of Sony.

Ibuka began as an obscure inventor after graduating in engineering at Waseda University in 1933, and has always been strongly interested in research. He has more than fifty patents to his credit. Unlike most inventors, he was fortunate enough to find a business partner early on who had an equal flair for finance and salesmanship. They met during the Second World War on a Japanese navy research project, and in 1946 set up operations in a single room in a bombed-out Tokyo department store building. Their starting capital was only £200, but their venture was grandly named The Tokyo Telecommunications Company. Raw materials were scarce and, Ibuka told me, 'we were forced to do everything just to live'. The experience taught him that 'it is easier to earn a living by doing something others are not doing'. It remained his guiding principle.

Ibuka's lucky break came in 1952 when, on a business trip to the United States, he first saw the transistor and recognized its commercial possibilities. Western Electric, which held the patent, opposed him when he told them of his plans to make transistors for radios, but he went ahead all the same. The task proved far more difficult than he had expected. But he pressed on. Like Honda Ibuka decided, at an early stage, that his strength lay in finding and developing new ideas and that the business side ought to be left to others. Like Honda, he greeted me in overalls. 'In my field,' he said, 'research and development cannot be left to a department. This is one of the big mistakes so often made in Europe. I take the view that the president, or chairman, must be directly in charge of it. He must recognise its importance, and push it in the right direction.' He showed me his latest products and talked enthusiastically about the future. Leisure? 'I love golf, but I haven't had much chance to play lately. I also like to go to the cinema, but I'm lucky to make it once a month.' He had no serious regrets, though. 'I still want to do so much,' he said.

It is a comment I have heard countless times since. If there is such a thing as the 'millionaire mentality' – as Paul Getty insists there is – this willingness to forgo everyday pleasures is certainly a major part of it. You may find it distasteful, and you may even feel sorry for them, but it is patently absurd to dismiss people like Honda and Ibuka (or, for that matter, Lew Grade and Charles Forte) as the grasping, greedy money maniacs of popular fiction. They sincerely believe that they have a strong creative urge – the kind of absorbing, highly individual need for self-expression that drives on painters, sculptors and good writers. They do not chase money as such.

In Hong Kong, early in 1976, I met another typical example: Run Run Shaw, the man who launched the Kung-fu cult. Shaw (Run Run, he explained, means 'square, sincere, honest' in Chinese) is a shrewd, tough multi-millionaire who has spent fifty years in show business and, today, is one of the world's most successful film-makers. He and his brother, Runme, who looks after the Singapore end of a business that also takes in 141 cinemas and theatres, amusement parks, real estate concerns, hotels, banks and insurance companies, were born into a theatrical family in Shanghai in 1907. Their parents owned and operated one of the live theatres there. In 1929 the brothers left for Singapore, where they bought their first cinema. Run Run went to Hong Kong in 1959 to set up Shaw's Movie Town. His first film was a musical called *Kingdom and Beauty* and it proved to be an instant success. The Chinese film industry was in poor shape at the time. Most films were badly made: they were shot in seven days and released only at third-rate theatres. Naturally the revenue was also low: in Hong Kong Chinese films produced only 10 per cent of the total revenue of all the movie theatres. Shaw decided to make better films and to concentrate on all-out action. 'I am convinced,' he says, 'that action pictures are what people in this part of the world want to see. In the West there was a time when Biblical pictures were all the rage. Then it was the James Bond type action and the traditional Westerns boosted into modern sagas. In our case we had the sword fights and, more recently, Kung-fu. They are action pictures presented in a different way. People like excitement.'

Shaw's Movie Town has a permanent staff of 1,500 and covers sixty acres bordering on Clearwater Bay. Run Run Shaw makes the final decision on all the scripts, the cast and the budget. Each production calls for a minimum of forty days shooting. By Hollywood standards the cost is still remarkably low: the annual outlay on all forty films equals some $10 million (US), all of which comes from the Shaw family's own resources. His critics accuse him of underpaying his stars, and indeed Western stars like Paul Newman and Steve McQueen would be appalled by the kind of money he offers. So would American and European trade unions. 'Here,' Shaw says happily, 'I don't have to worry about unions.' A phenomenal worker himself, Shaw likes to be at his desk by 7.00 a.m., after spending an hour or so reading scripts in bed ('It's the best time to read scripts') and he works until late in the day. 'I don't find work a hardship,' he says. 'I enjoy it.' He does, however, insist on taking a short nap after lunch and, at 69, he is a keep-fit enthusiast. 'I do half an hour's shadow boxing every morning,' he told me. 'And I do a thousand arm swings. Yes, a *thousand*. It's what kept Mao fit for so many years, did you know that? Here, let me show you. Stand with your legs slightly apart and bend your knees. Keep your body straight. Now swing your arms back and forth – 30 degrees at the front, 70 degrees at the back. Got that? Start with 100 swings at first. You'll be amazed how good you'll feel after a few weeks.'

Apart from the film business, the amusement parks, the hotels and banks, Shaw is involved in all kinds of charitable organizations, and they take up an increasing amount of time. He is, among other things, President of the Hong Kong Red Cross and Chairman of the Arts Festival. Launched in 1972, the Festival is now a firmly established feature of the Hong Kong scene and draws visitors from farther afield, especially from India, Thailand, and Japan. The standard is impressively high, and Shaw is very much an involved and active chairman, as well as a generous financial supporter. He has been keen to introduce a much greater Chinese content into the festival, to involve the Chinese community and to 'activate a process of cross-fertilisation'. East and West do meet at festival time.

Shaw's films, which help to finance this cultural beano, have no aim other than to entertain. While Moura Lympany was playing Rachmaninov and Keith Michel declaimed Shakespeare at City Hall, Shaw's studios were filming a Kung-fu film and a story about turn-of-the-century prostitution. In Shaw's offices I saw posters with typical titles: *Spirit of the Raped*, *Forbidden Past*. Critics say there is too much sex and violence. The films I saw did indeed seem to be extraordinarily bloodthirsty. But this, it seems, is how Chinese audiences like it – and there is a Government censor to keep an eye on the whole business.

Shaw wears sober grey business suits and quiet ties, even on Sundays, and talks so quietly that it is sometimes difficult to hear what he has to say. He looks more like a shy bookkeeper than a successful tycoon: if you met him on one of Hong Kong's crowded buses you wouldn't give him a second glance. Shaw says he likes it that way. He hates pretence, dislikes making speeches, and makes a point of sitting unobtrusively among film-goers at the opening of every one of the forty films his studios make each year. 'This business,' he says, 'is all guesswork. You have to keep in touch with the tastes and attitudes of ordinary people. It helps to watch an audience, to listen to their comments. Perhaps I'm lucky; I guess a little better than others.'

We went down into the basement of his house, where he has a comfortable and well-equipped cinema. It was party time. Shaw, a restless and attentive host, had invited local friends and members of the Chichester Festival Theatre to lunch and a private showing of a British film, *Conduct Unbecoming*. Watching films, he said in that soft voice, was his only hobby. Rumour has it that he is also fond of female company, and, of course, there is no shortage of glamorous girls at Shaw's Movie Town. But he refused to be drawn on that one. 'I am very happy with my wife,' he said, pausing only seconds before adding: 'I have two sons who have graduated from Oxford and two daughters who have graduated from Brynmawr University, Philadelphia. I have nine grandchildren. I have a happy family.' He also has five homes (two in Hong Kong, one in Singapore, one in

Penang, another in Kuala Lumpur) and a fine collection of Chinese porcelain, paintings and jade.

I asked him if, at 69, he had given any thought to retirement. 'No,' he said. 'I don't think one should retire. I am so used to working ... I couldn't live without work.' But didn't he think that, perhaps, he ought to slow down? 'I don't see why. I'd like to do more charitable work ... my brother and I have created the Asian Foundation and want to expand that side. We have given a lot of money to hospitals, schools, and other institutions. We want to give more.' (One recent gift, not mentioned by him, was a cheque for more than a million US dollars for Hong Kong's new Arts Centre.) No doubt there are people – in Hong Kong as elsewhere – who would like to see the Shaws of this world replaced by state corporations, turning out propaganda films. There is no shortage of them in communist China, a short distance away. But there is nothing to stop a state corporation competing with Run Run, just as other film makers compete with him now. He has made a fortune, to be sure, but in doing so has given pleasure to millions of people and provided talented performers with a chance to shine. How many of us can say the same?

It may be that, in thirty or forty years time, entrepreneurs will no longer have a place even in Hong Kong. All the odds seem against them. More and more Asian countries are turning communist, and in Hong Kong the lease on the New Territories runs out in 1997. If Peking wanted to grab the colony it could do so right now: the few thousand British troops still stationed there would not be able to stop them. And yet Shaw, like most of the colony's wealthy entrepreneurs, is not fussed about the future. 'We just don't talk about it,' he told me. The tiny colony, half the size of an English county, buys some £700 million worth of goods from China every year and the money enables Peking to buy needed Western technology. The need is likely to continue for some time to come; as Shaw sees it, this is the best possible guarantee against a sudden acquisition.

To visitors, the Hong Kong of today seems to come closer to Adam Smith's concept of pure capitalism than anywhere else. Its formula is simple: low taxes, few controls, hard work, and quick profits. The pace of life is as hectic as in New York and communist China is, paradoxically, very much part of it. Peking has learned all the capitalist tricks and doesn't hesitate to put them on display: it operates more than fifty Hong Kong department stores and a number of banks and insurance companies, publishing houses and restaurants. (The manager of the Bank of China keeps a benevolent eye on the whole business from a plush penthouse overlooking the swimming pool of the Hong Kong Hilton.) There are slums, of course, but the same is still true of Shanghai and the Hong Kong Government is making strenuous efforts to solve the housing problem. Much of the $4\frac{1}{2}$ million population – an impossible number for so small a place – consists of refugees from the mainland. They all came of their own free will and they prefer to stay. By Western standards, people are still overworked and underpaid but by Asian standards they are not doing at all badly: wages are estimated to be the second highest, after Japan. Labour disputes are the exception rather than the rule.

It would be easy to write a critical book about Hong Kong, if one wished, but not even the most severe critic would deny that this is a remarkably vigorous community – living evidence of what Chinese talent and energy can achieve under a free enterprise system. It *ought* not to work, in the turbulent seventies, but it does. I have visited Hong Kong four times in the past fourteen years, and on every occasion I have marvelled at the ingenuity, industry, and vivacity of the people. I have also, to be honest, enjoyed the benefits free enterprise has to offer: excellent service, decisiveness, and encouraging receptiveness to new ideas.

Next to Run Run Shaw (or ahead of him, according to one's taste) the most noteworthy entrepreneur produced by the colony is, by general agreement, a shipowner called Y.K. (for Yue-kong) Pao. In just over two decades in the business he has built a seagoing empire that is larger than the fleets of either the legendary golden Greeks, Stavros Niarchos or the late Aristotle Onassis; before long, he will own more ships than both of their lines combined. And in terms of total tonnage, Pao is on the verge of amassing a fleet that approaches the size of the entire Soviet merchant marine. Pao began his working life in pre-communist China as a bank clerk, rising to number two in a big Shanghai bank not long before the People's Republic came into being in 1949. He recalls his undistinguished school-days in Ningpo, a seaport near Shanghai, where he was born in 1918, saying he was not a good student 'but very ambitious to be a very good sportsman'. When the communists took over mainland China, Pao and his family escaped to Hong Kong with enough capital to start anew. By 1955, aged 37, he made the momentous decision to plunge into a profession in which he frankly concedes he had no experience and absolutely no expertise. 'My father was very much against it when I proposed to do shipping,' he says. 'He would like me to do real estate business.'

Pao sent away to London for basic books on ship chartering and maritime banking and a bevy of how-to-do-it manuals on running a ship. Armed with his new knowledge, he bought a 27-year-old, second-hand coal-burning steamer which he optimistically named *Golden Alpha* – and promptly chartered it to Tokyo's Yamashika Line to carry coal from India to Japan. Unlike other shipowners, who often branch off into sidelines, he has stuck with single-minded purpose to tankers and bulk carriers, a field of expertise that is compact enough to allow him to oversee virtually every aspect of his operations. Totally dedicated to ships and shipping, he is on call twenty-four hours a day, fifty-one weeks a year (with only Christmas off for a holi-day with his wife, Sue-ing, usually in Hawaii). Pao's travel sche-dule would leave most people exhausted: he spends up to three-quarters of his time visiting distant points of the globe, and he combats jet-lag simply by forcing himself to adapt to local time whenever he lands. And wherever he is, he gets in an early morning swim (another jet-lag antidote) and, as he proudly points out, he takes his skipping rope everywhere.

For all his activity, friends find Pao a surprisingly relaxed man who never shows signs of strain or rush. 'He has remarkable powers of concentration,' his son-in-law told *Time* not long ago. 'For five minutes he will concentrate on a personal problem; in the next five minutes he will straighten out an engineering hitch and five minutes after that he will be working on the complexities of an insurance contract.' And Pao himself gives every indication of revelling in his work. 'Very exciting; every day different; banking, charters, staff, customers, ships. As things get bigger, more complex, they get better.' He is, of course, a multi-millionaire but says he can't remember when he made his first million or, indeed, how many millions (be it sterling, US or Hong Kong dollars) he is worth today. He doesn't carry cash around in his pocket – 'I always borrow money from my driver to pay for my haircut' – and doesn't throw his money around in the flamboyant style of an Onassis. As he puts it: 'It's better, I think, not to remember how much money you have, so you still have to work hard.'

Chapter Four
Do It Now!

Desire is the beginning of all human achievement.
W. CLEMENT STONE

Clearly, then, F. Scott Fitzgerald was right: the rich *are* different. But the people he had in mind were different again from those we have discussed. The rich, he wrote, 'possess and enjoy early, and it does something to them, makes them soft where we are hard, and cynical where we are trustful, in a way that, unless you were born rich, it is difficult to understand. They think, deep in their hearts, that they are better than we are because we had to discover the compensations and refuges of life for ourselves. Even when they enter deep into our world or sink below us, they still think that they are better than we are ...'

Fitzgerald was referring to inherited wealth and, of course, in the California of his day there was no shortage of people who fitted his description. Nor is there today. But it certainly doesn't apply to the rich as a whole. In the USA alone, some 5,000 people become millionaires every year (according to the Internal Revenue Service) and most of them get there by their own efforts. The economic environment has become more and more difficult as the twentieth century has progressed – personal taxes have increased enormously and business laws have been tightened – but there are still men making fortunes. Most of them will spend the rest of their lives protecting and, if possible, expanding the business they have built, giving themselves little time to enjoy their new-found prosperity.

I have no wish to stop them (they do, after all, provide prosperity for many others in the process) but my sympathies lie with the people who see money as a means to an end, not an end in itself. 'Increased means and increased leisure,' said Disraeli in 1872, 'are the two civilizers of man.' It doesn't always work that way, but one can't quarrel with his basic premise. 'Increased means and increased leisure' has enabled generations of rich people to devote time and care to beautiful things: magnificent houses, splendid gardens, great paintings. We still derive enormous benefit from their enthusiasm. Walk around any museum and look at the treasures they have left us, and ask yourself what there would be to see if communism had arrived a few centuries earlier. Socialists can sneer at the 'toys of the rich', if they like, but the world would be a poorer place without them. Medici money financed the work of some of the greatest artists in history; Rockefeller money has financed some of the finest work of the twentieth century *and* paid for the restoration of places like Colonial Williamsburg. The whims of the rich have often been delightfully impractical. Who would build the Taj Mahal in India today? Who in Britain would construct a Hampton Court or a Blenheim? Who would commission artists and craftsmen to paint the ceiling of the Sistine chapel, or pay a goldsmith to devote years to creating a magnificent church door? Compare the modern work in any gallery or museum in Moscow, Leningrad, Budapest, or East Berlin and you can't help regretting the demise of wealthy, eccentric individualists in those so-called civilizations.

I accept that we can't all lead a leisurely life devoted to art but it is one of the great merits of the free enterprise system that each and every one can acquire the means to try. The idea that the worker is excluded from this is a socialist myth. Countless rich, successful men have come from humble beginnings – as Andrew Carnegie, Andrew Mellon, Henry Ford, and Joseph Kennedy did before them. Many left school at an early age. Lower down the financial scale, countless people have made a modest fortune and devoted the rest of their lives to developing whatever artistic talents they have. It is clearly impossible for everyone to do the same, and not everyone even wants to try. But it's important that the opportunity should exist.

By Disraeli's standards, we have all come a long way since 1872. Increased means have bought not only cars but increased leisure. 'Man' – a term which we may safely assume includes both miners and professors – has indeed become more civilized. If we do not always acknowledge that this adds up to progress it is partly because we tend to measure progress by the balance of payments or the GNP. 'Increased means and increased leisure' are taken as signs of decadence rather than of advancement. If a worker wants more money, he is 'rocking the boat'. And if he uses his extra pay to buy more leisure (just as rich men use their leisure to buy freedom from work) he is 'wrecking the country'. We don't applaud him for making the most of his short life; 'laziness' is portrayed as a sin. I have always thought this absurd, and still do so. There is no merit in hard work as such: men do not live to work, but work to live. I am on the side of anyone who chooses to lead a fuller life, *providing* he does not attempt to do so at my expense.

It means, among other things, that I am also on the side of rich men who pass on money to their children – and children who accept it. I see no reason to condemn a millionaire for looking after his family. Tax him, by all means, but don't pass moral judgments. Most of us would behave exactly the same if we were in their shoes. Youth should be enjoyed. My father was a poorly paid civil servant for most of his working life, so I had to fend for myself after leaving school at 15. But I certainly would not have rejected the opportunities that wealth can provide: a round-the-world trip at 21, say, or five years devoted to studying a non-commercial subject like painting. And I am not envious of those who enjoy the privileges money can buy. Being born rich is not always an unqualified blessing. To 'possess and enjoy early' may lead to a good deal of unhappiness – difficult marriages, drug or alcohol addiction, alienation from parents and childhood friends. The life stories of Doris Duke and Barbara Hutton show what can happen if one inherits too much, too soon. Even at work, being the boss's son is not necessarily the great boon people imagine. Indeed it may be a handicap: you may have to work twice as hard to overcome the natural scepticism of your colleagues. Nepotism, like everything else, is not what it was. 'This is my son,' the caricature chairman tells the office dogsbody. 'I want him to start at the bottom and work his way up. Make sure he is in the boardroom on the twelfth floor by five o'clock.' It still happens, of course, but not nearly as often as you may think. A lot of rich young men spend years trying to prove – to themselves, to their friends, and above all to their fathers – that they are as able and competent as people who have made it on their own. It often means working longer hours, for less pay, than the rest of the staff. Self-made millionaires expect a lot from their sons: ask David Rockefeller.

C. Northcote Parkinson has argued (in *Punch* and therefore not too seriously) that an even greater handicap than being born rich is to be the product of 'respectable parents in Ealing'. Never to have known the spur of poverty, he says, 'is an initial disadvantage, made insurmountable for the poor fool who rebels half-heartedly in hippy style. Add to this the fetters of a university degree and financial success recedes in proportion to the grade achieved. What finally kills all initiative is the legacy from Aunt Hilda. For who would dare gamble with the money saved over his lifetime by the late Uncle Oswald? It is not so much a legacy as a trust for the next generation. Who are we to squander what we know to have been so laboriously earned? There is nothing in the world to stop the able boy from the comfortable home becoming an admiral, an ambassador, a vice-chancellor or a bishop. Success in many a different guise may be within his grasp. All this, however, has nothing to do with making money. When it comes to the pursuit of wealth he is crippled at the outset, lacking sufficient incentive and manacled by the fear of losing what he has. To the question of why I'm not rich my short answer is that I came from too respectable a home.'

As excuses go, this is as good as any I have ever heard. But there are plenty of people who have managed to overcome even this particular handicap. The reality – still – is that anyone can join the race if he has a mind to. One's background is obviously a factor, but you don't *have* to be rich, poor, or respectable to have a go.

Let us, for a moment, look at some of the advice handed out by the rich themselves. The late Paul Getty maintained that no one could achieve any real and lasting success or get rich in business by being a conformist. A businessman who wants to be successful 'cannot afford to imitate others or to squeeze his thoughts and actions into trite and shopworn moulds. He must be an original, imaginative, resourceful and entirely self-reliant entrepreneur.' Characteristically, Getty had always looked upon bad times as periods of great opportunity. He recalled buying the Hotel Pierre, on Manhattan's Fifth Avenue, for a bargain price, at a time when 'the gloom-and-doom chaps were too busy titillating their masochistic streaks with pessimistic predictions of worse times to come to recognise such bargains as this when they saw them'. The majority, he counselled, is by no means omniscient just because it is the majority. 'In fact, I've found that the line which divides majority opinion from mass hysteria is often so fine as to be virtually invisible ... the majority often has a tendency to plod slowly or to mill around helplessly. The non-conformist businessman who follows his own counsel, ignoring the cries of the pack, often reaps fantastic rewards. There are classic examples galore – some of the most dramatic ones dating from the Depression.'

Aristotle Onassis, anything but a conformist, offered this formula: 'Keep looking tanned, live in an elegant building (even if you're in the cellar), be seen in smart restaurants (even if you nurse one drink) and if you borrow, borrow big.' Onassis was 16 when the Turkish army ravaged his home town, but showed enough ingenuity to obtain freedom of movement from both the Turkish and the United States authorities as well as to save his father from almost certain execution. A year later he arrived in Argentina with $60 in his pocket. His first job was working for the British United River Plate Telephone Company. By 1929, still only 23 years old, he had set up in business as a tobacco importer and, on a visit to Athens, persuaded the Greek Prime Minister to make him Consul-General in Buenos Aires. This consular post gave him a chance to meet and exchange with many Greek ship captains who aroused his interest in shipping. In 1930 he took advantage of a world slump to buy for $120,000 six Canadian cargo ships which had cost $2 million to build ten years earlier. Within one decade he was the owner of a sizeable merchant fleet and had taken delivery of his first oil tanker. During the war he rented his ships to the Allies and most of them were lost. However, victory brought its reward: he was allowed to buy from the United States twenty-three surplus Liberty ships at a low price. This deal and his marriage to Athena, daughter of Stavros Livanos, the leading shipowner, finally confirmed the newcomer in that exclusive maritime club of the Golden Greeks. He went on borrowing – borrowing *big* – and followed his other maxims to the end. Marrying Jacqueline Kennedy in 1968 was very much part of the formula.

I'm not sure about the tan (it may be taken as proof that you are excessively fond of the frivolous pursuit of pleasure) but I can see why one should live in an elegant building. The right address still carries a lot of weight. And I suppose that if you patronize smart restaurants there is always a chance that you will make the acquaintance of someone like Onassis, which can speed things up a lot. A natural extension of this is to belong to the right golf club and to take your holidays in places favoured by the rich. Some of the biggest business deals of the past decade have begun with a casual remark on the fairway. Merchant bankers, stockbrokers, and advertising agencies have acquired some of their best clients while blasting out of a bunker. Industrialists have celebrated some of their most profitable *coups* over drinks at the club house. And, of course, many ambitious executives have landed highly-paid jobs, over the heads of better qualified rivals, by subtly developing a golf partnership. You can ring a partner up, a week later, and he will remember you. He may even invite you to his own home – where, of course, you will do your best to impress him with your business talents. Or he may ring you, with a request that you should meet to discuss that casual remark. Holidays in places like Cannes or Palm Springs may offer an even better opportunity to develop the right sort of contacts. Hire a nice comfortable villa and find the bars and beaches your millionaire neighbours use. You will soon get to know them. You may even end up marrying into a fortune; many people do. (Marriage is still the quickest way to acquire wealth – for both sexes.)

Conrad Hilton had another guiding rule: 'Never give up, and never under any circumstances deceive anybody. Have your word good.' Hilton's father was a small-town shopkeeper in New Mexico and when he died the young Conrad was left an inheritance of $2,000. He dreamt of becoming a banker but went to Texas and bought a small hotel instead. 'Right there,' he recalled many years later, 'I made up my mind I didn't want anything else ... what really did it was going over there and seeing the bustle, having the owner tell me about all the business that he was doing, how the trains were coming in there at night and the money that he was making. When he showed me his books, I figured that I could get all of my money back in one year. We didn't have any income tax then; so what a deal that was! Today you have to figure on getting it back in twenty years. That is what it takes us with taxes and labour costs.' Hilton went on to buy other hotels, but had a hard time during the Depression. He refused to give up. 'In the first place, I wouldn't give up because that isn't the way I am constituted. And I figured that I would be able to work this situation out sooner or later. At that time hotels were going broke all over. In fact, I think the record shows that about 80 per cent of all hotels in America went broke. And at one time I was $500,000 in debt and nothing coming in. But I worked out of it.'

Hilton had what another American multi-millionaire, W. Clement Stone, calls PMA – Positive Mental Attitude. Every adversity, Stone insists, contains the seed of an equivalent or greater benefit, and all things are possible to those who cultivate PMA. A guilt feeling is also useful: 'It even motivates persons of the highest moral standards to worthwhile thought and actions.' Stone has devoted much time and energy to spreading the gospel of PMA. He has distributed millions of inspirational books (including two written by himself), magazines and records to young people, employees, company shareholders, schools, hospitals, veterans' organizations, and inmates of correctional institutions. Some say his publishing ventures are cynically designed for money (though he hardly needs it). Others say he sincerely believes in PMA and genuinely wants other men to succeed as he did. I interviewed him once, for the BBC, and his enthusiasm was infectious. It was also embarrassingly corny. Stone, a little man with a Ronald Colman moustache and a penchant for colourful bow ties and flashy rings, tends to talk in folksy clichés and the methods he outlines seem more appropriate to a classroom in Peking than to a sophisticated industrial society. He uses phrases like 'Tear Down the Unseen Walls' and 'Little Hinges Swing Big Doors'. Trouble, he says, is 'opportunity in work clothes'. When the going gets tough, 'the tough get going'. But there is ample evidence – including his own life story – that they work.

W. Clement Stone was born in Chicago and brought up in a poor, run-down neighbourhood. As a six-year-old he helped support his impoverished family by selling newspapers. He was thrown out of one restaurant several times but kept sneaking back with more papers to peddle. The customers were so amused by his nerve that they finally persuaded the owner to 'let him be'. He never had trouble selling papers there again. Some years later his mother (the father had died when he was very young) invested her modest savings in a small insurance agency in Detroit. 'She pawned her two diamonds to get sufficient cash to add the money she did have to buy the agency,' he recalls. The entire staff consisted of one woman – her. The agency prospered and in the summer before his junior year of high school the teenage Clem went to try his luck as a salesman. His mother instructed him to go to a certain office building and cold-canvass it from top to bottom. He was frightened. But his days as a newsboy came back to him, and he persevered. 'I found,' he says, 'that if I spoke loudly and rapidly, hesitated where there would be a period or comma if the spoken word were written, kept a smile in my voice, and used modulation, I no longer had butterflies in my stomach. Later I learned that this technique was based on a very sound psychological principle: the emotions (like fear) are not immediately subject to reason, but they are subject to action. When thoughts do not neutralize an undesirable emotion, action will.' He sold two policies that day, four the next day, and six the day after. His career was under way. He continued to sell health-and-accident policies during time off from school and, before long, had boosted his sales average to twenty. Then came a day in school when he was sent to the principal's office to discuss some minor infraction of the rules. Stone left there and then. (He later continued his studies, part-time, at YMCA schools and began, but didn't finish, a college law course.) He roamed all over the state, selling for his mother's agency, and at the age of 20 moved to Chicago to set up his own one-man insurance business with a capital of $100, no debts, and desk space rented at $25 a month. The firm prospered and by the late twenties he had more than 1,000 men operating from coast to coast. The Depression hit insurance sales, and at one time it seemed as if Stone's business might be among the casualties. But he pulled through ('Sales,' he told his staff, 'are contingent on the attitude of the salesman, not the prospect') and by the end of the thirties Stone was a millionaire. He decided to buy an insurance company of his own, rather than just sell the policies of others, and managed to acquire the Commercial Credit Company of Baltimore. By 1956 it had grown into the largest accident and health insurance company of its kind in the United States; the Stone family fortune was estimated at $400 million.

How does one acquire PMA? You start, Stone told me, by repeating slogans to yourself—'self-motivators', as he calls them. You recite them every morning and night and at odd hours through the day. They float about on the surface of your mind for a while. Then, after sufficient repetition, they begin to sink in and become integral components of your psyche. From then on you barely need to think about them. In the midst of any business situation, the correct self-motivator will assert itself and will automatically guide you in the direction of success. The key phrase, Stone went on, is 'DO IT NOW!' Whenever the symbol DO IT NOW! is flashed from your sub-conscious to your conscious mind, *act* immediately; with practice you will develop a reflex response so powerful that you will take action come what may. Many or most people fail to develop all the useful self-motivators naturally as they grow to adulthood. Confronted with an opportunity which involves some element of risk they tend to back off. They prevaricate. The opportunity evaporates before their eyes. They then blame a capricious fate for their bad luck. This kind of experience, repeated over and over again, confirms them in the belief that they are born losers. A man with this crippling attitude rooted in his psyche, Stone pointed out, obviously will not succeed except by accident. Since he has failed to develop the right self-motivators naturally while growing to manhood, it's necessary to implant them in him artificially by the technique. If the technique works, he will eventually reach a point where his immediate reaction will be 'Do it now' instead of 'Well, maybe next week'.

Stone's books have inviting titles like *Success through a Positive Mental Attitude* and *The Success System that Never Fails*. Not surprisingly, they are best-sellers. But they are not, by any means, the only inspirational books on the market – or even the first. People like Horatio Alger were there before him. Born in 1834 at Revere, in Massachusetts, Alger was the son of a pious Unitarian Minister. He went to divinity school and was ordained at the age of 30; two years later he quit the ministry, went to New York and tried to earn a living as a journalist. He sold a serial story called *Ragged Dick* to a boys' magazine and it was such a hit that a Boston publisher immediately commissioned him to write several books about the same character. Stone says he came across Alger's stories when he was twelve. 'I'll never forget the first day I went upstairs to the attic ... at least fifty of his books, dusty and weather-worn, were piled in the corner. I took one down to the hammock in the front yard and started to read. I read through all of them that summer. The theme in each: from rags to riches. The principles in each: the hero became a success because he was a man of character – the villain was a failure because he deceived and embezzled.' No one knows how many Alger books were sold – estimates range from 100 to 300 million – but their influence on young Americans like Stone was, without doubt, enormous. Ironically, Alger himself died in 1899 flat broke.

I don't know whether Bernie Cornfeld read Alger in some dusty attic as a boy, but I am sure that he studied W. Clement Stone. The sales techniques adopted by IOS could hardly have been more positive. Cornfeld, too, implanted the 'right-motivators' in his salesmen and his career would have made splendid material for an Alger novel. That his empire collapsed, in the end, was not due to any lack of PMA but simply reflected the basic flaw in his product. In the long run one's sales talk has to be matched by performance and Cornfeld never had much chance of doing so. His career is often cited as proof that the capitalist system is evil – the man, it seems, not only duped countless poor widows and orphans but lives to enjoy the fruits of his duplicity. He is invariably photographed, even now, surrounded by nubile Young Things and obedient servants. It doesn't seem fair. I hold no brief for Cornfeld, but I have always thought that his story was more of a comment on the gullibility of people who want to have something for nothing than on the capitalist system as a whole: there is a world of difference between the kind of attitude which led him to success and the determined, hard-working individualism of self-made businessmen. Cornfeld's victims, if that is the word, were not so much widows and orphans as middle-class people out to make some easy money. His basic idea was almost childishly simple. Mutual funds (or unit trusts, as they are known in Britain) had been popular for some time, as a way of allowing people with modest means to invest in industry. You pool the money, put it into a broad and wisely chosen range of stocks, and watch your investment grow. It is a sensible enough approach and, indeed, a great many people have benefited from it. But, of course, there is no guarantee of success and salesmen rarely bother to tell a potential customer how much it is going to cost him. Commissions, management fees and other charges can add up to 10 per cent or more of the original investment. As long as there is capital gain it doesn't really matter; it's only when the market goes down, as it so often does, that people start to complain. Cornfeld took the whole process one stage further. He created a Fund of Funds, which invested in other mutual funds. In short, he persuaded people to put up money to buy investments which they could easily have acquired for themselves. And, of course, he charged them for it. The scheme worked so well for a while that, at one time, the IOS empire had total funds of $2,500 million dollars under its control.

Cornfeld – born in Turkey and brought up in Brooklyn – built up a fortune, much of it on paper, estimated at some $150 million. His sales conferences had an almost religious atmosphere. I first met him in the early sixties, at a convention of his UK salesmen. He had hired the Festival Hall in London and invited me, as City Editor of the *Evening Standard*, to address the faithful. It was all very well done, and I'm afraid I rather spoiled the occasion by delivering a gloomy speech on the future of the British economy. The speech was received in deafening silence and Cornfeld's UK managing director desperately tried to repair the damage by telling them, *à la* Stone, that sales were contingent on the attitude of salesmen, not the prospect. Cornfeld, dressed in a trendy Mao-style jacket, made no attempt to conceal his anger. As far as he was concerned I had been hired, for a substantial fee, to help spread The Word. And here I was, an outsider, putting a damper on the proceedings. He shook my hand, briefly, and then disappeared. The Great Man, an aide explained, was Not Amused. I made things worse, I fear, by writing an irreverent piece about it afterwards.

There have always been Cornfelds and I have no doubt there will be more, though Government control is nowadays so strict that it's harder than ever before to fool people for any length of time. Financial journalists can warn their readers, within the limits of the laws of libel, but they cannot compel them to listen.

Readers make a free choice; the loss, if any, is theirs. It is absurd to blame the system for their mistakes.

Can one grow rich through financial deals? Yes, obviously. Some of my colleagues will tell you that it's the *only* way to make a fortune. And, of course, a lot of people have done it. People like Charles Clore, for example. Clore shook the British establishment in the fifties with a series of spectacular take-over deals, based on a keen appreciation of the true value of other people's assets. He thought big and took calculated risks, buying shares in the market over a period of many months before making a bid and then offering considerably more than the market price. If the bid flopped, the other side's efforts to justify rejection to shareholders boosted the value of his holding to a point where he could sell at a useful gain. Clore argued that his activities were forcing complacent managers to become more efficient and, of course, they had precisely that effect. His tactics have been used by others since (though here, too, regulations have been tightened considerably) and will no doubt be used again. The same goes for property deals and other gambits, including stock market speculation.

The stock market is widely seen as the easiest touch of all, a quick and painless way to wealth. The notion is encouraged by financial journalists and authors who write books with titles like *How I Made $2 Million In The Stock Market* and *The Way to a Fortune*. The Stock Exchange itself is looked upon as a rich man's gambling den; its more important function, that of providing capital for industry, tends to be ignored. It would be futile to deny that fortunes have been made (and lost) in the stock market but in my experience it is a great deal more difficult than most people think. If it were easy, the people who are so free with their advice would all be rich.

I wrote a stock market column myself for many years and I always found that telling people what *not* to buy was much easier than the wretched business of tipping. There is, inevitably, a considerable element of hit-and-miss about the whole business and even experts get caught. On Wall Street, some are nowadays trying to keep ahead with all kinds of unlikely aids: chartcraft, ESP, tarot cards, numerology, and witchcraft. You'll find astro-economics, corporate horoscopy (with the company's date of incorporation or founding conveniently substituted for birthdays), mass telepathy, clairvoyancy, and market-predicting ghosts who, it seems, make a habit of adopting certain humans as pets. You will be urged to study sun-spots, analyse dreams, and watch the ups and downs of hemlines. There are experts who swear they can forecast market trends by the number of dog licences issued (the theory being that people do not buy dogs unless they are confident of the future) and respectable investment managers who belong to spell-casting witches' covens. A book I picked up in New York last year quoted a futurologist as saying that she sees things symbolically. 'When I'm thinking about the stock market, I get a vision of a bull and a bear playing around a moving conveyor belt. It's always this same vision. The bull and bear climb over it and under it, jostle each other, try to push each other off. Sometimes one of them rides on the belt while the other sleeps underneath. They seem to have a life of their own. I don't control them with my mind. I just—well, watch them. And whatever I see them doing is what the market will do in the future.'

I never went in for bear-watching, and somehow neglected to join a witches' coven—which, I concede, may well explain why I'm not rich. Indeed, I never went into the market at all. My reasons were two-fold: I could see all the risks (no PMA, you see) and, secondly, I felt that financial editors who played the market were too easily tempted to abuse their position. A leading London businessman once offered me an attractive deal—he would put up £30,000 and I would gamble with it, losses to be taken care of by him and profits to be shared. It wasn't hard to say no, because I would not have remained a financial editor for long if I had agreed.

A financial editor has several advantages over the outsider—though not necessarily over stockbrokers, merchant bankers and others in his parish. He is close to the market, he occasionally gets inside information, and he is well placed to influence the movement of share prices. Much of the 'inside information',

I hasten to add, is overrated. There is an old Wall Street saying:
'The surest way to lose money is to have a fat bank account
and some inside information.' People tend to be so impressed
by the source that they don't pause to consider why the news
should have been leaked, or to evaluate what they have been
told. The Stock Exchange, each day, retails the most extraordinary rumours. Some are circulated solely to exploit the gullibility of greedy amateurs. A broker who finds himself stuck with
a dud share, for example, may tell everyone that a take-over
bid is on the way. People move in, the price goes up, and he
is out before anyone else. Or someone close to a company chairman may hear of some impending development, such as the
loss of a large contract or a sharp downturn in profits, which
is certain to hit the price of the stock. So he tells people that
good news is on the way, dumps his stock on the market, and
watches the poor dumb outsiders buy it up. There are dozens
of gambits like this, and dozens of ways in which a professional
can cover his tracks. A financial editor learns to recognize all
this. But even he gets caught out occasionally, not least because
it's often difficult to check information. So there is always a risk
that he will mislead readers – and if he happens to hold shares
in the company concerned, people may conclude that he is
doing so deliberately.

Some tipsters have such a wide following that almost any
recommendation they care to make will move the market. If
a particular stock is in short supply, the move may be quite
dramatic. It is possible, therefore, to make money buying a
share, tipping it, and selling again as soon as it goes up. Many
people think that financial editors do this all the time, but it
isn't so. For one thing, the chances of being found out are high.
In one case, many years ago, market professionals noticed that
each time a certain stock was tipped, the same broker appeared
just beforehand with a buying order and re-appeared again just
afterwards to sell. Inquiries were made, a complaint was lodged
with the Stock Exchange Council, the Council informed the
man's editor, and the editor sacked him on the spot.

Some people will go to remarkable lengths to discover what

an influential columnist is going to tip. When I was City Editor of the *Sunday Express*, printers were offered bribes to hand over proofs of my column and, once, someone tried to get at the contents of my wastepaper basket. Like my predecessors, I took extensive precautions against this sort of thing. The column was never written until Friday, and when I went out to lunch I not only locked the sheets of paper away in my desk, but also stuck a strip of Sellotape over the lock. No one saw my tips until late on Friday night – when, of course, the Stock Exchange was closed. Other people will go to equally remarkable lengths to secure favourable mention of a particular share. A company which is about to raise new capital, or to make a share-exchange offer for someone else, clearly has a vested interest in seeing its own stock 'talked up'. Financial editors will find themselves plied with drink, taken to lavish lunches at the Savoy, invited on free trips, and occasionally offered splendid presents. They may also find themselves wooed by friends and colleagues. It is, nevertheless, comparatively rare for an editor to get himself involved in any deliberate deception. His reputation is far too valuable an asset.

This is not a book about the stock market or about get-rich schemes, but we shall touch upon the subject again later on. We have looked at the careers of capitalists who have made fortunes in business, rather than by market speculation, and who have contributed to the well-being of the community in the process. Let us now consider what a former British Prime Minister, Edward Heath, once called 'the unacceptable face of capitalism'.

Chapter Five
The 'Unacceptable Face'

Maybe it takes a gang to do that.
RICHARD NIXON

'Unacceptable' is one of those convenient shorthand labels which can be used – and interpreted – in whatever way one likes. To someone on the extreme left all private enterprise is unacceptable; a man on the far right will feel the same about all kinds of state interference. Definitions vary considerably from one country to another, and are subject to constant – and sometimes sudden – change. Washington and his fellow revolutionaries insisted that 'all men are by nature free and independent' but excluded slaves because they were 'property'. In Victorian England it was politically acceptable to send 12-year-old children down a coalmine. In the Soviet Union of the 1970s they shoot people who take bribes; in the Middle East they may shoot you if you forget to bring one.

It would clearly be absurd to suggest that all the various faces of capitalism are totally acceptable. It would, for that matter, be equally absurd to suggest that all the faces of communism meet with approval – but more of that later. No one approves of swindles or child labour. Governments do not approve of tax evasion, currency smuggling and, in most cases, the sale of arms. There is, today, such a vast network of prohibitions in force or in the pipeline that most people break the law at some point in their lives, often without knowing it. And, of course, everyone nowadays feels entitled – indeed compelled – to make moral judgments. It is, against this background, infinitely more difficult to take the public for a ride than it was even twenty years ago. Most of the practices – and swindles – which got capitalism such a bad name would be hard, if not impossible, to repeat today. But of course this is not the image developed and sustained by novelists and scriptwriters: they prefer, for very understandable reasons, to show businessmen as scheming liars.

The then British Prime Minister Mr Heath, as it happens, was making a *moral* judgment on what used to be regarded as a logical – and reasonable – business arrangement. A boardroom row in a company called Lonrho had revealed that company directors enjoyed sundry 'perks' in addition to their salaries. Perks are a popular feature of our system, not because British businessmen are essentially dishonest but because the level of taxation is one of the highest in the world. Inevitably, they vary in scale. At one end, we have free trips for transport workers. At the other, company yachts. In between are cars, boxes at Ascot, theatre seats, apartments, and financial help with sending children to fee-paying schools. Some executives have their home telephone bills paid, and a number of companies operate share-option and profit-sharing schemes. Most of these perks go to senior management but several trade unions have also taken to negotiating fringe benefits for their members. The tax authorities keep a close watch on all these arrangements, as they do in every other country. The comments, in the press and elsewhere, on the Lonrho case therefore contained a sizeable element of hypocrisy. Hardened journalists claimed to be shocked and astonished that 'this sort of thing goes on' – this sort of thing being provision of company houses and payment through tax havens. Where, one wondered, had they been all these years? Were not journalistic expenses claims known throughout the profession as 'swindle sheets'?

Lonrho had hired a former Colonial Secretary, Duncan Sandys, as a consultant because he had valuable contacts in Africa, where the company does most of its business. He later became chairman, and Lonrho's energetic chief executive, 'Tiny' Rowland, offered him compensation for loss of the substantial consultancy fee. He also suggested, apparently, that a large payment of the compensation could be made in the Cayman Islands. Sandys refused to accept it, but it was enough

85

that the offer had been made: this, according to Mr Heath, was 'the unacceptable face of capitalism'. Lonrho had not broken any existing tax laws: it was simply making use of a loophole. The law makes a clear distinction between tax evasion and avoidance. Evasion is a deliberate fraud – you know you ought to declare, say, a capital gain on a stock market operation, but do not do so. Avoidance is to know the nature of the tax, and ways of getting around it through full use of allowances and one or another of the many complex financial schemes – all legal – thought up by clever tax accountants. But few journalists and politicians bother to make the distinction. An awful lot of nonsense is talked about the allegedly despicable behaviour of people who choose to arrange their affairs in such a way as to suit themselves rather than the taxman. Film stars who make their home in Switzerland rather than the country of their birth are frequently accused of being unpatriotic. And there is much criticism of wealthy people who find perfectly legitimate ways of minimizing estate duty. Yet the law is explicit enough: 'No man in this country,' a Scottish judge declared many years ago in an edict which still holds good, 'is under the smallest obligation, moral or other, so to arrange his legal relations to his business or his property so as to enable the Inland Revenue to put the largest shovel into his stores.'

Inevitably, the law has been tightened further since then. So have our exchange controls. Few major industrial countries – certainly not Germany and the United States – maintain a more elaborate system of controls than we do. There are so many regulations that even the people who are employed to enforce them admit they don't know them all. The stated purpose, of course, is to save foreign currency but no one knows for sure how much this form of protectionism is really worth to a trading nation like Britain. One suspects that most of the currency saved by policing foreign investments, travel, and the like is promptly spent on importing foreign cars and other products. Germany has shunned exchange controls for more than thirty years and, as we all know, its currency is one of the strongest in the Western world.

Tax havens have lost much of their attraction for British residents, but they continue to attract considerable funds from elsewhere. Switzerland, of course, remains the best known haven: its unique combination of political stability, banking secrecy, highly developed financial expertise, and low rate of taxation make it an understandably popular choice. But there are many others: the Bahamas, Bermuda, Liechtenstein, Panama, the Channel Islands. In some cases, it is their Government's chief source of income. There is little worth taxing within their own borders and it pays to abolish local taxes, and sacrifice the modest revenue they would yield, in order to encourage the highly taxed citizens and companies of the industrial nations to establish residence or set up trusts. Many have copied the Swiss bank secrecy laws and there is no doubt that these laws are sometimes used to hide so-called 'dirty money' – money which is the product of a criminal act. We have all read novels about Mafia leaders and Latin American (or African) dictators with large Swiss bank accounts and no one has ever denied that they exist. And those stories about Italian businessmen smuggling currency and gold bars across the border into Lugano are unquestionably true. But the amount of 'dirty money' deposited by organized and white-collar criminals is reckoned to be only a small part of the total volume of clean foreign money sent to the same Swiss banks in the course of the year. There is no guarantee of secrecy if the prospective client has robbed a bank (which, understandably, is considered a most dreadful thing to do) or is known to have taken part in a criminal fraud. This became apparent when the question of fraud was raised in the Clifford Irving case: the bank concerned readily agreed to co-operate with American and Swiss investigators. Tax evasion and attempts to dodge currency controls come into a different category; the Swiss do not regard it as their business to administer laws imposed by less tolerant governments, especially totalitarian states. The secrecy laws, they point out, were passed in 1934, at a time when a lot of Jewish money was beginning to leave Germany and Nazi agents were trying to discover where it was going. Countless political refugees have benefited from them ever since. The unacceptable face of capitalism? It depends on one's point of view.

Critics are on stronger ground when they attack the Swiss and other tax haven governments for facilitating that other controversial gambit: bribery. Much has been said and written about the subject in the last few years, chiefly because of Watergate. People were understandably appalled by the disclosure that the President of the United States and his legal counsel had been discussing, among other things, ways of buying the silence of criminals. There was an extraordinary conversation early in 1973 between Richard Nixon and John Dean which the President was foolish enough to tape: it referred to methods of 'washing money' and included Nixon's suggestion that 'Maybe it takes a gang to do that'. The episode and its aftermath focused attention on the whole business of corruption, and public opinion underwent a considerable change, as the board of Lockheed and others have since discovered to their cost. Officials in America and elsewhere are under closer scrutiny than ever before; so are corporations. To some people the various disclosures have seemed like final proof of the capitalist world's moral decay – as if corruption were confined to the West. To others, such as myself, the recent purges and subsequent reforms have been encouraging evidence of the capitalist system's willingness to identify its shortcomings and do something about them.

'Corruption' is such an emotive word that it might be as well to get a few basic points out of the way. There are cases where it may well be justified and even some where it merits applause. Governments themselves frequently break the corruption laws. America's Central Intelligence Agency is just as quick to bribe people who can be useful as the Soviet Union's KGB. The national interest, they say, requires it. One cannot, obviously, judge the validity of that argument without knowing the details of each case, but it isn't hard to imagine circumstances where it makes excellent sense. If it takes a bribe to unmask someone who is stealing defence secrets, for example, then it probably is money well spent. There are other, more personal, occasions when you and I would not hesitate to corrupt. Imagine that a close relative had been arrested, on some trumped-up charge, in a totalitarian state like the Soviet Union or Uganda. An official hints that he is willing to let the matter drop in return for cash or some other material incentive. Would you hesitate? It happens far more often than is generally supposed: for obvious reasons most cases never find their way into the press. 'God,' the German playwright Bertolt Brecht once wrote, 'is merciful and men are bribable and that's how his will is done on earth as it is in Heaven. Corruption is our only hope. As long as there's corruption, there'll be merciful judges and even the innocent may get off.'

Commercial bribery is a different matter, but here we may offend without knowing it and, for that matter, without doing any harm. Under British law, almost anything worth having is illegal. The 1906 Prevention of Corruption Act makes it an offence corruptly to receive or give 'any gift or consideration as an inducement or reward' in industry or commerce; the 1889 Public Bodies Corrupt Practices Act make it an offence corruptly to receive or give 'any gifts, loan, fee, reward, or advantage whatsoever in local Government'; ancient Common Law makes it an offence to bribe a policeman, magistrate, judge, or any other official. Strictly speaking, then, you are in trouble if you accept a bottle of Scotch from a business contact at Christmas. Public relations people break the law all the time. Among journalists, free trips and other inducements offered in the hope of a favourable mention are by no means uncommon. (Some of the loudest complaints about bribery tend to come from people who have never been offered anything: it is vaguely insulting not to be considered worth bribing.) And corruption need not necessarily take the form of cash or a deposit in some Swiss bank account. An offer of a knighthood or peerage, in return for favours, also qualifies as 'an inducement or reward'. So does an ambassadorship; American presidents have always used their patronage to buy support. Another, more subtle approach is to promise lucrative directorships to senior public servants when they retire—or to politicians after they leave office. The understanding, seldom voiced and certainly not committed to paper, is that favours granted now will be well rewarded later on. The favour may be anything, from a word in the right ear, or biased advice, to the actual awarding of a contract. All difficult to prove—but, more often than not, much more important than a cheque.

In Britain, journalistic attempts to find our own Watergate have sometimes produced pure farce. There was, for example, the Affair of the Silver Coffee Pot. A builder called John Poulson, later jailed for his involvement in all kinds of corrupt practices, was found to have presented the pot to a Minister back in 1966. The minister, Tony Crosland, had written a nice thank you note. Sinister? The British press certainly thought so. Crosland himself behaved as if he'd been caught with a kilo of heroin. 'It's been lying in the cupboard for seven years with a lot of other lunatic things and has never been used,' he told reporters. 'All I want to do is to get rid of the bloody thing.' The episode mystified our friends abroad: how could anyone believe that Ministers could be bought with such a trivial gift? In Italy, it is the kind of present which parents give to teachers to make sure their children pass their school examinations. In France you spend that sort of money on town councillors and policemen. Ministers come much more expensive. Poulson said he hadn't been trying to buy anything; Mr Crosland had opened one of his new buildings and the pot had been a modest token of appreciation. The press was, nevertheless, reluctant to let the story go. Our scandals have always tended to be more concerned with sex than money; it was exciting to have something else to write about for a change. But, of course, the whole affair was utterly absurd. It is common practice for ministers who launch ships, or open schools, to be presented with a memento of the occasion. It may be a plaque or a silver coffee pot. Jim Callaghan, now Britain's Prime Minister, was once given an alarm clock and it still wakes him up every morning. It would be churlish to reject such tokens; with foreign dignitaries it could even lead to awkward incidents.

The Lockheed affair, which hit the headlines in 1976, is

something else. Lockheed is one of the world's top manufacturers of aeroplanes and America's leading defence contractor. Developing planes is an expensive and risky business, and success depends heavily on the response from foreign as well as domestic customers. To get some of those customers Lockheed, like many other American companies, resorted to bribes. Not that anyone actually used the word. Executives preferred to talk about gifts, commissions, and agents' fees. (Some of Lockheed's men had an even more cosy label: 'sugar'.) Help them to sell their product and you got a commission or fee. Nothing wrong with that—as long as it is done openly and doesn't involve public officials. I had lunch with Dan Haughton, then Lockheed's chairman, in Washington just before the story became big news. If he had offered me money to use my influence I should certainly have accepted. But somehow he neglected to do so, and I forgot to ask him whether he had brought his cheque-book. Life is full of missed opportunities like that. The chairman spent most of the lunch talking about *his* financial problems. Or, rather, his company's problems. 'The aeroplane business,' he said, 'is a great business and an exciting business. If only it were a business we could make some money in, it would be perfect.'

Like other defence contractors, Lockheed has found Government work a distinctly mixed blessing. A few years ago, for example, it ran into heavy financial weather over its cargo-carrying C-5A Galaxy, the world's largest aeroplane. The C-5A can carry any piece of equipment required by an army division, from tanks to helicopters—up to 265,000 pounds of payload at a time, or the equivalent of nearly ten railroad boxcars fully loaded with household appliances. As a technical achievement the plane deserved, and got, the highest praise. But costs were something else. Other problems followed, including the financial troubles of Rolls-Royce, and in 1971 Lockheed had to be bailed out with a massive Government loan guarantee. The guarantee helped Haughton to press on with other programmes, including the production of the splendid Tristar passenger plane. But there was no chance of making a profit, or even recouping all the money invested over the years, without selling a considerable number of planes. Haughton had long taken the view that the end justified the means: if payola could secure the sales needed to get a return on their investment then it was cheap at the price. One had to take the world as one found it, not as one would like it to be. Besides, the total amount expended on commissions and fees would add up to only a fraction of the overall development cost. Foreign sales would provide employment for American workers and help the country's balance of payments; bribes were therefore as much in the national interest as the CIA's handouts. For much of the 1960s Haughton followed this particular line, and most of the allegations made in 1976 arose from payments made during this period. Watergate showed Haughton that others might not share his simple business logic. Lockheed became more cautious, but by then it was too late.

It is easy to condemn people like Haughton, who has since resigned. But one can also sympathize with their desire to do the best job possible, especially if it involves worthwhile technological achievement. Would you rather let your company go bust, or drop some ambitious project? The fault, arguably, lay not so much with enthusiasts like Haughton as with the generals and public officials who took their 'sugar'. Nothing could excuse the conduct of corrupt military officers in Colombia who deliberately falsified their Government's national defence estimates to favour an otherwise unjustified purchase of Lockheed equipment. 'In certain parts of the world,' the London *Times* observed after the Lockheed affair came to light, 'the businessman is faced with a simple choice. Either he allows a bribe to be paid, or he does not get the business . . . there is some evidence that the excessive fastidiousness on the part of British businessmen and governments, in the face of other European competitors, is having the effect of losing contracts.' A similar view was expressed by Lord Shawcross, an eminent lawyer who heads a Commission set up by the International Chamber of Commerce to look at 'unethical practices'. There were, said Shawcross, about a dozen countries (including the UK) where corruption was quite exceptional and was regarded with grave legal and social disapproval. But in many other countries corruption was 'almost a way of life' with no adequate measures to prevent it. One could not do business without 'greasing someone's palm' so one had to make sure that 'those accepting money were punished'. The Commission, he went on, might ask the UN to bring pressure to bear for the introduction of legislation which 'might even suggest a code of conduct for companies operating internationally'. An international agreement on a legal definition for bribery and corruption might be needed before any general law and penalties could be drawn up to stop the practices. Then there would remain the problem of enforcement.

Lord Shawcross was too diplomatic to say so but it is no secret that some of the worst offenders are countries which have officially renounced capitalism. They include several iron curtain countries and a number of developing nations which are supposed to be socialist. Before independence, their leaders denounced capitalism in passionate speeches. It soon emerged, however, that they really meant colonialism, which is certainly no longer an exclusively capitalist institution. They couldn't wait to get their hands on the material benefits so generously distributed by both communist and capitalist governments in their earnest endeavour to win friends. If the West was squeamish about bribing the new masters – with cash, tanks, and planes – then the East was only too willing to oblige. African countries have been particularly eager to play this kind of game, but the Arabs have been close behind: in the Middle East, bribery is certainly part of the 'way of life'. Oil has given the Arab world enormous spending power and the business goes to those who are willing and able to provide the greatest 'incentive'. You can refuse to oblige; that is your privilege. You can try to tell them that bribery plays havoc with industrial efficiency; contracts should go to the most efficient firms, not to those with the deepest purse and the darkest secrets. They, in turn, are free to tell you to take your business elsewhere – and probably will.

The chairman of Shell, one of the companies which has admitted making 'unauthorised payments' in several countries, told a T-V interviewer in 1976: 'I would like to ask some of the people who are becoming close to sanctimonious humbugs just what they would do if they had $200 million invested in a country and a politician, with a death warrant in his pocket, came along and said give me $10 million or else – and the 'or else' can take several forms. Would they pay it or would they refuse to pay? And if they did pay, would they say it was a bribe or would they not call it by its proper name – extortion?'

It may well be that the world-wide publicity given to the Lockheed affair will lead to further changes in public opinion. Looking back over the last two decades it is remarkable how much change there has been already. The idea that corporations, however large, can do what they like is a myth: their ideas and methods of operation have never before been so strongly challenged. On every issue, from wage rates and planning to consumerism and the environment, the businessman is forced to consider broader interests than his own. He certainly has to pay far more attention to the press, the consumer, the academic world, and the political opposition than his equivalent in totalitarian states is called upon to do. In the financial world, the conditions which enabled earlier generations to carry out spectacular coups – like the South Sea Bubble and the great Salad Oil Swindle – have long disappeared. If anything, we have gone too far the other way: there are too many rules and regulations thought up, and passed into law, by people who have no practical business experience. There will, no doubt, be other scandals and both journalists and politicians will continue to make 'amazing' discoveries. But recent events have again underlined one of the great strengths of the capitalist system: its ability to adapt without, at the same time, destroying human freedom.

Chapter Six
Why Marx was Wrong

The theory of communism may be summed up in one sentence:
Abolish all private property.
KARL MARX

Milton Friedman, the Chicago economist, says that two authors
who are read the least but who have influenced mankind most
are Karl Marx and John Maynard Keynes. Perhaps, but there
the resemblance ends. Marx sought to destroy the private enterprise system; Keynes tried to improve its functioning so that
it might survive.

It is easy to see why most laymen should find Marx unread-
able. His theories are complex and his prose is, for the most
part, surprisingly turgid for someone who tried to earn his living
as a journalist. It is equally easy to see why his work should
have such fascination for intellectuals and those who like to be
thought of as intellectuals. Marx was the kind of man many
academics would love to be – a historian/philosopher/socio-
logist/economist who formed a new basis of thought which later
became the basis of a powerful movement. He was shrewd,
energetic, far-sighted, and involved. He dealt in epochs rather
than generations, let alone decades. He was a realist, or at least
thought himself a realist, who treated fanciful utopian schemes
with contempt and considered all religion an intellectual fraud.
He was a humanist who believed in the 'free activity of men' –
and who would be utterly appalled by what societies like the
Soviet Union have done, and are doing, in his name.

Marx was born in Treves of German–Jewish parents. His
grandfather, Marx Levi, had been a rabbi and it was his father,
Heinrich, who took Marx as a surname when he embraced
official Lutheranism, a year before Karl was born, in order to

avoid the civil disabilities upon Jews. (Karl Marx never seemed to mention that he was a Jew. He once wrote a pamphlet on the Jews in which he explained, and by implication justified, anti-semitism because the Jews were 'usury' and 'merchant' capitalists.) He studied in German universities and got his doctorate of philosophy while under the influence of the leading German philosopher of the day, Friedrich Hegel. He wanted an academic career but his democratic views got in the way; instead he earned a precarious living as a journalist. His first benefactor, a rich radical publicist named Moses Hess, talked about him in glowing terms:

'Dr Marx – that is my idol's name – is still very young (about 24 at most) and will give medieval religion and politics their *coup de grâce*. He combines the deepest philosophical seriousness with the most biting wit. Imagine Rousseau, Voltaire, Holbach, Lessing, Heine and Hegel fused into one person – I say fused, not thrown together in a heap – and you have Dr Marx.'

Hess provided Marx with a newspaper platform – the *Rheinische Zeitung*. Within a year the paper was suppressed by the autocratic Prussian Government. Then, having recently married a girl of aristocratic family who had been his childhood playmate, he moved to Paris where he met sundry anarchist and socialist leaders with whom he had long and heated arguments. He also made the acquaintance of his lifelong friend, patron, and collaborator, Friedrich Engels, son of a mill-owner with interests in Manchester. Marx's journalistic efforts in Paris, dealing largely with the German situation, annoyed the Prussian Government which managed to get him expelled from France. He then settled in Belgium.

A secret international organization calling itself the League of the Just thought in 1848 that the opportunity of exploited labour had arrived, and decided to proclaim its views and head the revolutionary movement. They asked Marx and Engels to draft their proclamation, and the result was the celebrated *Communist Manifesto*. It asserted the existence of a class struggle between capitalists and workers, claimed that everybody would be liberated with a final victory of the working class when it took over the means of production, and ended with a slogan which has outlived countless others: 'The proletarians have nothing to lose but their chains. Working men of all countries, unite!'

The manifesto also ridiculed the ideas of the Utopian Socialists. It wasn't difficult to do; some were truly bizarre. (Charles Fourier, famous French socialist, announced publicly that he would be at home every day at a certain hour to await any philanthropist who felt disposed to give him a million francs for the development of a colony based on Fourieristic principles. For twelve years thereafter he was at home every day, punctually at noon, awaiting the generous stranger, but alas, no millionaire appeared.) The Utopians, Marx and Engels noted, 'want to improve the condition of every member of society, even that of the most favoured. Hence, they habitually appeal to society at large, without distinction of class; nay, by preference, to the ruling class. For how can people, when once they understand their system, fail to see in it the best possible plan of the best possible state of society? Hence, they reject all political, and especially all revolutionary, action; they wish to attain the end by peaceful means, and endeavour, by small experiments necessarily doomed to failure, and by the force of example, to pave the way for the new social gospel ... to realize all these castles in the air, they are compelled to appeal to the feelings and purses of the bourgeois.'

It was this 'appeal to the feelings and purses of the bourgeois' which particularly angered Marx and Engels. For them the change to the new society was to be brought about by the revolutionary action of the working class, not through the efforts of the ruling class. But talk of proletarian revolution was premature, and after the collapse of the movement Marx moved to London, where he spent the rest of his life elaborating the doctrines foreshadowed in the *Communist Manifesto*. He lived meagrely, supported partly by Engels and in part by writing a regular column for the New York *Tribune*. Marx never visited the USA and his articles were mostly about European or Asian politics, but once he strayed off into concern about the working conditions of the Western wrangler, or cowboy. Immediately he recognized this romantic movies hero of our age as one of the oppressed – suffering from dietary deficiencies on his diet of beans; wracked by haemorrhoids and arthritis from his saddle-sore unsocial working hours on horseback in the cold open air; exploited without security of job, sickness benefits or pensions by his employers.

The first volume of *Capital* was published in 1867. It seems to have given him quite a lot of trouble. In January 1851 Engels is urging him to 'hurry up'. In April, Marx is replying: 'I am so far advanced that in five weeks I will be through with the whole economic shit.' By June, Marx is still complaining that the work has 'so many damned ramifications' that 'I will not be able to finish for six to eight weeks.' In December, Engels is writing back 'show a little commercial sense this time'. Seven years later, Marx is still hopefully promising it will now be 'only four weeks'. This might be any contemporary author's letter file. The first volume of *Capital*, when it finally appeared, didn't make him a fortune; it would have been an ironic twist if it had. (The rest took him all his life and, in fact, was never finished in his lifetime. The second and third volumes were published by Engels in 1885 and 1895 respectively, after Marx had died.)

It was in England, of course, that large-scale capitalism first developed and Marx lived and worked at a time when the Industrial Revolution was producing truly staggering advances: production of cotton, iron, coal, any and every commodity, multiplied at an unprecedented rate. But capitalism also proved to be a disruptive force on an equally staggering scale. And exploitation of labour was in fact not fancy. There were, as Disraeli noted in his *Sybil*, 'two nations; between whom there is no intercourse and no sympathy; who are as ignorant of each other's habits, thought, and feelings as if they were dwellers in different zones, or inhabitants of different planets; who are formed by a different breeding, are fed by a different food, are ordered by different manners, and are not governed by the same laws'. The division was not new, but with the coming of machinery and the factory system the borderline became more marked than ever before. Marx's distaste for the system – and the ruling class which administered it – was therefore understandable. He became the most active and influential member of the International Working Men's Association – the First International – established in London in 1864, and wrote countless pamphlets, manifestoes, articles, and letters on 'the coming struggle'. (He also found time for other unconventional pursuits. After an evening's drinking in his old Soho haunts he would relax by knocking out the lamps along the way home up the Tottenham Court Road. And somewhere between the British Museum Reading Room and cosy Sunday picnics on Hampstead Heath he managed to father a son on his wife's German maid, becoming, as Alan Brien has put it, 'the first NW 3 progressive to make the *au pair* pregnant'.) *Capital* is based partly on the ideas of others; Marx took the thoughts of many of his predecessors, both capitalist and socialist, and combined them with ideas of his own. Engels describes the end result in these terms:

'In this system – and herein is its great merit – for the first time the whole world, natural, historical, intellectual, is represented as a process – i.e., as constant motion, change, transformation, development; and the attempt is made to trace out the internal connection that makes a continuous whole of all this movement and development. From this point of view the history of mankind no longer appeared as a wild whirl of senseless ideas ... but as the process of evolution of man himself.'

History, Marx argued, is predictable, producing a sequence of inexorable events. The thinking comes from his old mentor, Hegel. A major tenet of Hegel's was that change takes place through a so-called process of 'dialectics'. For every positive there is a negative; for example, white and black, good and evil, high and low. Ideas, beliefs, systems of thought are arranged in opposite pairs. Every positive Hegel calls a 'thesis', its negative an 'antithesis'. These two interact to produce a synthesis, embracing parts of each. The synthesis becomes a new thesis and the cycle is repeated. Thus the change from slavery to feudalism to capitalism, each stage bearing within itself the seeds of its own destruction.

Marx gave a number of reasons why he thought capitalism would destroy itself in the relatively near future, perhaps during his own lifetime. They ranged from 'the growing concentration of wealth in the hands of the few' and 'the increasing misery of the masses' to 'the recurrence of periodic breakdowns in the system – crises – each one more devastating than the last'. And, most important, the fundamental contradiction in capitalist society as he saw it: the fact that labour produces and capital appropriates. There is a passage in *Capital* which sums it all up:

'One capitalist always kills many. Hand in hand with this centralization, or this expropriation of many capitalists by few, develop, on an ever-extending scale, the co-operative form of the labour process, the conscious technical application of science, the methodical cultivation of the soil, the transformation of the instruments of labour only usable in common, the economizing of all means of production by their use as the means of production of combined, socialized labour, the entanglement of all peoples in the net of the world market, and this, the international character of the capitalistic régime. Along with the constantly diminishing numbers of the magnates of capital, who usurp and monopolize all advantages of this process of transformation, grows the mass of misery, oppression, slavery, degradation, exploitation; but with this too grows the revolt of the working class, a class always increasing in numbers and disciplined, united, organized by the very mechanism of the process of capitalist production itself. The monopoly of capital becomes a fetter upon the mode of production, which has sprung up and flourished along with, and under it. Centralization of the means of production and socialization of labour at last reach a point where they become incompatible with their capitalist integument. This integument is burst asunder. The knell of capitalist private property sounds. The expropriators are expropriated.'

The distinguishing feature of communism, Marx said, was

not the abolition of property generally, but the abolition of private property. Modern bourgeois private property was 'the final and most complete expression of the system of producing and appropriating products, that is based on class antagonism, or the exploitation of the many by the few'. He went on to address the people who were to be expropriated: 'You are outraged because we wish to abolish private property. But in extant society, private property has been abolished for nine-tenths of the population; it exists only because these nine-tenths have none of it. Thus you reproach us for wanting to abolish a form of property which can only exist on condition that the immense majority of the members of the community have no property at all. In a word, you accuse us of wanting to abolish *your* property. Well, we do! Your contention is that the individual will cease to exist from the moment when labour can no longer be transformed into capital, money, land rent; from the moment, in short, when it can no longer be transformed into a monopolizable social power; from the moment, that is to say, when individual property can no longer become bourgeois property. You admit, therefore, that when you speak of individuals you are thinking solely of bourgeois, of the owners of bourgeois property. Certainly we wish to abolish individuals of that kind!'

And how was it to be accomplished? 'The communists disdain to conceal their views and aims. They openly declare that their ends can be attained only by the forcible overthrow of all existing social conditions. Let the ruling class tremble at a communist revolution.'

Which, in some countries, they eventually did, though not in the manner which Marx had envisaged. Oddly, his doctrine contained almost no plans for the society which would arise after the workers took over. He just seemed to assume that all would live happily ever after. He suggested no new antithesis for the new thesis which would come into being with the end of capitalism; the cycle of social evolution, by which he set so much store, was apparently going to come to a stop. The word 'planning' is hardly mentioned, nor is there any guidance on socialist distribution of income, or of money and prices under socialism, or how a socialist society would allocate resources and conduct foreign trade. For a time, Marx said, order would be provided by the 'dictatorship of the proletariat' and then the post-capitalist society would 'move into a higher place in which true communism will prevail'. The state would wither away, 'for the only function of the state is to hold down the exploited class'. The old bourgeois society, with its classes and class conflicts, 'will be replaced by an association in which the free development of each will lead to the free development of all'.

This lack of concern with future policy, beyond a few naïve assumptions, has always bothered many of those who like to call themselves Marxist. But reading Marx today, one can see the appeal of his message not only to those of his contemporaries who understood it but also to people like Lenin and Trotsky and to would-be revolutionaries of the 1970s – students, trade unionists, Marxist academics, and Socialist politicians. It's heady stuff for those who, like Marx and Engels, hate the idea of collaboration and compromise. And Marx's analysis of capitalism appears so impressively supported by subsequent events. The growing concentration of wealth in the hands of the few ... the crushing of the many small producers by the big ones ... the recurrence of periodic breakdowns in the system ... here is a prophet who, it seems, simply couldn't help being right.

Or could he? The truth, rarely if ever acknowledged by his followers, is that Marx was wrong on so many counts that it's hard to know where to start. Perhaps one should take some of his key points one by one.

The value of a commodity is determined by the social labour-time necessary to produce it.

According to this theory, the basis of communist economic thought, everything is the product of labour. A thing has value because labour is expended on its production. But the owner manages to sell it for more than it costs him, therefore he is the recipient of surplus value. What the employer has to pay the worker is only enough to keep the worker alive (the 'iron law of wages', borrowed from another economist, David

Ricardo). What he collects from the customer is the true value of the labour put into the article. The capitalist, in the process of accumulating wealth for himself, therefore robs and exploits the worker.

The doctrine has a certain crude appeal but it has little to do with economic reality. Like so much of economic theorizing it makes assumptions which are not justified by fact – in this case, perfect competition. Perfect competition doesn't exist; it is merely an analytical 'model' of the pure form that a market would take. The theory of value assumes stationary economic processes and, worse, it assumes that workmen, like machines, are being produced according to rational cost calculations which, of course, is nonsense. No allowance is made for the natural differences in the quality of labour and the quality of work performed; details of this kind would have got in the way of Marx's argument. But you don't have to be an economist to spot the flaws. Gold is not valuable because men dig for it, but men dig for it because it is valuable. The 'iron law of wages' is no longer valid, at least in advanced capitalist countries, because trade unions have the bargaining power to override it. And surplus value is by no means guaranteed: many firms can and do make a loss on their operations. Workers are not asked to share in losses, even though they may be the outcome of factors outside the employers' control; indeed, employers are nowadays expected to keep unprofitable operations going, if need be with borrowed money, in order to provide continued income for employees. Some exploitation!

The material misery of workers will increase, and so will their alienation.

Material misery has *not* increased inside the capitalist world. On the contrary, the working class has enjoyed, in most industrial nations, a substantial improvement in their economic conditions ever since the middle of the nineteenth century. There have been severe depressions and unemployment (and, of course, one can find misery even in the midst of general prosperity) but the trend of advanced capitalism in the twentieth century has been against Marx's prediction of increasing material misery. Most of the benefits which the *Communist Manifesto* promised would follow the seizure of power have long since been achieved by so-called capitalist societies: shorter working hours, social insurance, and so on. Not surprisingly, Marxists have shifted the emphasis from material misery to the second part of the argument, alienation. They have a case. Many people do feel alienated from the process of their work. Marx could be (and often is) echoed by any modern sociologist. For many factory workers the job is just that – a job. It isn't a source of self-fulfilment. And the worker's activity is controlled by others: 'It is not his work, but work for someone else ... in work he does not belong to himself but to another person.' But Marx was wrong to attribute this to capitalism alone and as such. Much the same has happened in communist countries; it is a consequence of mass industrialization itself. Does anyone imagine that turning out sprockets, or whatever, on a vast production line in Warsaw or Moscow is any more self-fulfilling than doing it in Hamburg or Detroit? Does anyone believe that the individual on the production line in Warsaw and Moscow feels that in work he belongs to himself and not to another person? It is an elementary fact of economics that specialization and exchange, under a division of labour, makes a level of productivity possible which otherwise would not be remotely attainable. In earlier centuries when a man's well-being was limited by the goods which he himself could produce with his own limited tools, an unconscionable amount of time was needed to make or acquire the simplest necessities, and the general standard of living was dismally low: human existence was a continual struggle against imminent starvation. (It still is in our more primitive societies; an Indian peasant would gladly trade his 'self-fulfilment' for some of the advantages enjoyed by, say, the American or German car worker.) Mass production has given people a better life. And, of course, it supports a vastly increased population. In short, there are substantial benefits to be set against the drawbacks.

Property as a source of income is the objective criterion of class: within capitalism the two basic classes are the owners and the workers.

Another typical oversimplification. Marx insisted on defining the position of men within capitalist society solely in terms of their relation to the means of production, to the source of their income. He brushed aside considerations like status, power, occupation. Doctors, lawyers, university professors, civil servants, scientists, managers, and others who, in most cases, are no more owners of the means of production than factory workers (and sometimes receive less income) are put together with the latter and treated as one stratum, on the criterion of property alone. And at the other end, the small shopkeeper, the farmer and the restaurateur is included in the same hated 'ruling class' as the wicked landlord and the proprietor of a coal mine. Marx knew better, but it suited him to stick to a simple 'them and us' classification. Countless trade union leaders and labour politicians have continued to do so ever since. In the 1970s, of course, it is even more misleading than it was a hundred years ago because effective control of so many companies – indeed whole industries – has shifted from owners to managers. Marx's tendency to oversimplify in order to prove his case led him to make other errors. He claimed, for example, that the 'natural laws' of capitalist development would continue to lead to the elimination of neutrals in the class struggle, so that a relatively few capitalists on one hand would confront a propertyless working class, or 'proletariat', on the other. The proletariat would compromise all but a tiny majority of the population and would unite to overthrow the oppressor. The facts are different. The middle class, far from vanishing, went on to enjoy unprecedented prosperity and even now, despite the boom in mergers and acquisitions, independent businessmen and self-employed people vastly outnumber big capitalists. Wage-workers in advanced capitalist countries have not combined with the middle class to overthrow the 'owners'. Indeed, a 'proletarian revolution' of the kind Marx had in mind has never happened. The revolutions made in his name have occurred in types of society quite different from those he had in mind; what now goes by the name of communism has won its victories chiefly in backward regions. There is no instance of a pure Marxist state which has come to power by the votes of the people and none of those which have come into being by force have ever been willing to submit themselves to electoral trial by free votes. (In Britain the Communist Party has no more than 30,000 members and has failed to get a single seat in Parliament.) Communism has been successful only when concealed under the cloak of nationalism: from Mao to Castro and Ho Chi Minh all Marxist leaders who have been swept into power by their own people have proclaimed the chief aim of their struggle to be not the establishment of communism but the liberation of their country from foreign domination.

Within capitalist society, the workers cannot escape their exploited conditions and their revolutionary destiny by winning legal or political rights and privileges; unions and mass labour parties are useful as training grounds for revolution, but are not a guarantee of socialism.

Tell that to any labour leader in Britain, Germany, France, Italy and the USA. Trade unions have not only secured varying degrees of control over working conditions in factories, but have also secured an impressive list of rights and privileges, both political and economic, within the capitalist system. This is particularly true of Britain, where Marx composed these 'inexorable' laws. Marx never thought much of the British working class; they disappointed him, just as they disappoint today's Marxists. 'Prolonged prosperity,' he wrote late in his life, 'has demoralized them. The ultimate aim of this most bourgeois of lands would seem to be the establishment of a bourgeois aristocracy and a bourgeois proletariat side by side with the bourgeoisie.'

The ending of class oppositions within the nations will end the mutual hostilities of the nations.

Tell that to the Chinese, who are busy warning Western leaders that their fellow-communists in Moscow may start the next world war. Tell it, for that matter, to the European countries under Kremlin domination. If their Governments are not hostile it is only because dissenters are not allowed to survive in office: ask Dubcek or the Hungarians.

Capitalism is involved in one economic crisis after another. These crises are getting worse. So capitalism moves into its final crisis – and the revolution of the proletariat.

This seems to many people the most persuasive of all Marx's predictions. Economic crises are, indisputably, a fact of modern life and although there is a tendency to exaggerate (*everything* nowadays seems to qualify as a crisis) capitalism undoubtedly has had some bad moments. Marx was one of the first – some say the first – to recognize the existence of the boom-slump cycle, and for this he deserves due credit. But it takes no genius to prophecy crises (they happen even in communist countries, as we shall see) and they do not prove that Marx's theories were right. Indeed, there now seems to be general agreement among economists that if capitalism does break down it *won't* be for the reasons he stated. We shall look at the subject in far more detail later on; for the moment let us confine ourselves to the comment that Marx clearly underrated the capitalist system's capacity to adapt to ceaseless change. He did so quite deliberately because to do otherwise would have undermined his belief in the eventual 'revolution of the proletariat'. He and Engels sneered at the 'sham improvements' introduced by the bourgeoisie; socialists who participated in such programmes were branded as traitors regardless of the immediate benefits they might bring to the poor, downtrodden workers. The capitalism of the 1970s is not the capitalism that Marx knew or thought might come into existence. It is very likely that his challenge, and the influence it has had on others, helped to remove, or at least substantially to diminish the injustices which so aroused his passion. One should certainly not dismiss Marx for his errors or his wishful thinking. But it won't do, either, to leave his followers free to present his teachings as gospel. Marxism is more than economic theory; to the believers it is a religion. The students who shout slogans outside American embassies see Marxist ideology as a more than satisfactory substitute for the teachings of Christ. And *some* of the politicians who spout Marxist platitudes at public meetings really do believe that it is the key to paradise on earth. Somewhere in between are Western academic Marxists who maintain, with justification, that

Marxism did not end with Marx: it merely began with him. We shall include their arguments at various points in this book because some are clearly relevant. Meantime, though, it seems pertinent to look at the one European post-capitalist society which has come closest to the prophet's dreams: Russia.

Capitalism means exploitation of man by his fellow man.
In socialism, it is precisely the other way round.
MOSCOW JOKE

If Marx were alive today, and went to Moscow to urge the proletariat to overthrow the ruling class, he would be sent to a
labour camp or, more likely, to a psychiatric hospital. In Stalin's day he would have been shot. That is the reality, Soviet
Style, behind the slogans, the brilliant theorizing about the way
men should live, the stimulating intellectual debates. The
Soviet 'superstructure' has ways of dealing with would-be revolutionaries.

I don't know how many Western trade unionists, Socialist
politicians, and Marxist academics have read Solzhenitsyn's
Gulag Archipelago or Sakharov's *My country and the World*. They
should: it might make them pause, in future, before they start
talking about the glories of the workers' Jerusalem. Sakharov
calls Soviet society 'a sea of human misery, difficulties, animosi-
ties, cruelty, profound fatigue, and indifference'. After close on
sixty years of attempted Socialism, Russians have shorter holidays than Westerners, and work a longer week for less pay.
There is no right to strike, and pensions are low. Housing
remains bad; many cities do not even have modern sewerage.
The quality of education is low. Soviet medicine is losing its
early gains. People are not free to move around the country
or to take trips abroad. They drink three times as much alcohol
per head as they did under the Tsar, and in the Russian republic
alone 10,000 drunkards a year collapse and freeze on the streets.
And, says Nobel prize winner Sakharov, Soviet science has been
strangled. 'It is no accident that all the great scientific and tech-

nological discoveries of recent times – quantum mechanics, new elementary particles, uranium fission, antibiotics, most new drugs, transistors, computers ... happened outside our country.'

Marx condemned press censorship because, he thought, 'it leads to hypocrisy, the greatest of vice ... the government hears only its own voice ... surrenders to the illusion that it hears the voice of the people ...' It isn't hard to imagine what he would have to say about the tightly controlled, sycophantic Soviet press. In the Soviet Union even a Minister in office is not supposed to ventilate *any* opinion of his own, let alone criticize anyone except when and if the régime instructs him to do so. And even then he cannot use a single word that the régime has not approved for usage. Dissenters have no officially approved outlets. Their views and observations are published abroad, but you won't find them in Moscow itself unless, perhaps, you happen to come across them in the form of typed manuscripts. (Circulated from hand to hand, they are clandestine publications which frequently get their authors into trouble.) Throughout the Soviet Union every duplicator or photocopying machine is kept under lock and key, its use licensed by the political police in case anyone tries to duplicate unapproved news or views. 'The system,' says Valentin Turchin, chairman of the Soviet branch of Amnesty International, 'tends to eliminate those who are capable of independent thought. The Party doesn't want such people. Our system is awful for anyone who has any brains, you know. It is very difficult to hide your cleverness, to hide your soul in this system. No one in the West understands to what extent our situation is like the situation described by Orwell in *1984*.'

It is hardly surprising, in the circumstances, that Soviet intellectuals no longer show much interest in Marxism. They are too close to the end product. Western Marxists who visit the Soviet Union tend to find, to their surprise and dismay, that few of the people they meet want to discuss Marxist theory. Karel van het Reve, who is Professor of Russian Literature at the University of Leyden, and served as a foreign correspondent in Moscow for a year during the 1960s, says, 'Nowadays believers in the official doctrine are exceedingly hard to find ... it is hardly a great exaggeration to say that more university professors in Paris and Tokyo are convinced Marxists than in all of Russia.' (In *Encounter*, February 1974.) The Communist Party, of course, still professes Marxism – combined with Leninism – as its sacred ideology. But it is largely a pretence. The legacy of Marx and Lenin serves one purpose and one alone: to justify in terms of various elements drawn from it the decisions, and actions, of a great power state.

It is interesting, but useless, to speculate what might have happened if Lenin had lived longer. It was Lenin, more hardheaded than Marx but no less romantic, who gave the Russian revolution its special character. But he died, at the age of 56, only six years after the new state came into being. Already in 1922, two years before his death, he was horrified by the growth of bureaucracy, the conversion of the organs of state 'from servants of society to lords of society'. According to Trotsky, he was preparing a struggle against the faction of Stalin, which had made itself the axis of the party machine as a first step towards capturing the machinery of state. In the Lenin Museum in Moscow, a few years ago, I was shown the famous letter, written by him, in which he warned colleagues against Stalin – and, indeed, before he died he recommended that Stalin be dismissed because he was arrogant, conceited, and too contemptuous of those below him. In 1926 his widow, Krupskaya, said in a circle of Left Oppositionists: 'If Ilyich were alive, he would probably already be in prison.' Most of his closest associates were killed by Stalin, who was not beyond quoting Lenin to justify his deeds – thus setting an example followed to the present day. Lenin, he recalled, had laid down that 'whoever in the least weakens the iron discipline of the party of the proletariat (especially during its dictatorship) actually aids the bourgeoisie against the proletariat.' It followed that 'the existence of factions is incompatible with party unity and with its iron discipline'. For factions read critics and possible rivals; for dictatorship of the proletariat read dictatorship by one man – Stalin.

Much has been said and written about Stalin's thirty years as leader of the party and the country, and there is no need for me to go over it again. The facts speak for themselves. The state did not wither away: it became all-pervasive. Man's inhumanity to man did not end with the abolition of private ownership, private business, private profit. The state became a master more greedy, more brutal, more ruthless than any bourgeois exploiter. Lenin had argued that 'there is no need of a special machine, a special apparatus for repression. This will be done by the armed people themselves, with the same simplicity and ease with which any crowd of civilized people even in contemporary society separate a couple of fighters or stop an act of violence against a woman.' Stalin thought otherwise.

There are many Marxists, today, who maintain that the end justified the means. Stalin took over a backward agricultural country and, within a relatively short period of time, turned it into a modern industrial state. It was worth sacrificing two or three generations of Russia's intellectuals in order to enter the twentieth century; it was worth turning the Soviet Union into an autocratic police state, ruled by terror, in order to catch up with the most advanced industrial nations. Stalin himself, of course, always used this argument. As Khrushchev put it in his famous speech before the 20th Congress in 1956: 'Stalin was convinced that this was necessary for the defence of the interests of the working classes against the plotting of the enemies and against the attack of the imperialist camp. He saw this from the position of the interest of the labouring people, of the interest of victory of socialism and communism. We cannot say that these were the deeds of a giddy despot. He considered that this should be done in the interest of the party; of the working masses, in the name of the defence of the revolutionary gains. In this lies the whole tragedy!'

Stalin's approach was very much in line with the Marxist doctrine that economics is everything and the rest 'superstructure'. It shows the dangers of allowing economists to draw up blueprints for a new society: moral considerations invariably

112

take second place. (It also, of course, shows the dangers of allowing one party, and one man, to decide what is good for the rest of the 'proletariat'.) Khrushchev tried to put the Stalin era in its proper perspective, but in the last two years there have been efforts to rehabilitate Stalin, to portray him as a great, much misunderstood man. No doubt the same will, before long, be tried with Hitler. He did, after all, build the autobahns and rescue Germany from the misery of mass unemployment. It's always easy to write off generations if you and your relatives and friends are not, and have not been, part of them. It is even easier, for those who don't have to live in totalitarian states, to argue that liberal traditions of free speech, free association, and freedom to change institutions by democratic means are luxuries which backward nations cannot afford.

Was it worth it? Can *anything* excuse the suffering, the deceit and corruption, the degradation, the brutality and vileness which marked the Stalin years? Where, if anywhere, does one draw the line? Whatever Stalin's motives may have been in the early years there can be no doubt about his later reasons: the purges, the fabricated charges, the false accusations of conspiracy and treason against his countrymen, the branding of friends and party colleagues as 'enemies of the people' and their subsequent annihilation were the direct product of his own paranoia. To quote Krushchev again: 'In the situation which then prevailed I have talked often with Nikolai Alexandrovich Bulganin; once when we two were travelling in a car, he said: "It has happened sometimes that a man goes to Stalin on his invitation as a friend. And when he sits with Stalin, he does not know where he will be sent next, home or to jail." ' Is *that* worth it? And even if one thinks it is, is it *necessary*? There is no question that the Soviet Union made immense industrial progress during the Stalin years. It carried out its own industrial revolution in record time. But contrary to Soviet propaganda it did not have to start from scratch. Industrial development was already well under way when the Soviets took over. It was a late start, to be sure, but this wasn't necessarily a disadvantage: it enabled industrialists to eliminate the experimental stage and concen-

113

trate on the most up-to-date technology. When Stalin asked his economists to devise the first Soviet five-year plan they looked for, and found, the files of a tsarist industrial plan drafted on the eve of the war, and based their own programme on a revised version. Stalin speeded up the process, in a way in which perhaps no other man could have done, but he was by no means the first to recognize the need for industrialization. No one can say with any degree of certainty what might have happened without him. It is unlikely, though, that the economy would have stood still under Lenin or some other leader less addicted to brutality. And there is at least one important area where Stalin's crash programme proved a miserable failure – agriculture. Between 1928 and 1930 he drove millions of peasants from their homes and into hungry exile in Siberia and Central Asia. How many died, either from deprivation or at the hands of Stalin's bullyboys, no one has ever been able to estimate. Cattle, livestock, pigs, and horses died as well. The peasants slaughtered their animals and fowl rather than turn them over to the collective farms – his state-enforced, state-dictated co-operatives. And in 1953, a few months after Stalin's death, Khrushchev revealed the truth: in Stalin's last years, nearly four decades after the Revolution, the grain harvest was averaging almost 10 per cent below the totals reached in pre-war tsarist Russia in 1913. The census of farm animals was not equal to that of 1916, the last year of the Romanovs. Stalin must have known the figures, but as Khrushchev says he was by then 'a man divorced from reality'. He never went to any village after 1928. 'He knew the country and agriculture only from films. And these films had dressed up and beautified the existing situation in agriculture. Many films so pictured *kolkhoz* life that the tables were bending from the weight of turkeys and geese. Evidently Stalin thought that it was actually so. . . . Facts and figures did not interest him. If Stalin said anything, it meant it was so – after all, he was a "genius" and a genius does not need to count, he only needs to look and can immediately tell how it should be. When he expresses his opinion, everyone has to repeat it and to admire his wisdom.'

Stalin died in 1953, but his farm policy has produced recurring problems for those who have come after him. (Successive crop failures played a key part in Khrushchev's downfall.) The history of Soviet agriculture since his death has been one of relatively heavy, but still insufficient, investment in fertilizers, irrigation, electrification and machinery, and of scheme after scheme to improve production within the framework of the collective farm system. But the root of the trouble is in the people who work the land – who have no chance to develop initiative – and their supervisors, too often ignorant and idle, interested only in getting up under the glare of the party secretaries from whom they take their orders. To make up the shortfall the Kremlin has repeatedly been forced to buy large quantities of grain from America and Canada. The public are, for the most part, kept unaware that some of the bread they are eating has been made with flour produced by the much-abused capitalists. Not that it really matters; capitalist flour tastes just as good as communist flour.

If you visit Moscow during the winter, as I did on the first of my two lengthy trips to the workers' paradise, one of the first things which is liable to catch your eye is the shortage of fresh fruit and vegetables. A Russian journalist took me to a classy restaurant, and at the end of a meal which included handsome portions of caviar and smoked salmon the waiter brought a few apples. My companion thanked him profusely and urged me to help myself. I declined, saying that I'd had more than enough to eat. He look amazed. 'But these are *apples*,' he said. 'Yes,' I replied, not sure why that should be so significant. 'Well,' he added, still puzzled, 'if you are not going to eat them put them in your pocket.' I did. He later explained that apples were harder to come by than caviar; sometimes one didn't see them for months. On my second visit, some years later, another journalist accompanied me to Tblisi in Georgia. This is the garden of the Soviet Union and we had all the fruit and vegetables one could wish for. Georgian hospitality is justly famous, and when we left to fly back to Moscow we were both presented with crates of – well, you guessed it, apples. This time I knew

115

better than to refuse and we arrived at the airport laden like mules. Most of the other passengers, we discovered, were similarly blessed. Some, indeed, had done better: they were accompanied by live, cackling chickens which they insisted on keeping on their laps throughout the return journey. After this, I was not surprised to learn of the existence of a bit of free enterprise – the so-called collective farm markets, where peasants are free to bring their privately grown produce and sell it for whatever they can get. The Government, I was told, recognized that it was an anomaly but said nothing because the markets met an obvious need.

There are other things which catch your eye. The architecture for example. Pretentious neoclassic piles left over from the Stalin era; standardized, utilitarian five-storey walk-ups built, at great speed, when Khrushchev ruled in the Kremlin; blocks and blocks of unrelieved identical suburban apartment houses. Moscow still has a housing shortage, so people take whatever 'living space' (the official term for rooms) they can get. And then, in remarkable contrast, the metro stations, built of marble, look like palaces and have dazzling chandeliers instead of strip lighting. It's the most extravagant subway in the world and was designed to show Muscovites and visitors what the future could, and would, be like. Outside, the streets are wide and mercifully free of traffic jams; the car remains a luxury. You walk down Gorky Street and, inevitably, make comparisons with New York's Fifth Avenue and West Berlin's Kurfurstendamn. There is no colour, no grace, no style. Moscow is, in many ways, a fascinating city and there have been considerable improvements over the last decade. The present rulers are kinder to consumers than Stalin, or even Khrushchev, used to be. But there is still no warmth, no *joie de vivre*. For all the Kremlin's gloating over the problems of the West, the Soviet Union remains a land of empty shops and of warehouses filled with goods so shoddy that buyers cannot be found for them. It still takes a worker on the minimum wage two weeks to buy a decent pair of shoes and at least a month to buy the cheapest winter overcoat. And a man going on the dole in England might be dismayed if his living standard dropped to that of many fully-employed Soviets.

Krokodil, the Russian humour magazine, makes fun of Moscow's interminable queues ('you even have to queue to get into a queue,' one of its editors said to me), and of the difficulty of getting spare parts for state-produced goods like tractors and TV sets. One regular gag shows hardware coming off the assembly line and being carried straight over the road to a shop labelled 'repairs'. There are a lot of cartoons about drunkenness, the housing shortage, and the endless waiting one has to do in restaurants. (If you eat out, you must be prepared to wait half an hour or more before you are handed the menu, and even a simple lunch takes at least two hours. Waiters have no incentive to move faster and there is nothing you can do to speed them up. You simply have to learn to be patient – or go hungry. I used to take a book. Marx, I supposed, would write another chapter on the evils of profit.) Muscovites also tell a lot of jokes which don't find their way into print. The one quoted at the beginning of this chapter is a fair sample. Another goes like this: 'Soon every Russian citizen will have his own helicopter. What for? Well, for example, you hear in Moscow that in Kursk you can get matches or shoe-laces, so you jump into your helicopter and buy some.' Then there is the question-and-answer type of gag. Question: 'What was the nationality of Adam and Eve?' Answer: 'They were Russians. They went around naked, didn't have enough to eat, didn't have a proper roof over their heads, and yet they insisted they were living in Paradise.' During my last visit, the Kremlin was conducting one of its periodic campaigns against tipping, which is called 'an insult to the worker's dignity'. Muscovites went around asking each other, 'Can I insult you?' and foreigners like me were informed that 'all kinds of monetary humiliations are welcome'.

The staff of *Krokodil*, with whom I spent some time, are actively encouraged to attack bureaucracy and inefficiency. Readers' complaints about pompous officials, corrupt shopkeepers, shoddy products and countless other irritations are followed up, and if they prove to be justified the magazine uses

117

its own brand of attacking satire to cut the offenders down to size. Any small-time official picked on for backsliding is always named and usually denounced. Punishment in the form of demotion frequently follows. The editor maintains that as the bureaucratic set-up *is* the Government, *Krokodil* can be regarded as a vigorous opponent of the State machine. Since the attacks stop at a certain level this is debatable, but one only has to spend a few days in the Soviet Union to see why he likes this side of his job. The endless form-filling, the arrogance of petty officials and their unwillingness to take even minor decisions are some of the most depressing (though hardly unexpected) features of everyday life behind the Iron Curtain. For most Russians the real oppressor is not some shadowy figure in the Kremlin, but the little dictator strutting about in a scruffy office down the street. The inefficiency of central buying and selling organizations, and of anything remotely connected with the service industries, is equally notorious. And doing business with Government officials -- the representatives of State Trading Corporations -- can be a frustrating experience. Letters often don't get answered for months and, because everyone is reluctant to make decisions for which they might be held to blame at some future date you may not actually get results even if you are there on the spot. Some deals are done in three days but more often than not it takes up to three years.

One of the oldest – and, you may feel, most illuminating – things one comes across in Moscow is the immense regard everyone has for the dollar (so vigorously attacked in the cartoons) and other Western currencies, like the German mark, the French franc, and even the dear old British pound. The big hotels all have shops in which one can buy goods not available in Russian stores, providing one has foreign currency. Prices are given in dollars, and the story is told of an out-of-town Soviet couple who walked into one of these shops, delighted with the unexpected array of goodies, and produced their Russian roubles. 'Roubles,' they were curtly told, 'are no good. You must have dollars.' The husband looked puzzled, and then asked: 'And where can I get these dollars?' Inevitably there is a black market in 'hard' currency. In Leningrad I was twice stopped in the street by young men who asked if I could sell them pounds, marks, or dollars. They offered more than double the rate available in the hotels. I refused; currency dealing is a criminal offence in Russia and one never knows whether the offer comes from an ordinary citizen or an *agent provocateur*.

It doesn't, apparently, strike the fellows in the Kremlin as ironic that the hated symbol of capitalism should be king in their own capital. Or if it does, they don't care. Like most communist countries, the Soviet Union is permanently short of 'hard' currency with which to pay for American grain and sophisticated Western machinery. The *élite*, in any case, don't go short. Their many privileges include the right to shop at special stores. Here they can get Russian delicacies like caviar and all kinds of foreign goods that the proletariat never sees – Scotch whisky, French perfumes, American cigarettes, Japanese stereo sets. And there are other perks which help to make life at the top pleasant, including ample 'living space', servants, special clinics, country *dachas*, and chauffer-driven limousines which speed down the special centre lane of main avenues, the lane reserved for VIP cars. Still further benefits are gained by using influence or pressure: high officials, for example, get their offspring into universities and institutes and place them in good jobs afterwards. Hedrick Smith, a former Moscow bureau chief of the New York *Times*, says the privileged *élite* is a sizeable class, well over a million and, counting relatives, probably several million. And he tells a story which has been making the rounds in Moscow for some years. Brezhnev, so the story goes, brought his mother in from the Ukraine to show her how well he had done in the capital. He took her around his ample town apartment, ordered a chauffeur-driven car to take them to the airport, and flew her to his *dacha* in his personal helicopter. He escorted her through the banqueting room, into the gun room, and finally when he settled the troubled and ill-at-ease old lady in the lounge, he asked: 'Tell me, Mama, what do you think?' The old lady hesitated: 'It's good, Leonid. But what if the Reds come back?'

Whatever else the system may have done, it certainly hasn't produced a classless society. It has merely replaced one class with another; status and power have taken the place of profit. (Though even profit is not excluded. A Soviet citizen may own a house, a car, and so on, and there is no law against selling such possessions for more than he paid.) The new class, drawn from the political-economic bureaucracy which runs the vast machinery of state, is more secure than its capitalist predecessor because, if experience is anything to go by, there is no road back to freedom from Marxism. Leon Trotsky, who was first exiled by Stalin and then assassinated, saw it all coming many years ago. This is what he wrote in 1945:

'In its intermediary and regulating function, its concern to maintain social ranks, and its exploitation of the state apparatus for personal goals, the Soviet bureaucracy is similar to every other bureaucracy, especially the fascist. But it is also in a vast way different. In no other régime has a bureaucracy ever achieved such a degree of independence from the dominating class. In bourgeois society, the bureaucracy represents the interests of a possessing and educated class, which has at its disposal innumerable means of everyday control over its administration of affairs. The Soviet bureaucracy has risen above a class which is hardly emerging from destitution and darkness, and has no tradition of dominion or command. Whereas the fascists, when they find themselves in power, are united with the big bourgeoisie by bonds of common interest, friendship, marriage, etc., the Soviet bureaucracy takes on bourgeois customs without having beside it a national bourgeoisie. In this sense we cannot deny that it is something more than bureaucracy. It is in the full sense of the word the sole privileged and commanding stratum in the Soviet society.'

The command extends to every sphere, including education and the arts. Bureaucracy and party hacks determine what is 'safe' for young people to study, and what authors should be allowed to publish. They don't hesitate to distort and/or lie if it suits their purpose. History is subject to 'correct' interpretation – the struggle of the masses against the oppressive 'ruling circles'. Wars are either imperialist (bad) or of 'liberation' (good). Awkward facts, like the Stalin–Hitler pact of 1939, are ignored. Science is safe, technology is safe, but the humanities are something else. As for writers, they are supposed to be servants of the State whose only function is to give expression to what will serve the State best. They are not meant to indulge in what Khrushchev once called 'emotional self-expression'. Write a novel about a tractor driver who finds True Happiness in Siberia, or about a patriotic milkmaid who consistently fulfils her five-year plan twelve months in advance, and you may very well wind up a Hero of the Soviet Union. (Mind you, even that is far from guaranteed. Forty years ago Alexei Stakhanov hewed fourteen times more coal than normal from a Donets mine in one shift, and became a hero overnight. The Stakhanovite movement was launched to exhort all Soviet workers to follow his lead. But Stakhanovism is becoming increasingly unpopular: not long ago the authorities criticized one modern Stakhanovite, who had been milling ten times more parts in a Leningrad factory than is customary, for behaving in a vainglorious, money-grubbing, underhand and anti-socialist fashion.) Write a book on, say, the Soviet invasion of Czechoslovakia, or the power struggle in the Kremlin, or the positive side of capitalism, and it is unlikely to see the light of day. Western books which deal with controversial subjects have no chance of being published in the Soviet Union. You can't buy any Western newspaper or magazine in the Soviet Union other than reliable communist publications like Britain's *Morning Star*. (Here again the *élite* is the exception: one important sign of status is whether you qualify for the list of subscribers to the *Economist* and *Playboy*.) Painters, too, are expected to flatter the State and romanticize the common life of its people. You will, nowadays, find paintings by Picasso, Matisse, and others in the art galleries of Moscow and Leningrad, along with works from the Tsarist era. And, as one might expect, there are some superb exponents of modernism in the Soviet Union itself. But the bulk of art is still devoted to what Mayakovsky called 'heroic realism' – paintings of Lenin is heroic stances, memorials of the revolution and the Second World War, happy workers on a collective farm. The famous Hermitage Museum in Leningrad is full of them: so are the museums and galleries I have toured in Budapest, East Berlin, and other satellite cities. If you want to please the bureaucrats, young man, paint half a dozen brawny workers – men and women – carrying the red flag through knee-high cornfields. Everyone else seems to be doing it.

The usual reaction of Soviet officialdom to comments of this sort is that they are exaggerated and artificially selective. There is, they insist, no such thing as censorship in the Soviet Union, just as there is no such thing as an *élite*. The lie is dutifully echoed by trusting Marxist trade unionists and socialist politicians in the West. But the facts are plain enough – and they have ample backing from the small but growing number of writers who no longer feel able to stay silent. The mass of the people is, inevitably, apathetic. Like ordinary people everywhere, they simply want to improve their standard of living. And since they are deliberately cut off from comparisons with, say, America and West Germany (except for highly coloured official versions) they judge progress in terms of the past. Life is getting better; what more could one ask? But even ordinary citizens have reached the stage where propaganda is viewed with great scepticism. Slogans no longer produce the hoped-for response. Fanciful targets are not taken seriously. In agriculture, as we have seen, the collective system has produced a kind of passive revolt, with peasants concentrating on their private plots at the expense of the collective as a whole. In industry, the work-ethic is out of fashion: Soviet workers have become experts in the art of doing as little as possible. You don't have to take my word for it, or even that of the dissidents. The Kremlin leadership admits as much. In 1965 Aleksei Kosygin, the Prime Minister, announced major reforms designed not only to give managers more elbow room – to make them a little less like bureaucrats and more like entrepreneurs – but also to provide workers with more incentive. In future, he declared, the main criterion of success would be profitability. Salary bonuses would be directly tied to the profits of an enterprise, and a whole range of social services which Soviet enterprises provide for their employees, including housing and paid holidays, would also be financed from funds built up from accumulated profits. 'The advantages and opportunities offered by the socialist system of economy,' he told the Party's Central Committee, 'are still far from being utilized to the full.' More recently, the chairman of the State Planning Committee has lashed out at widespread inefficiency, wastage and delay in adopting modern methods, bad co-ordination in building construction, and lack of improvement in the quality of consumer goods. Only improved performance in work, he indicated, will net Russians higher salaries and a better standard of living. Privately, some Soviet economists have gone even further. A select group of Western specialists in communist affairs were surprised to hear a highly-placed economist observe, the other day, that what Russia really needs to improve economic productivity in the coming years is 'a pool of unemployed'. Efficiency, he added, was being undermined by 'an excess of job security'. What he might well have been hinting at is a quiet order to supervisors to get rid of the most persistent laggards who would then be systematically denied any other work. Or the hapless labourer could be advised that his only hope for getting hired would be to go off to some distant and unappealing place.

It is very possible that, as affluence increases, the Soviet Union will move further towards state capitalism and away from Marx's 'higher state in which true communism will prevail'. The scope is obviously limited, from the Kremlin's point of view, by the fact that any real diminution of central control would inevitably mean a decline in party influence – exactly the same experimental course that brought Nikita Khrushchev to political grief. The leadership also has unhappy memories of Czechoslovakia's drift to 'socialism with a human face', which they brought to a sudden end precisely because they feared that it might catch on in the Soviet Union itself. There is little chance that all the demands made by dissidents like Sakharov will be met. They want, among other things, freedom to strike,

123

a multi-party system, full amnesty for all political prisoners, and a law guaranteeing freedom to leave the country and to return to it.) But there is obviously a case for broadening the reform of 1965 and for partial denationalization in the area of services (repair shops, hotels, restaurants), in retail trade, in education, and medical care.

Whatever happens, the gap between the Soviet Union and the world's other communist state, China, is likely to grow still wider. For all its progress, China remains a comparatively poor country and is, therefore, more willing to try undiluted Marxism. The Soviets don't like what the Chinese are doing, and the Chinese say Moscow has betrayed Marx and his prophets. Relations between the two have deteriorated rapidly over the years; insults which were once reserved for capitalists are now traded between fellow communists with unfailing regularity. (China's favourite label for their comrades, these days, seems to be 'Soviet Social Imperialists' and Moscow's brand of Marxism is denounced as 'phoney goulash communism gone bankrupt'.) There are Western economists who believe that, ultimately, the Chinese way of life will triumph – that a hundred years from now we shall all live like Mao's robots. Their arguments are considered elsewhere, but this seems as good a point as any to state my own conviction that they are talking nonsense. At least, one hopes so. It has been fashionable, in recent years, to go on a whirlwind tour of Peking and Shanghai and to return with songs of praise for the dedicated, disciplined, spartan barrack-room existence of Mao's masses. How delightfully different it all is from the troubled West! No strikes, no struggles with the bosses, no tiresome disagreements with official policy. Just one big, happy, egalitarian family, with everyone wearing the same jackets and using the same chopsticks. 'One of the characteristic sights of Peking,' the resident correspondent of the London *Times* wrote recently, 'is the small army of Western visiting radicals, loping around in the spanking new cotton tunics and peaked caps which they are permitted to buy without the normal ration coupons at the city's big "Friendship Store". Their guides, trained propagandists, explain that rationing is just a temporary inconvenience and they nod approvingly. We'd have fewer problems in the West if we, too, brought back rationing. The guides tell them about Maoist innovations like "social courtyards", with ten residents appointed to supervise (and, if need be, to denounce) between thirty and forty families, and they readily agree that, yes, this is the way to enforce official control. (Hitler had the same idea, but Hitler was not a Marxist.) The guides add that one of the main purposes of the courtyard is to persuade families how excellent it is for children to be sent, often for life, to work in communes far away from home, often as far as the border regions of Sinkiang and Tibet. The visitors smile and say yes, this is how planning should work. It would do Western children good to be subjected to the same discipline. The guides say that extra-marital sex has been outlawed and that a further duty of the courtyards is to see that the residents breed as slowly as possible. The visitors express their admiration for the way China is handling the population problem, and promise to pass the idea on to their own governments. The guides point out that individual expression is a thing of the past – that painters, writers, designers, architects, and sculptors have all learned to suppress their individuality and are toiling feverishly to please the masses. The visitors say, yes, it's a good thing that awkward individualism should be suppressed. The guides explain that violent crime has been eliminated and that the bands of armed militia who patrol the streets at night are merely out on a training exercise. The visitors say they understand – how *could* there be crime in such a happy, well-run country?'

I don't know about you, but if this is happiness I'd rather be on the moon. China really is Orwell's *1984* in action: the mindless obedience, the fully-automated conformism, the dreary slogans, the numbing sameness of it all, add up to a bad nightmare.

The gap is even larger in the case of Hungary, Poland, Rumania, East Germany and other European communist countries. The installation of Marxist régimes in these countries was not the result of any internal revolution, proletarian or otherwise. All but one – Czechoslovakia's – were imposed by Russian arms after the defeat of Hitler. And although communist rule is firmly established today there is, in most cases, even less enthusiasm for Marxist ideology than in the Soviet Union. In Hungary, and later in Czechoslovakia, totalitarianism has had to use tanks to defend itself against the local people. In Poland, the shipyard towns of Danzig and Gdynia went on a rampage of strikes and violence that brought down the blinkered communist boss Gomulka and won higher wages and much better living standards. In Poland and Hungary the Government allows nowadays some private ownership in service trades like restaurants, cafés, and petrol stations. Yugoslavia has gone its own way since 1948 and now has the most westernized economic system in the socialist world. 'Our system,' says one of its leading economists, 'is built on the basis of two fundamental concepts. The first is that no central leadership, however wise it may be, is capable of directing unaided economic and social development whether in general or in detail. The second is that the effort and initiative of the individual is not increased in proportion to the rigour of the directives, controls, and checks exercised upon him ... to us the principle of self-government by the producers is the starting point of all democratic socialist policy, of every form of socialist democracy.' Yugoslavia, he goes on, has a 'free market within which enterprises compete one with another. Market success is determined by quality and price. The beneficial influence of competition upon pricing and quality, combined with considerable dependence of the material welfare of the whole working collective and even of the community upon the market success of the enterprise, provide a more potent stimulus toward quality and volume of production than could any form of administrative control ...'

Communism, with its emphasis on central control, has undeniably produced some notable economic successes – though the rate of post-war growth in capitalist countries like Germany and Japan has far outstripped that of the Soviet bloc. It isn't difficult to understand its attraction to underdeveloped countries. To reject communism, as I do most emphatically, is not to make out a case for capitalism. But as an alternative system for countries which possess, in any high degree, liberal traditions of free speech, free association, and freedom to change their institutions by peaceful means, it is utterly repugnant. Despite the well-advertised problems of the capitalist world, the rulers of the most prosperous country in the Soviet bloc - East Germany - continue to shoot fellow citizens who try to escape to the West. Wherever people have the opportunity to cross the border between communism and freedom, they choose freedom.

I mistrust anyone under thirty who isn't
a socialist and anyone over thirty who is.
GEORGE BERNARD SHAW

According to Engels, Marx in 1847 adopted the term 'communist' in preference to 'socialist' because socialism had by that time acquired a flavour of bourgeois respectability. But the word 'communist' rarely appears in official language: the Soviet Union is called the Union of Soviet Socialist Republics, and China is known as the People's Republic of China. Socialism is such a widely used label, and is open to so many different interpretations, that it might be as well to consider a few definitions. Hitler's Nazi party was called, officially, the National Socialist German Workers party, and indeed it fell within the technically precise meaning – a society in which the state exercises control over the means of production. But there is obviously a vast difference between the 'socialism' of Hitler's Germany and that of, say, Yugoslavia, or between the socialism of China and that of Sweden or Britain. There are at least as many types of socialism as of capitalism. In some countries earnest young men will tell you that socialism means 'bread for everyone'; in others middle-aged men will argue that socialism means *any* kind of state interference in economic affairs. Neither of these oversimplifications will do. It won't even do to define it solely in terms of economics: socialism, as we have seen, has all kinds of cultural as well as economic goals.

There are two fundamental differences between communism and the socialism generally practised in the West. The first is that Western socialist parties are *democratic*: they aim to install socialism in advanced capitalist countries having parliamentary systems. Secondly, social democracy is a thesis about means as well as ends. Communist societies believe that all the means of production, distribution, and exchange must be in the hands of the State. Social democratic countries are less emphatic: they put more faith in the individual and leave more room for private enterprise. Most of the arguments, between countries and between different sections of each socialist party, are about the *degree* of control to be exercised by the State.

Western socialism has always been based on good intentions. It is the practice which, as I hope to show, tends to go wrong. In the 1840s, as noted earlier, all kinds of groups and utopian colonies existed under the name of 'socialism'. One of the best known of the early socialists was Robert Owen (1771–1858). Born in North Wales into the family of a small businessman, he left school at the age of nine, continued his own education by reading, and at nineteen borrowed £500 from his father to set up his own business as a cotton spinner in Manchester. Before he was 30 he had bought the New Lanark Mills, near Glasgow, employing about 2,000 people. The prevailing condition of mill workers shocked him, and he decided to do something about it. He reduced hours, raised wages, built model housing, introduced free education, and placed in the schools all children under ten, whom he would no longer employ. In order to provide decent food and clothing at low prices he opened a company store. Recreation was provided, and insurance funds were set up. When, later, the mills were shut down for four months because of depression he paid his employees full wages. No one else had ever thought of doing such things. Conditions in the town improved and distinguished visitors came to see the 'miracle'. But industry as a whole failed to follow his example, and his partners demurred when he tried, as a next step, to limit profits to 5 per cent. The firm was dissolved. But he succeeded in finding new partners, among them the celebrated social philosopher, Jeremy Bentham. In 1825 Owen founded two co-operative communities, one in Scotland and the other in New Harmony, Indiana. Neither worked out well, and they consumed most of his wealth.

To Marx and Engels people like Owen were dreamers because they believed that society could be changed without revolution. But Owen helped to organize trade unions and his inspiration had a considerable effect on the British labour movement. In 1883 another small but influential group emerged – the Fabians. Like Marx and Engels they were bourgeois intellectuals; unlike them, they worked for improvement rather than revolution. They lectured to working-class and middle-class crowds, wrote pamphlets, and campaigned for individual policies. In short, they concentrated on goals which seemed within practical politics. At the same time, trade unions grew stronger and became more actively involved in politics. The Independent Labour Party made its début in 1893. (Keir Hardie, its founder, shunned the word 'socialist' and most of his successors have done so ever since. Harold Wilson even tried to have it removed from the party's manifestoes. To some people socialism is a holy crusade; to Wilson it is 'essentially a pragmatic conception, related to the needs of the age and the world in which we live'. An astute politician, he also recognizes that the word 'labour' ensures the loyalty of many workers who would not necessarily vote for the party if it were socialist.) Eighteen years earlier, the first purely socialist party of consequence had been formed in Germany and in the 1890s it became the main force in international socialism. The outbreak of war in 1914 put paid to another Marx theory: that the worker 'has no country' and that class war is the only war which concerns him. German socialists fought British socialists without the slightest hesitation, and vice versa. In Germany, they helped to create the mess which eventually brought Hitler to power. In Britain, they helped to administer capitalism. The Second World War also had a major effect on socialist fortunes, especially in Britain where voters elected a Labour Government the moment it was over. The story of British socialism since then has been one of continuous tug-of-war between the 'left' and the 'right' of the party, conducted against a background of more or less permanent economic crisis. Like Owen, everyone means well. Left and right both claim to be desperately concerned with the Common Good. It's just that they can't agree what the Common Good is, or should be, and how it should be served. The arguments are passionate and often bitter; hell hath no fury like a socialist who disagrees with his fellow man. And they cover not only economic subjects but a wide range of other issues as well: education, defence, immigration, welfare, press freedom, Europe, medicine. Somewhere in between – no one knows quite where – stands the man who led the party for thirteen years, Harold Wilson. His life's work has been to accommodate them all, from Marxists who are only in the Labour party because the Communist alternative doesn't work, to socialist lords, resplendent in the plush robes of the aristocracy.

Tony Crosland, a leading Labour politician who is generally regarded as being on the 'right', has given a lucid definition of the middle-of-the-road position. To begin with, there are the good intentions. 'The word "socialism" is not in any way an exact descriptive term, connoting a particular social structure, past, present, or even immanent in some ideologue's mind. Rather it describes a set of values, of aspirations, of principles which socialists wish to see embodied in the organization of society. What are these values? First, an overriding concern for the poor, the deprived, and generally the underdog, so that when considering the claims on our resources we give exceptionally high priority to the relief of poverty, distress, and social squalor. Secondly, a belief in equality. By equality we mean more than a meritocratic society of equal opportunities, in which unequal rewards would be distributed to those most fortunate in their genetic endowment or family background. We also mean more than a simple redistribution of income. We want a wider social equality embracing the distribution of property, the education system, social-class relationships, power and privilege in industry – indeed all that is enshrined in the age-old socialist dream of a "class-less society". Thirdly, strict social control over the environment – to enable us to cope with the exploding problems of urban life, to plan the use of our land

131

in the interests of the community, and to diminish the growing divergence between private and social cost in the whole field of environmental pollution.'

And how is all this to be accomplished? By taking over the means of production? No. 'We reject the Marxist thesis that socialism requires, depends on, and indeed can be defined as, the nationalization of the means of production, distribution and exchange. The ownership of the means of production is not now, in our view, the key factor which imparts to a society its essential character. Collectivism, private ownership or a mixed economy are all compatible with widely varying degrees of equality, freedom, democracy, exploitation, class feeling, industrial democracy and economic growth. We can therefore pursue our goals within the framework of a mixed economy, with public ownership taking its place as only one of a number of possible means for attaining our objectives. Indeed, I would go further. A mixed economy is essential to social democracy. For while a substantial public sector is clearly needed to give us the necessary control over the economy, complete State collectivism is without question incompatible with liberty and democracy.'

This was very much the line taken by the 1964–70 Wilson Government. The Keynesian revolution, it was argued, had shown ways of exercising economic sovereignty without the need for ownership, which had become an irrelevant nuisance. None of the Labour Ministers seriously felt that his problems arose from lack of control over private industry. Mr Wilson made considerable use of taxation, prices and incomes legislation, regional planning and direction, and the State's formidable purchasing power. Nationalization was hardly ever mentioned. It re-appeared in the party's next election manifesto, but Mr Wilson took pains to stress, on television, that the commitment to public ownership amounted to 'only a few sentences' in a policy document of 70,000 words. Needless to say, this lack of enthusiasm infuriated the 'left'. Mr Tony Benn, its self-appointed leader, declared that State ownership would be extended regardless of what the party leader might say. The

National Executive Committee and the annual party conference made supporting noises. The left-wing *Tribune* said there was 'no future for Mr Crosland's socialism'.

Ironically, the 'left' has since had considerable help from an unexpected quarter – the capitalist world itself. Economic hardship has driven one company after another into the arms of the State. Businessmen who, for years, have claimed to be stout champions of free enterprise have embraced socialism at the first sign of serious trouble. Appeals for financial help have poured in at a record rate, and the Government has spent staggering amounts of public money on propping up companies – indeed whole industries – which its own advisers insist have no commercial future. Like it or not (and people like Tony Crosland clearly do not) the State has become a major shareholder in all kinds of hopeless enterprises. (According to John Kenneth Galbraith much the same trend has emerged in America. The tendency, he claims, is 'to say to hell with principle when the prospect is for losing money and go for any port in a storm.') Ministers defend their actions chiefly on the grounds that the need to save jobs takes priority over everything else, but privately the 'right' expresses deep concern about the direction in which such short-term and narrow considerations seem to be taking them. It is one thing to nationalize public services like the railways, the Post Office and electricity. There *is* a case for state control in fields where wider community interests are clearly more important than financial gain. It is another thing, though, to saddle the state with all kinds of 'lame ducks' (a term coined by a Conservative Minister who later fell from grace) merely because the alternative conflicts with the party's good intentions. Too often public involvement arises not from logic but from an emotional refusal to accept unpalatable facts. The capitalists go 'for any port in a storm'. So do left-wing politicians and, of course, trade unionists. Nationalization is widely seen as some kind of a miracle cure, and instant solution to every financial and economic problem. Mortgages too dear? Nationalize the building societies! Trouble in the car industry? Nationalize Ford's! Shipbuilders finding it hard to compete with the Japanese? Nationalize the shipyards!

The emotional response is backed by a reckless attitude to public money. It isn't *real*; it's more like the little blue and gold chips they hand you in casinos, except of course that Government millions are used for a worthy cause. The causes multiply as fast as the millions so there is no risk that the Government will ever find itself with a money glut. I am a cause, you are a cause, they are a cause. There is no lack of champions and, because it's only Government money, no lack of support from the public. Free goldfish for old age pensioners? Why not! Pills for dogs, subsidies for parish magazines, free train rides for ex-Prime Ministers? Certainly! Let no one say the British aren't generous. Politicians would not be politicians – or, at least, successful politicians – if they were not tempted to go along with it. Blood, sweat, and tears make fine rhetoric but it's promises which win elections. And, after all, it's not their money they are spending. Do you think that Harold Macmillan broods, in retirement, over the millions he authorized when he was Premier? Do you think that Edward Heath, counting the royalties from his sailing memoirs, bothers about the chits he signed when he wasn't busy arguing with trade unionists? Politicians, even more than company chairmen, quickly become willing victims of the numbers game.

There was a time when the favourite unit of currency in Britain was the groat, and there have been other periods when people paid their bills with iron bars, or with the noble, the royal, the angel, the ora, the teston, the farthing, the half-crown, the golden guinea and the florin. I am old enough to remember sophisticated post-war currencies like the Clothing Coupon and the Packet of Woodbines. They have vanished, all of them. Today the Principle Unit of Account is the Million. The million is generally referred to in the plural, such as '£300 million' and, for the sake of headline writers, it is customarily abbreviated to 'm.' In recent years a new denomination, the billion, has come into general use. The abbreviation here is 'bn.' Thus one reads in the *Financial Times* that 'public sector borrowing requirements in the present financial year are now well into the £7bn.–£8bn. range'.

But let's stay with the smaller unit. The million has become so popular that scant attention is given to lesser amounts: it can't be long now before old-fashioned terms like 'hundred' and 'thousand' disappear from circulation.

No one, to the best of my knowledge, has ever actually seen a million, let alone a billion. Some people even question whether it exists. But the question is academic: we have travelled a long way since the days of the groat. No one expects Ministers to carry a sackful of notes and coins when they go shopping for companies. They merely sign a piece of paper – and, lo, we have another £50m. The medieval alchemists who spent all their time trying to find a recipe for gold never realized that a far simpler solution was right under their noses. (In 1450 a hopeful Englishman called Bernard de Treves mixed 2000 egg yolks with equal parts of olive oil and vitriol, and boiled this concoction for a fortnight. Like others before him and since, he was simply wasting eggs: you won't catch socialist politicians indulging in such tomfoolery.) Because it is invisible, the million is easy to multiply – you merely add a few more noughts – and even easier to spend. It also dispenses with the need to worry about words like 'deficit'. It is as difficult, these days, to get people worked up about a £60 million increase in the trade gap as it is to get them excited about a £60 million fall. It's not, after all, as if the bailiffs are going to come in tomorrow to take away the washing machine. Nor are you likely to get a letter from the managing director of the International Monetary Fund requesting your share of the nation's overdraft by the end of the month. Payments deficits are abstract concepts, far removed from the cares of everyday life. Let the Government worry. Something will turn up; it always does.

In Germany, where people are much more aware of what this attitude leads to, the socialists have exercised rather more restraint. In the twenties their predecessors took this game to its logical conclusion. A single dollar would buy you thousands of millions, and eventually, millions of millions of marks. Wages and salaries were paid daily, and soon twice daily, with the sums carefully worked out by means of a key based on the rise of the dollar. Wives used to come into the office in the morning, and again in the afternoon, armed with their shopping baskets as well as briefcases to hold the bundles of banknotes which had to be spent without delay. Children were sent round the corner with a 500 million mark note and came back with a bit of shopping and 70 million of change. Britain has not yet reached that stage and, hopefully, will never do so. But the thinking which produced this tragic state of affairs has become much more firmly entrenched than seemed possible fifteen or twenty years ago.

Britain's nationalized industries have been losing money at a terrifying rate. In the first thirty years of State control their aggregate deficits came to well over £9,000 million, and since 1962 some £4,000 million of capital debt or accumulated losses have been written off. The men who run these white elephants blame successive Governments which, they say, have forced them to operate under circumstances which make any other result impossible. 'The main problem,' says Sir Frank McFadzean, Chairman of British Airways, 'is that most Ministers can't keep their grubby fingers off.' Sir Monty Finniston, until recently Chairman of British Steel, claimed that 'if private industries had to put up with the restraints, constraints and irrationalities we do, they'd all be bankrupt'. And Sir Richard Marsh, a former Labour Minister who for several years headed the undisputed loss leader, British Rail, bluntly said, 'This business has never made a profit since nationalization and in my view it never will.'

The original nationalization statutes of the first post-war Labour Government enjoined state industries to do no more than 'break even, taking one year with another'. There was much talk of 'social' obligations which, they were told, would be taken into account in considering their financial performance. But these obligations were not properly quantified and could, therefore, be used to justify whatever losses they happened to make. At the same time, Ministers refused to let state industries raise their prices to realistic levels – ostensibly to 'set an example' to the private sector in the perpetual war on inflation, but in fact often to buy the housewife's vote by attempting to usher in a period of phoney relative price stability. The repeated tolerance of losses, inevitably, reduced the incentives to management to run their affairs efficiently. The game of running a nationalized industry largely became one of trying to calculate and achieve the level of losses for which plausible excuses could be found and which the Government of the day would be forced to accept. In the last resort the nationalized industries could not go broke – the safety net of additional public funds was always there. This freedom from bankruptcy was naturally seized on by the unions as a splendid device for securing higher wages and protection for employment. Nationalized industries have, over the years, been appallingly bad in their management of human resources. Short term sentimentality in crude job preservation, the interventionist role of Government as direct employers of nationalized-sector labour, and a system of placing by patronage rather than competition in most key posts, have combined to wreck managerial efficiency and good labour relations. Consumers all have their favourite anecdotes to support the charge of overmanning. They range from the story of the six different engineers who came on successive days to mend a gas leak, to the fact that there are 7,000 former steam-engine firemen employed by the railways to provide the engine drivers with cups of tea. And patronage did, under Mr Wilson's Government, reach scandalous proportions. The growth of State intervention in every field of activity created more public jobs on boards, corporations, commissions, and councils than at any time in British history.

To many people outside Whitehall and Westminster the range of jobs at the Government's disposal may come as a surprise. They may be aware that it includes prestigious posts like the governorship of the Bank of England, the chairmanship of the National Savings Movement and of nationalized industries like the Post Office, British Airways, and British Rail. They may also have heard that the Prime Minister decides who should head the BBC and IBA, or who should run organizations like the Central Office of Information. But others are a little more unexpected. The Prime Minister, for example, also appoints bishops and, in many cases, the heads of colleges and universities. And the Home Secretary, like other Ministers, has more than a hundred appointments within his gift, including the chairmanship of the Race Relations Board, the Community Relations Board, the Gaming Board, the Horserace Betting Levy Board, and the Horserace Totalisator Board. Then there are all those paid political advisers recruited by the Labour Government and the various people inquiring into this and that, with a knighthood or a peerage at the end of their labours. Whitehall keeps lists of suitable candidates (known as the lists of 'the Great and the Good') but Ministers have their own favourites, and lucrative appointments are often made on a whim. This was certainly true of Mr Wilson himself. His paranoia made him particularly susceptible to assiduous (and intelligent) flattery, and he tended to place personal loyalty above all else, including ability. In turn, he went to great lengths to ensure his friends a comfortable seat on the gravy train. It has never been difficult; today the immense power of the State machine makes it child's play.

The Conservative party did astonishingly little about nationalization (or, for that matter, State intervention in general) during its long periods of office. MPs complained, to be sure, and the steel industry became for a time a political shuttlecock. But Ministers showed themselves reluctant to initiate major changes – presumably because they, too, found the situation convenient. Passionately opposed to nationalization during the Attlee years, they made no serious attempt to alter the organization of state industries or to return them to the private sector. Pressure for closer financial discipline came not from politicians but from the Treasury, which grew tired of throwing good money after bad. The Conservatives, under their new leader, are pledged to 'put a stop to further nationalization', improving efficiency, and finding ways of selling shares in State concerns to the public. Another suggestion is that the brief of the Monopolies Commission should be extended to cover the State sector, and that it should be encouraged to use its power to break up the largest State corporations into much smaller and more manageable competitive units with a minimum of central common services and a maximum of local and regional attachment. But there is no question now of wholesale denationalization: where would one find investors mad enough to buy shares in British Rail or the Post Office? It is more likely that still more companies will fall into the Government's hands. The hope must be that socialist governments mean business when they promise, as they have done lately, that a more 'realistic' attitude will prevail in future.

The post-war experience with nationalized industries is not, alas, the only example of good intentions leading socialists astray. Public spending generally has grown at an incredible rate. Here again Ministers have promised, under pressure from Britain's creditors, to be more 'realistic' from now on. The fact is, nevertheless, that in 1975 the Government achieved the dubious distinction of being the biggest spender of all time: despite all those warnings that the country is in desperate trouble the Cabinet managed to spend a staggering £12,000 million more than it actually had.

Where did that record spending go? Who benefited from the Government's largesse? In part, as already noted, it went to private companies in financial trouble—companies which did not actually become State property. Every Government in the last thirty years has offered grants, subsidies, loans, and handouts in a well-meant but often futile attempt to 'get things going again', but Mr Wilson's Cabinet carried the game to new heights. At one time, early in his stewardship, his Ministers were innocently offering cash grants to non-British shipowners who were building ships in foreign yards for operation by non-British crews under non-British flags-of-convenience. As Robert Heller has pointed out in his splendid book, *The Common Millionaire*,* 'All that lucky Greeks needed was a plaque on the door of a

* Weidenfeld and Nicolson, London 1974.

139

London office. Some £60 million is supposed to have plopped into Greek and other foreign pockets before the civil servants in Whitehall, as ever reluctant to spoil the perfect symmetry of a scheme by correcting a ludicrous error (it never occurred to them that London shipping firms weren't necessarily British) were persuaded to block the drain.' Heller cites an even more bizarre situation: In Belfast 'the Government was busily pouring £50 million or more into a shipyard, one with a notorious appetite for cash, which it didn't even own. Half of the benefit of this enormous State expenditure will go to the outside shareholders, of whom by far the largest is a conspicuously non-greedy Greek, Aristotle Onassis.' I could add umpteen cases observed when I was a financial editor: the 'advance factories' built in neglected regions which no one wanted to use; the millions offered to smart operators who offered to implement the grandiose reorganization schemes of Whitehall planners (and who, of course, became millionaires in the process); the subsidies given to enterprises which everyone, including the most stupid junior Minister, knew to be doomed. One of the most grandiose schemes of recent years, the Concorde project, has cost the British taxpayer more than £1,000 million and there is no reason to believe that we will ever get a penny in return. On the contrary, we are expected to pay out several million pounds in subsidies just to keep the plane in the air. There is, as usual, a great deal of fancy talk about British technological achievement (though the French, co-sponsors of the project, naturally claim it as a French achievement) but it is hard to get away from the basic fact that staggering sums of public money have been spent, with the active backing of a Socialist Minister in whose constituency the Concorde just happened to be built, on a venture which will never benefit more than a privileged few. More recently, we have had the example of the *Scottish Daily News* – a worthy venture, to be sure, but nevertheless one which any businessman without access to public funds would have recognized as futile. And Chrysler – like other rescue operations of this kind, chiefly a case of short-term job preservation.

Then there is the Welfare State. The British have always had a particular fondness for the Welfare State because in a real sense they pioneered it. It was Bismarck, of all people, who gave the first big boost to socialist ideas of welfare throughout Europe with his social insurance scheme, but it was a British Government which laid the foundation of State paternalism as we know it today. The biggest advance came with the implementation of the war-time Beveridge Report, and particularly the introduction of the National Health Service in 1948. Economists applauded welfare spending, not so much because they felt deep concern for their fellow-men but because it fitted in with fashionable 'Keynesian' ideas on economic management. Unemployment benefits and other handouts, it was argued, would prove to be a useful stabilizing device during recessions, preventing incomes and spending from falling as drastically as they would do otherwise.

There are conservatives who still oppose the whole principle: to them the welfare state is nothing more than a mechanism by which governments rob the productive members of society in order to distribute benefits to people who are too lazy to fend for themselves. This harsh view is more prevalent in the United States, but it has plenty of followers in Europe, including Britain. I am not, of course, among them. You can see the Welfare State as an obligation we owe, as a community, to the less fortunate among us, or you can see it as a form of protection money – cash distributed by the State to ensure, as far as possible, that unscrupulous and/or disillusioned people don't burgle your house or mug your children. But you can't condemn it wholesale. There are 680,000 pensioner householders who, according to Whitehall, don't claim the benefits to which the law says they are entitled. I salute them – but I would defend to the death (well, almost) their right to change their mind. It is right and proper, in a modern society, that the State should provide a safety net for those who are truly in need. On this there is broad agreement among all the parties and of course it is a view shared on the continent.

What one can and should do, though, is to question whether

the system is properly run. Here there is much more scope for valid criticism. British welfare services have in many respects fallen well behind those prevailing on the continent, even though the public sector has accounted for a steadily increasing share of the economy. Figures published by the European Commission reveal Britain second from the bottom of the nine-member league on social spending (as a percentage of net income). Only Ireland spends less. This largely reflects the much more rapid economic growth rate in other European countries since the war. But there is no doubt that the system suffers from a wasteful and inefficient structure. The indiscriminate, across-the-board welfare services we have come to know not only cost too much, and force taxation up to dangerous levels, but make it impossible to concentrate the benefits where they are most needed.

A giant propaganda machine exists in order to persuade us that whatever we receive we have the right to get. In parks and public lavatories, on buses and in tube stations, in libraries and surgeries, in newspaper and television ads the Welfare State announces its careful benefactions. VD clinics and supplementary allowances, ante- and post-natal care, rent rebates and reduced fare travel, free legal advice and council housing lists, contraceptive facilities and library lectures – in theory there should be nobody who cannot be feather-bedded by the taxes and rates they do not have to pay. All of it is useful; certainly *not* all of it is necessary. And, inevitably, there is considerable abuse. Newspapers like the *Sunday People* and the *News of the World*, who delight in exposing 'scroungers', never have much difficulty in finding impressive-looking evidence. In 1975, claimed the *News of the World*, '13,000 people were taken to court for Social Services benefit claim frauds'. It went on to tell the story of a man called O'Hara, who had been on the dole for fifteen years, and of an unemployed builders' labourer who spent £150 on a holiday in Switzerland and Austria, and then wrote to Downing Street complaining that his benefit of £9·80 was stopped for his holiday week. The *Sunday People*, not to be outdone, had a go at 'Britain's crackpot council house set-up'. It told of the man with a gleaming Rolls-Royce Silver Shadow who moved into a council house, of the out-of-work labourer who had a refund on his rent even though he hadn't been paying any, and of the Asian enjoying 'cheap living in council homes, subsidised by the taxpayer' who was a landlord too. Tory MP Mrs Jill Knight chipped in with the tale of another Irish builders' labourer with eleven children who hadn't done a full week's work since he arrived in England in 1970. She thought we must be 'raving mad' to permit this kind of thing, but the *Daily Mail* quoted the Irishman as saying: 'Why pick on me? There are scores of families here in the same boat.' Other newspapers regularly focus on people drawing unemployment money every week but still working for cash in all sorts of trades throughout the country. The *Financial Times* has even published figures showing that people can be financially better off unemployed than at work over a wide range of incomes.

Not surprisingly, some of the sharpest criticism of the Welfare State comes from working-class people themselves. They are, after all, closest to the evidence. They resent having a sizeable slice of their income deducted to finance 'scrounging' and see, better than most, that the needy often lose out. The administration of the Welfare State has become a complex, as well as costly, business. The people at the bottom, for whom it was designed, find it a huge maze, full of one-ways and no-entries, mystifying hold-ups, and returns to Square One. Many do not even try to work their way through it. Again, middle-of-the-road socialists like Tony Crosland acknowledge that somewhere along the line things have gone wrong.

'We have made the painful discovery that a shift from private to public spending does not necessarily increase equality. We rightly saw that public spending could distribute goods according to need rather than to income. For example, a National Health Service could in principle provide the services of the best surgeon to the patient with the most need for his services, rather than the one who could afford to offer him the biggest fee. But we drew from this the mistaken conclusion that public

143

spending was *ipso facto* egalitarian – that it was always financed by the rich while its fruits were consumed by the poor, and therefore that the faster it increased, the more equal a society we should create. This has turned out to be an oversimplification. In the social services, much of the spending has gone on creating large bureaucracies of middle-class professional people. Where we once were sure that better education would enable working-class children to catch up with the children of the middle classes, we now know – thanks to the work of Jencks and his associates in the United States – that "the character of a school's output depends largely on a single input, namely the character of its entering children. Everything else – the school budget, its policies, the characteristics of the teachers – is either secondary or completely irrelevant." Moreover, we underestimated the capacity of the middle classes to use their political skills to appropriate more than their fair share of public expenditure. They demand more resources for the schools in their areas; they complain vociferously if they have to wait for their operations; they demand that the State intervenes to subsidise the price of the rail tickets from their commuter homes to their work. Too often these pressures have been successful; and in consequence the distribution of public spending has been tilted away from the areas of greatest need towards those which generate the loudest demands.'

Having made this honest and, for a socialist, remarkable admission Crosland goes on to ask: 'Should we then abandon our belief in high public expenditure?' The answer, he says, is No. 'For the principle remains valid; it is the practice which has gone wrong.' There you have it, straight from a man who has been a guru of many socialists for more than two decades. The trouble is that the practice *always* seems to be going wrong. Society is overturned, new taxes imposed, private medicine destroyed, the educational system changed beyond recognition, debts piled up at a frightening rate and at the end of it all the only people who really gain are 'those which generate the loudest demands'.

144

There's always got to be Them and Us.
MIDLANDS SHOP STEWARD

In the front ranks of that noisy group are, of course, the people who are supposed to be a Socialist party's closest allies - the leaders of trade unions. Not surprisingly, some of the strongest criticism of their activities nowadays comes from socialist intellectuals who resent their power and the way that power is being used. 'Trade unionism,' says Paul Johnson, 'is killing socialism in Britain, and it is time socialists did something about it.'

Johnson, a former editor of the *New Statesman*, argues that, from the moment the Labour party was founded in 1900, 'the emphasis should have shifted progressively from the outmoded sectionalist methods of unionism to the universalist methods of political socialism'. It hasn't happened. Britain's trade unions 'have not only rejected the idea of a progressive abdication, and the shift of their social and economic function to the political process, but they have flatly declined to allow the smallest diminution of their power to press the sectional interest they represent. Indeed they have steadily, ruthlessly and indiscriminately sought to increase that power. And in recent years, and particularly in the last five years, they have exhausted or beaten down any opposition and have finally succeeded in making themselves the arbiters of the British economy.'

Mr Johnson and his fellow idealists should not have expected anything else. Trade union leaders have always had one overriding objective: to get more money for their members. The union is not a socialist instrument, and the automatic assumption that every trade unionist must be a socialist, and vice versa, has never been supported by the facts. A survey published by the *Economist* in 1975 showed that only a bare majority of British trade unionists are Labour supporters: a third support the Conservatives. It reflects not only the growing affluence and aspirations of rank-and-file members, but also the fact that the movement not long ago ceased to be purely working class. Union activity nowadays extends to all kinds of middle-class trades and professions.

Even more inaccurate is the widespread claim that trade union leaders are anarchists. Exactly the opposite is true. To the true anarchist, the Trades Union Congress, with its endless committee meetings and squabbles about composite resolutions, block votes and election procedure, is anathema. Trade union leaders sit in the House of Lords, serve on Royal Commissions, and put on their best suits for those cosy Buckingham Palace luncheon parties. They are far more concerned with barriers, and if possible erecting new ones, than with tearing them down.

'There is no question,' says Johnson, 'of the unions being motivated against capitalism as such. Their motives, indeed, are difficult to analyse on any rational basis, being a mixture of hatred of management, dislike of change of any kind, fear of unemployment, unwillingness to adapt to technological improvement, and an almost childlike faith that the system will somehow continue to provide for them.'

Trade union leaders tend to counter that they are merely doing the job they were elected for. The nation's welfare is not their concern. They represent wage earners, and wage earners are chiefly interested in increasing wages and protecting their position. A leader who ignores this simple fact will soon find himself replaced. It's not for him to lecture his members on the need for social responsibility. It is an attitude which British governments feel compelled to challenge, from time to time, with varying degrees of courage and success. In 1969, the Labour Government decided to introduce an Industrial Relations Bill designed to curb the power of the unions. The Prime

Minister insisted that it was vital to Britain's survival and his Minister of Labour, a life-long socialist, readily agreed. At one point during the lengthy arguments which followed, Mr Wilson told union leader Hugh Scanlon that he did not intend to become another Dubček. 'Get your tanks off my lawn, Hughie!' Scanlon kept his tanks where they were. So did the others and, in the end, the Prime Minister suffered a humiliating defeat. The party (and, in particular, the large number of trade union-sponsored MPs) faced him with a simple choice: drop the bill or lose your job. The bill was dropped. In 1974 it was the Conservative Party's turn to discover who was boss. This time the Prime Minister, Edward Heath, refused to budge and the party was promptly thrown out of office.

I have always sympathized with the basic aim of trade unions to improve the lot of their members. If you believe in the profit ethic, as I do, you cannot demand that it should apply to business only. In America, this is much better understood than in class-conscious Britain. A worker is not 'wrecking the country' just because he wants a little more money for himself and his family. It is a practical issue, not a moral one. Strikes, too, are an entirely legitimate weapon. Industrial dispute is as old as industry itself, and is certainly not limited to us. Continental countries like Italy regularly outdo our own unions. But it is hard to sympathize with the other familiar features of British trade unionism: the class prejudice, the bloody-mindedness, the determination to maintain an elaborate network of restrictive practices, the reckless use of monopoly power, the incessant bickering among different unions, and the bullying, arrogant tone of their pamphlets, resolutions, and speeches.

The 'hatred of management' mentioned by Paul Johnson is by no means universal (many companies enjoy excellent labour relations) but it is certainly more common, even today, than it is in other countries. The foreign press invariably blames Britain's class structure, and there is no doubt that, by and large, this still plays a bigger role than it does elsewhere. 'This battle,' a Midlands shop steward told *Time* magazine not long ago, 'will continue when I have finished. This will always be the case.

147

There will always be people like myself to carry on and do this. There has always got to be us and them.' A great deal of the hatred, though, is based not so much on class as on plain envy and self-important bloodymindedness. These are also the chief factors behind a phenomenon which has nothing to do with management at all: the demarcation disputes, the arguments about procedure, and all the other petty rivalries which are the cause of so much industrial disruption. The British trade union movement is so haphazardly structured that it is inherently unstable. It is far more fragmented than that of, say, the United States or Germany and therefore tends to be more competitive: unions compete with each other, national officials compete with shop stewards for the loyalty of the rank and file, and groups of the shop floor jostle with each other at every opportunity. Inevitably, the system perpetuates outdated and often ludicrous practices, wastes time and money and, increasingly, limits the freedom of individual members.

Let us, for a moment, look at this last point – the threat to freedom. It is not merely a matter of restricting a man's right to make use of the full range of his abilities, though that can be frustrating enough. What disturbs me, as it does many other people, is the whole approach to the subject of individual liberty. The structure of working life in the seventies is leaving less and less scope for the non-comformist. In the scramble for numbers personal preferences are being sacrificed to so-called workers' solidarity. The Tolpuddle Martyrs suffered for the right to form unions; today's big unions gladly make martyrs of those who either do not wish to join them, or prefer to decide for themselves which union they shall join. If you think that is an exaggeration, consider the recent debate about one of the most cherished trade union institutions – the 'closed shop'.

The principle of the closed shop has always lain at the heart of the trade union organization, since only by excluding non-union workers could maximum leverage on management be brought to bear. Only if the work force could be welded together into a single cohesive mass, subject to common discipline, and willing to act as one, with no defectors tolerated, could union power hope to prove a match for the power of capital. But there is a point at which the legitimate, and reasonable, claim of the work force starts to clash with the equally legitimate and reasonable right of the individual to control his own life. In Britain this point has been reached and passed.

One of the more prominent illustrations, in recent years, has been the case of the so-called Ferrybridge six – life-long trade unionists who lost their jobs because they dared to leave the established unions and join a new one. A tribunal held that they had been unfairly dismissed but declined to recommend their reinstatement: they were described as 'unyielding and irritant types' who were not showing proper 'responsibility' in refusing to be dragooned into the union which authority decreed. The press, for once, showed understanding and sympathy because, for the first time in British history, journalists were facing a similar dilemma. Journalism has always been a trade which values its independence: one of its great attractions to the individual is that it isn't presided over by self-important committees, councils, or unions. Yet here was the Labour Government telling us that we had better join a closed shop or else. The Ferrybridge six were about to become the Fleet Street thousand. The reaction of Tory columnists like the *Sunday Telegraph*'s Peregrine Worsthorne were predictable and caused some amusement among left-wing colleagues. Worsthorne announced that 'coming from a bourgeois background, with the appropriate education of that station, the idea of being forced to join the National Union of Journalists, with all that this implies in terms of accepting its rules and allowing it to speak and act on my behalf, is profoundly repugnant'. It sounded like a typical piece of aristocratic snobbery and Worsthorne characteristically acknowledged that it might be seen that way. 'Mine,' he said, 'may be a case of extreme, almost neurotic anti-trade union consciousness.' But his concern was, and is, shared by less aristocratic journalists including, I need hardly mention, me.

Journalism has changed a great deal since I first went into it at the age of 18. I got my first job, on a weekly magazine, through an advertisement in the *Daily Telegraph*. The magazine's editor, now Lord Ryder, didn't ask me whether I belonged to a trade union and I, in turn, didn't ask about my pension rights. Questions like that would have struck us both as irrelevant. I accepted a low salary because I was eager to get into a trade – of, if you like, profession – which I admired and for which I thought I had a certain aptitude. I worked long hours and, because the staff was small, took on all kinds of tasks which, had I gone into the printing trade, would have caused me no end of trouble. None of us knew the meaning of demarcation, so there was no cause – or time – for tedious disputes. My first brush with trade unionism did not come until years later, as Financial Editor of the *Sunday Express*, when I happened to pick up a block late one Saturday evening, and the Head Printer – a keen union man – promptly threatened to halt production of the paper. I thought he was joking but he was in deadly earnest. I, a fellow worker, had committed the ultimate sin. I had crossed the trade union line. It was a far more serious offence than writing a bad article or letting in for a costly libel action the paper on which both our futures depended. Since then, of course, I have learned to be more careful. Fleet Street is a classical example of trade union foolishness: so many of my colleagues would rather let the paper die than show a little common sense. And an 18-year-old beginner, however talented, now has little or no chance of joining a national newspaper. The closed shop system, as applied in the seventies, deliberately prevents many potentially good journalists from being got into the profession – and keeps many bad ones in it. It also presents a quite genuine threat to the freedom of the press. It is intolerable that editors should no longer be permitted to employ the best available talent and equally intolerable that the opinions of journalists – and cartoonists – should be subject to the censorship of trade union militants.

Don't get me wrong. I am not, as I hope I've managed to make clear, opposed to trade unionism as such. I have as little time for the emotional, sweeping condemnation of trade unions, so common in the Britain of the seventies, as I have for the equally emotional denouncement of managers and owners. I do not accept that the unions 'run the country'. The power they possess is less positive than that – it is the power to restrict choice and to obstruct, sometimes to veto, the initiatives of elected Ministers in the limited, but decisive, areas of our national life where industrial strength can effectively be applied. I would dearly like to see British trade union leaders become more flexible, more open-minded, more ready to acknowledge that, in many respects, the interests of employees and employers are the same.

There *are* trade unionists who fit the bill. People like Bill Sirs, general secretary of the Iron and Steel Trades Confederation – a dapper, deceptively mild-mannered man who insists that the 'them and us' approach has no place in the seventies. 'I don't see my relations with management that way,' he says. 'I like to feel that I appreciate their problems as they do mine. I am here to represent my members and that is my main job. What I try to do is represent them sensibly and that sometimes means the company can have a point.' It is the kind of comment that, in the past, has come from American or continental trade union leaders rather than their British colleagues and, one hopes, will be heard more often in the future. The impetus, according to many people on both sides of industry, will come from a comparatively new concept: participation.

How Much Participation?

Participation can take various forms, from profit-sharing to seats on the Board. And, inevitably, it is the subject of much controversy. Some people argue that worker participation represents an intolerable attempt to supplant the legal owners of a business, the shareholders. Workers, they insist, must be kept in their place. Others maintain that the whole idea is a capitalist trick – a means, as one of Britain's Marxist trade union leaders has put it, 'of propping up, perpetuating and retaining a corrupt capitalist system'. Both sides, however, are outnumbered by moderates anxious to bridge the gap between

151

Them and Us without going as far as the communist world has done in this century. Most, if not all, political parties now acknowledge the need for some form of participation: the real argument is over the question of degree. The progress made in this area over the last ten years would have amazed Marx and horrified Rockefeller. It is both an acknowledgment of trade union power and a tribute to the non-communist world's ability to adapt itself to changing conditions.

In its broadest possible sense worker participation means wider involvement and participation by a company's employees in the decision-making process of that organization. There are, however, two important points which must be emphasized about this definition. First, participation in decision-making is meant to include all employees; manual workers, middle management, and clerical staff, and not simply the unskilled and skilled worker on the shop floor. Secondly, there is an important distinction between *immediate* and *distant* participation. Immediate participation refers to workers' involvement in the day-to-day decision-making process of their work group, be it on the shop floor or among clerical workers in the office. This form has manifested itself in the last ten years in the development of autonomous work groups, job enrichment schemes and work restructuring. In this sense worker participation in management is seen as a means of improving the quality of the worker's life on the job. Distant participation, on the other hand, refers to the process of including company employees at the top management level of the organization so that they may be involved in decision-making on long-term policy issues, such as investment in new machinery, employment, and even in the types of goods produced.

Sweden is generally acknowledged to have led the way in immediate participation, and some of its experiments have produced impressive results. Take, for example, the group working schemes introduced by car firms like Volvo and Saab. The straight assembly line layout is modified so that a group of workers assumes responsibility for a sub-assembly of tasks with a visible end product. The pace and method of working can be adjusted by the group provided production schedules are met. The individual gains pride in his job; he feels *involved*. A similar approach has been tried in other industrial situations, with beneficial results. The Swedish employees' confederation has, on the basis of these experiments, laid down some broad guidelines. It suggests that three formal targets be placed before a group when it is first formed: (1) attaining a high and rapidly rising level of productivity, (2) stimulating interest in the job through a broadening of duties, and (3) creating security of employment. It is widely recognized in Sweden that job security depends on the firm remaining competitive, both through high productivity and by changing to meet new conditions. Some go so far as to say change is actually a prerequisite for job security.

The work, says the federation, should be organized to make full use of the workers' knowledge and experience and they should be encouraged to widen their activities by rotating jobs within the group. This implies that, as knowledge grows, the work will be reorganized – the whole concept is closely associated with growth and self-adaptation.

West Germany is the model of Western European countries for worker participation at board level or what they term 'co-determination of employee in economic enterprises' (*mitbestimmung*). At the foundation of this co-determination policy are the works councils, which are common not only in West Germany but in most of Europe. In Germany any company of five or more employees can form an all-employee works council which must be consulted or informed on manpower and production planning, safety regulations, and the general economic situation of the organization. Its approval is also needed on matters involving salary/wages, working conditions, recruitment, and dismissal. In larger organizations there is a two-tier board system. Control is divided between a 'supervisory board' which decides major questions of policy, and an 'executive board' of the directors who actively manage the enterprise. The supervisory board appoints the latter, has unlimited rights to information, and exerts influence by recommendations and suggestions. Its membership is divided between representatives of shareholders and employees *plus* at least one further member defined as 'an independent personality without common interest in either group'. The executive board must include a director for labour relations whose appointment is subject to the votes of the majority of employee representatives on the supervisory board. Supporters of the system claim that this new style of shop-floor democracy has produced both better labour relations and greater social equality. The weight of evidence is on their side but, of course, it isn't hard to pick holes in their case if that's what one is determined to do. Businessmen tend to say that it gets in the way of sound commercial decisions. Managers, they maintain, must be free to discuss policy without being preoccupied with the risk that what they say may be misunderstood and lead to confusion on the shop floor, just as workers' representatives must be free to meet on their own. If you put the two sides on the same board, they claim, there is a serious danger that meetings will become perfunctory with the real decisions being taken before and by managers alone. Trade unionists tend to argue that the system gives the semblance but not the reality of democratic control to the shop floor.

In Britain, particularly, the whole concept of participation has been treated with suspicion. British trade unions have always been wary of all measures which could have the effect of undermining worker solidarity by creating 'management-oriented' elements in their midst. (Self-interest also comes into this: officials are very conscious of the fact that rank-and-file involvement may undermine their own authority. Remember the profound comment that all power corrupts and even a little power is absolutely intoxicating.) The feeling is shared by many of the workers themselves. They are not interested in intellectual debates about participation: their sole concern is to secure the maximum amount of cash. All these fancy schemes, they suspect, are simply a dodge to make them work harder and for less money than they might otherwise get. Put a worker on the Board, they say, and in no time at all he will, inevitably, become one of Them. The temptation to lord it, to accept the willingly offered trappings of success, are too hard to resist. A company car? Tea with the chairman's family? Lunch in the executive dining room, and the key to the executive lavatory? Well, why not? It's all part of the job, isn't it? And even if he manages to resist the multifarious blandishments, isn't there bound to be a clash of loyalties? Boardroom discussions invariably centre around questions which most of the work force prefers to ignore. Closer acquaintance with a balance sheet, for example, may change his views about 'profit'. Or someone may come up with a scheme which will make the firm more efficient, but put some of its employees out of work. Who can guarantee that he won't take the employers' side? The habit of conflict is too deeply imbedded; there is still widespread support for the view, noisily propagated by the militants, that trade unions would be compromised by involving themselves in management, and weakened in their role as official *opposition* to management. The only answer, for those who genuinely believe that a free enterprise society should strive for an effective partnership between labour and capital, is to persist with efforts to bring the two sides closer together. 'Union bashing' not only misses the point but clearly strengthens the hand of militants who want to see private enterprise vanish altogether. There are, today, far more examples of partnership arrangements than is generally realized— arrangements which give the lie to the cliché argument that Britain is rigidly divided between two classes. But it is fair to argue that we have been slow to recognize the challenge, and even slower to do something about it. One inevitable result is that politicians have felt it necessary to impose their own ideas, regardless of the needs of a particular factory or plant.

Where should we go from here? There is no shortage of schemes, both for more 'immediate' and 'distant' participation. Some people claim that the most urgent problem is, very simply, better communications. Most companies, they maintain, still don't understand the distinction between telling their employees and consulting them. Merely telling people what is going on is a one-way flow of information of very little use (though better than nothing). Getting a two-way exchange of ideas going calls for real effort to break down old prejudices and suspicions, coupled with a willingness to share in actual decisions. There is, as one would expect, considerable disagreement about how far this two-way flow should go (do you *really* think that workers should have a say in what they produce, not just in how and for how much they produce it?) but the principle is nowadays accepted by most industrial groups. It isn't enough to publish brash 'house' journals and hold annual conventions or company dinners at which the chairman doles out patronizing praise. This, of course, is precisely the argument which led to the establishment of works councils and two-tier boards. People like Sir Bernard Miller, former chairman of the John Lewis partnership, have no patience with anything so half-hearted: Sir Bernard wants to abolish equity capital and transfer company ownership to the workers under trust arrangements aimed at combining managed and management in a joint responsibility. Peter Jay, Economics Editor of the *Times* and son-in-law of the present Prime Minister, also thinks the law should aim for a system of workers' co-operatives. Others are rather less ambitious. They want to see still closer involvement in decision-making and a significant extension in profit-sharing and share-ownership.

It's always fun to draw up plans for other people and, I dare say, even more fun to introduce legislation compelling them to put one's plans into practice. We shall deal with the issue of workers' control in a moment, but let us first consider the subject of profit-sharing and wider share-ownership. Profit-sharing schemes of one kind or another have a long history. There have always been entrepreneurs, from generals to property developers, willing to share the spoils with subordinates. Some did it because they had no choice: to deny a victorious army part of the loot, for example, might well have meant risking a mutiny. Others saw it as a way of spurring workers on to greater effort. There are countless different schemes in operation right now. Some take the form of an annual or twice-yearly 'bonus' distribution. Others consist of an annual handout of shares in the employees' own firm. The latter has been encouraged, for obvious reasons, by Conservative governments in Britain and elsewhere but has usually run up against one simple problem: recipients have sold the shares at the very first opportunity because immediate cash was more important to them than a stake in the future. (Companies have also had disappointing experience with another well-intentioned idea – 'share shops'. Counters were set up on factory floors at which workers could buy shares in their own company or any other they had their eye on. The scheme enjoyed an early boom, but it was soon discovered that the enthusiasm was linked directly to the fortunes of the stock market. When the market went down, and they made the painful discovery that speculation can involve losses as well as gains, the interest vanished. Few seemed to care about genuine long-term investment.) Companies have had more lasting success with the so-called deferred profit-sharing scheme, first developed by a German economist who died in 1850, J. H. von Thunen. Thunen thought that everyone should benefit from rising productivity but he wanted to know what was a fair division of the product between those who supplied the labour and those who supplied the capital. The key to his answer came from watching what was happening in America. The open frontier was continually luring people to strike out westwards, settle on virgin land, under the Homestead Acts, and build up their own capital. Employers farther east therefore had to pay a 'frontier wage' to encourage employees to stay where they were. Thunen's mathematics are used to demonstrate that in these circumstances of an open frontier, the fair or just wage, which brought maximum motivation and maximum reward to *both* labour and capital, would be the geometric mean between the basic subsistence wage which was commonly paid in those days and the net revenue per worker obtained from running the business after deducting all expenses except the rewards of capital. But at this 'frontier' level of wages it wasn't really possible to pay out the whole wage in instant cash. Part of it would have to be re-invested in the business, as a deferred profit-share, and paid out later. Anyone

157

receiving a 'frontier wage' would have to accumulate some capital, as was being done by the new settler who was actually at the frontier. If this was not done, productivity would not grow to give maximum return to both capital and labour.

Two years before his death, when Thunen completed his wage formula, he set up a system of deferred profit-sharing on his own estates. Employees were credited with a part of the profits which was invested for them in the business and they were paid a rate of interest. The accumulated sum was presented to them on retirement. There were, of course, no pensions in those days. The system continued successfully on the family estates for generations after his death. It is the primitive model for the deferred profit-sharing schemes which now exist in 175,000 American companies, including most of the giants. The system is spreading at the rate of 25,000 more companies a year, encouraged by favourable tax treatment. President de Gaulle was so impressed by it that on his initiative a law was introduced in 1967 applying a compulsory system of deferred profit-sharing, with favourable tax treatment, to all French companies with 100 employees or more. In Germany personal capital accumulation is run on a somewhat different basis, applying to civil servants and others, as well as to business employees. There have been three special laws passed about it, the most notable being one of 1965 which provided incentive for trade unions to negotiate with employers for capital accumulation at a place of work.

Predictably the various company schemes have come under socialist attack because they threaten to turn workers into capitalists. But there is impressive evidence that they produce beneficial results. In the United States, a major research project compared – over an eighteen-year period, 1952–1969 – the performance of a sample of companies with schemes for employee shareholding against the performance of similar firms without such schemes. The average rate of growth of the first was twice as fast as the second. Faced with surveys of this kind, trade unionists in some countries have come up with a different proposal – that governments should introduce systems which, in effect, would increase central trade union power through control of investment. The Danish scheme, for example, proposes that all employers, public and private, would contribute a proportion of their wage bill – $\frac{1}{2}$ per cent at first, rising to 5 per cent over nine years – to a central wage-earners' fund. Broadly, two-thirds of the contribution would remain as share capital in the company it came from, one-third would be freely investable elsewhere. Workers would get certificates of participation in the fund – equal for all, irrespective of wage levels – which could be cashed after seven years. It is reckoned that within seven years the fund would hold 35 per cent of total Danish share capital, though there was a provision that it could never hold more than 50 per cent of the company's equity. The fund would be controlled by twenty-four Government appointments and thirty-six appointed by worker organizations.

Similar ideas will no doubt sprout in future. They should be vigorously opposed: the last thing we need is monopoly trade union capitalism. But the British Conservative Party – and individual companies – would certainly do well to give the whole subject of employee shareholdings still closer and more vigorous attention. They may not always produce the hoped-for results, but all the evidence suggests that they can and do help to change the climate of industrial and political opinion. The amount of profit which a company has to set aside for buying shares for employees is relatively modest; it is typically 10 per cent of 'residual profits' after deducting dividends and any reserve needed for inflation. The gains, in terms of understanding and support, can be considerable. Meantime, employers might care to give a little more publicity to the fact that, in a round-about way, workers already have a massive stake in industry through the shares held by pension funds. This is as true of America as it is of Britain: US pension funds are reckoned to own more than one-third of the capital of all large and medium-base business, and a majority of stock in most of the 500 top corporations. In short, workers already participate to a much greater extent than is generally realized.

Which brings me to the subject of workers' *control*. Again, the basic notion is far from new: in Britain it goes back to the Industrial Revolution. Many people have long argued – generally with more passion than sense – that all would be well if only management would step aside and let shop stewards have a go. 'Power to the People' is an attractive battle cry. The most cruel answer, in a lot of cases, would be actually to let them do it. For, as a rule, it simply reflects a determined refusal to accept unpalatable financial facts. Never mind if a factory cannot sell the stuff it makes: production must be maintained regardless. The State can be relied upon to foot the bill. There would, I suspect, be a great deal less enthusiasm for the idea if one suggested that shop stewards should run the shipbuilding industry, say, or *The Times* newspaper, as an independent, unsubsidized operation. The prospect of sharing substantial losses holds little appeal. It certainly doesn't attract the people most directly affected – the workers employed at the plant. They are a good deal less interested in idealism than in the financial backing for their weekly pay packets. Redundancy pay is preferable to desperate last stands, and the majority would like nothing better than to maintain the *status quo*. It suits them to have bosses to complain to, and to have shop stewards to complain on their behalf. They don't want to be their own bosses. Trade unions, too, have proved far from eager. They know that the present system gives them far more effective control. Union strength today is such that few managements dare to brush aside the shop steward's wishes.

Some people would, of course, argue that all this is only so under a capitalist system. But communism is hardly better. Officially the worker controls Soviet industry. In practice, he does nothing of the sort. If he works for, say, the railways he finds that, as in Britain, control is firmly in the hands of the managerial class. Worse, the managerial class itself is dominated by the Moscow bureaucratic class. Not only is the worker far removed from real power, but the elaborate pretence that industry is being managed in his name deprives him of the right to use his most effective weapon – the strike. It is, the Kremlin insists, not 'necessary'.

Under capitalism, there is nothing to prevent a trade union or any group of idealists from setting up their own business and running it under workers' control. There are plenty of precedents – the experiments of Robert Owen and other 'Utopians'; Guild Socialism; the Co-operative Movement. Indeed, it would be easy to draw up a list of a dozen companies, in different parts of the world, which for some years now have been owned and operated exclusively by workers. In France and other countries, workers' co-operatives are commonplace. (I am including small farmers and wine-growers in the definition of 'workers' because that's exactly what they are.) The same is true of many other Western countries. There is no reason why this shouldn't be extended. I have, over the years, tried very hard to persuade trade union leaders to use their accumulated millions to make a public take-over bid for a prosperous going concern (say a large electronics group) and let the workers show what they can do if they are given a fair start. I have even offered to contribute £100 myself – and I hereby repeat the offer. The response, alas, has always been negative. Trade union leaders are reluctant to take on the challenge. And, of course, their Marxist friends and colleagues don't want them to do so: it might prove that the private enterprise system can be made to work after all. It's so much easier to attack big business – and to call on governments to pass laws which will allow one to requisition *other* people's property, ideally without a penny of compensation.

Chapter Ten
The Profit Motive

The smell of profit is clean and sweet, whatever the source.
JUVENAL

'Please,' a socialist Minister of Labour urged a British trade union conference a few years ago, 'stop equating profits with incest and lechery.' Incest? Lechery? Is that really how they talk about profits in the canteens and working men's clubs, or at the football match on Saturdays? I find it hard to believe, but there is no question that profit has long been one of the dirtiest words in the socialist vocabulary. Generations of ardent revolutionaries have made it synonymous with avarice and exploitation. Their campaign has been so effective that the London *Times* felt compelled to warn, not long ago, that 'it could well become the cross on which capitalism, and even democracy, might ultimately be crucified'. Losses, as we have seen, have always been regarded as much more acceptable.

I have no doubt that in this, as in so much else, there is a wide gap between the thinking of ordinary people and intellectuals. The ordinary person does *not* despise the profit motive as such. A survey published in 1976 showed that fewer than one in ten British workers think profit is a dirty word. There is a ready acceptance that, as Adam Smith argued, 'it is not from the benevolence of the butcher, the brewer or the baker that we expect our dinner, but from their regard to their own interest'. Common sense tells people that no one works for nothing – and, since most of them are not prepared to do so either, there is no serious disposition to regard profit as a deadly sin. The man who fills in a football coupon every week, or buys a lottery, does so in the hope of personal gain – just as the man who buys a shop, or opens a garage, will work eighteen hours a day, if necessary, because he hopes and expects that his efforts will make him more prosperous.

Intellectual resentment of profit, as such, arises partly out of envy – a teacher or a scientist has less chance of making money than a shopkeeper or a salesman – and partly out of the snobbish attitude which intellectuals have always had towards commerce. Deep down, they are in two minds about it. On the one hand, they want the benefits which profit produces both for mankind at large and their own world in particular. Intellectuals are always ready to claim their share of the spoils for whatever scheme or project is close to their big, pure hearts – a new art gallery, a new museum, a play, a college, a fellowship. It's rare for a college or university to turn down a millionaire's offer of financial help on the grounds that the cash represents immoral earnings; indeed, I have yet to hear of a single case of such touching self-sacrifice. Most intellectuals regard it as their *right* to share in the rewards of enterprise. It is the process which so offends them. Their sensitive souls can't stand the pursuit of profit, the values of the businessman, the manifestation of other people's self-interest. All they are really interested in is 'levelling wealth', which means taking from the rich and giving to those who, in their judgment, are more deserving. The rest is tedious detail.

The distaste for commerce and profit is strengthened by an old but still popular myth: that if someone gains, someone else loses. There is a simple and therefore widespread assumption that if two people engage in a transaction, and one of them is seen to profit from it, the other person must have been exploited. In other words, trade is viewed like a football game. Once the myth is accepted, many things follow. All business is seen as a frantic scramble to take something away from someone else, and all wealth is thought to have been accumulated by exploiting other people. The theory is extended to embrace whole groups and, indeed, nations. But you don't have to be an economist to expose it. Take this everyday happening. You walk into a shop and buy a suit. You do so of your own free will, and you gladly pay the price. The retailer has reason to

163

be pleased with the transaction – it shows him a profit – and so have you. Both of you have received an item of greater value to *you* than the value of the item with which you have parted. You prefer the suit to the money; he prefers the cash. Both of you have gained by the exchange. The same may just as easily be true of larger deals. The Soviet Union, faced with a disastrous harvest failure, arranges to buy millions of tons of grain from the United States. The farmers who sell it make a profit. The Soviet Union feeds people who might otherwise go hungry. Both parties gain.

The element which criticis invariably leave out of their argument is *risk*. There is no guarantee, under the free enterprise system, that the seller will be rewarded for the time, money and effort he has put into the process which leads up to the transaction. A dozen or more factors may be against him, including the weather, changes in fashion, Government regulations, and skilful competition.

Take another obvious illustration. A restaurant owner goes to the market and buys what he thinks he may need. But he cannot be sure how many customers will come to his place and, inevitably, there will be some waste. The actual meal he serves to you will make him a profit, but he has to make allowance for the waste as well. Many incautious restaurateurs have gone bankrupt because they have failed to do so. The larger business will have a better chance to spread the risk, but it is still there. And even if demand comes up to expectations, Government regulations will put a brake on the proceeds. At the one end it forces up costs; at the other, it makes it difficult, if not impossible, to charge whatever the market will bear.

Allowance also has to be made for trading setbacks. Conditions can and do vary considerably from year to year, and earnings with them. Indeed, it is by no means unusual nowadays to make a profit in one year and a loss the next. If it weren't for that year's profit the company might not be able to stay in business. Workers as well as the bosses would suffer. Then there is the need to buy new plant and equipment. A carpenter occasionally needs new tools; a restaurateur needs new cutlery and table linen; a newspaper needs new printing presses; a brewery needs new bottling plant. The most obvious source of finance is profit. (You can, of course, go to your bank manager and ask for a loan – but would *you* want to lend money to a business which runs at a loss?) Not least, profit promotes innovation. It finances research which may not pay off for some years and encourages the development of new ideas and products. Past profit provides the funds; the possibility of future profit adds the incentive.

All this is not to say that there is no such thing as exploitation, or that profits are always honestly come by. I am simply making the point that the emotional, one-sided view of the profit motive, so common among socialists, is nonsense. Even Communist leaders nowadays admit as much. So do socialist politicians who have held office, instead of merely making passionate speeches from the back benches. In 1975 the British Government published a long document on Industrial Strategy. It accepted 'as a major objective' that industry should 'earn a reasonable rate of return on capital' and promised that the Government would make it possible for industry 'to earn sufficient profits on its investment to spur managements'.

Ten or twelve years ago such a statement would have been considered political dynamite. It took Jim Callaghan two years, after he became Labour Chancellor, to concede that he was not against profits. George Brown, presiding over the ill-fated Department of Economic Affairs, told me during the same period: 'I don't work for profit; why should anyone else?' The Government's National Plan, launched with much ballyhoo, hardly bothered to mention the word. None of the Ministers, at that time, would have dared to speak out *for* the profit motive, let alone be seen to give public support to the argument that businessmen with a talent for making money should be encouraged because their enterprise would mean more jobs, higher wages, and greater economic growth. Ray Gunter, the Minister quoted at the beginning of this chapter, did not make his 'incest and lechery' speech until three years later. Whatever people like Callaghan and Wilson thought privately, it was

165

assumed that the rank-and-file wouldn't stand for anything which might look like approval of capitalism.

I thought this absurd, and said so. Having resolved to operate a 'mixed economy' they ought, as practical men, to have recognized that, like it or not, profit is a powerful driving force, a spur to efficiency and expansion. But they feared the wrath of the 'left' and of the trade unions. Personally I always found, as a financial editor, that trade unionists were much more sophisticated than they let on. It suited them (and still does) to use the word 'profit' as a weapon, but they had enough common sense to realize that profitability was in their own interest. If a company or industry made money it could afford to pay higher wages. It was also much more likely to invest in extra plant and, therefore, to create new jobs.

Workers, like everyone else, would rather tie their future to an enterprise which is successful than one which is not. It is unnerving, to say the least, to work for an organization which is constantly on the edge of bankruptcy. I have spent most of my working life in Fleet Street, which for the last decade or so has been staggering from one financial crisis to another. I resolved, early on, that if ever I were to be put in charge of a publication I would do everything possible to keep its balance sheet in the black. Not primarily because of concern for its shareholders, and certainly not for its own sake, but because experience has taught me that it is the best way to secure and maintain editorial independence. It is the weak publication, constantly in money trouble, which tends to hesitate before it expresses unpopular views. It can't afford the loss of sales and advertising which often result from unorthodox opinions. My socialist friends would no doubt argue that I'd be better off working for a Government-owned paper or magazine, but no one who has seen, at close quarters, what public ownership does to editorial freedom would seriously defend such a naïve approach. No journalist with self-respect could possibly claim to relish the prospect of acting as the mouthpiece of political masters.

When I became editor of *Punch* in 1968 it was losing money.

My colleagues and I worked hard to make it pay and, I am glad to say, it turned the corner within a couple of years and has remained profitable ever since. Other publications, such as *Nova*, have disappeared. There are times, of course, when one regrets that the profit goes to someone else. But one appreciates being left alone, and one certainly welcomes the willingness of proprietors to underwrite the bad years. There are, after all, far more profitable investments to be made elsewhere.

Why did Labour Ministers change their tune? Because events forced them to accept reality. Much of Britain's economic trouble since 1945 has been due to inadequate capital investment. It is commonplace to argue that the average Briton does not work hard enough. What we hear less often is that, over the last few decades, we have invested less in new plant and equipment, per person employed, than any of our chief industrial rivals. A high rate of manufacturing investment has always been essential if words like 'productivity' and 'modernization' are to mean anything at all. It was through rapid investment in the new industrial techniques of the nineteenth century that Britain became, for a time, the world's leading industrial nation. And it played a vital role in the 'economic miracles' performed by two other capitalist nations, Japan and Germany. There are people who argue, quite seriously, that they were lucky to have had so much of their industry destroyed. They had no choice but to go for a high rate of investment. We, on the other hand, were strongly tempted to make do with existing machinery – even though much of it was old-fashioned and inefficient. According to this theory, we should be angry with the Germans for not dropping more bombs on us during the war. But, of course, there was and still is a more civilized solution. Germany and Japan succeeded chiefly because they went for fast economic growth. This fast rate of growth produced high profits and they were ploughed back in the confident expectation of still higher profits. In Britain, successive governments have tried to achieve the same result by making speeches about Dunkirk. It hasn't worked, partly because we have never had a sustained period of expansion but also because exhortations are a poor substitute for profit. People will applaud patriotic speeches, and welcome grants and allowances, but what really counts in the end is confidence in one's ability to make new plant and equipment pay. You don't build a new factory unless you can be reasonably sure that you can get some return on your investment. For years Ministers refused to acknowledge this simple fact; they preferred to accuse businessmen of unpatriotic conduct and to bridge the gap by heavy public sector investment. Marxists still do, for obvious reasons. But there is, today, a greater willingness in Government to accept that profits are indispensable to economic progress, whether in a capitalist or a socialist society.

I have no doubt that this would be much more readily understood, by the public at large, if the term itself were properly defined. Strictly speaking it ought not to be called profit at all, but income, surplus or margin. A company, after all, still has to make allowance for tax, depreciation, loan stock interest, and other unavoidable charges – items which, taken together, tend to cut the figure by more than a half. To an accountant or investment analyst the most sensible yardstick, if one wants to see how a company is doing, is the return on capital employed. Add together fixed assets like plant and machinery, and net current assets – the difference between the total of items like cash, outstanding debts, and work in hand and the total of current liabilities like creditors, overdrafts, taxation and dividends. This is the capital employed. Work out how much the profit shown in the accounts comes to as a percentage of the combined figure. If it compares favourably with other companies in the field, it is a sign that the business is well managed.

Unfortunately, company directors themselves tend to prefer the simpler definition. It makes it easier to win the approval of shareholders and others they are trying to impress. You can buy up another company, add its profits to yours, and proudly announce a handsome increase in the year's total. It doesn't prove anything about your ability to manage assets, but who's to know? The important thing is that it looks good in the annual report.

I dare say that this, too, will change as time goes on. Businessmen have also begun to accept an important difference between the seventies and earlier decades: the *rate* of profit made by an enterprise is no longer a matter which concerns only company managers and their shareholders. Workers have a right to know how the money has been made and what the Board is doing with it. So do the customers. Governments *insist* on knowing. In countries where incomes policies of one kind or another are in operation, profit margins are under constant scrutiny. Public concern with inflation, the environment and other issues has introduced important new considerations. It is right and proper that companies should make profits; it is *not* right and proper that they should do so regardless of all other factors. A chemical manufacturer cannot, and should not, be permitted to ignore the effect his activities have on the environment. An oil company cannot, and should not, be allowed to make unscrupulous use of monopoly powers. A drugs manufacturer cannot, and should not, be permitted to corrupt the young, and endanger lives. There is a limit to the pursuit of maximum profits.

Companies are, on the whole, much more willing to acknowledge this than they are usually given credit for. Pressure groups have had a lot to do with this, and so have campaigns run by the press. Government legislation and trade union activity have imposed all sorts of obligations which didn't exist ten years ago. And, of course, the vast publicity given to the growing shortage of resources has not gone unnoticed in company boardrooms. Conventions and seminars nowadays include papers and discussions on 'corporations and the quality of life': I have taken part in several myself. There is, obviously, scope for more tangible expressions of concern. But attitudes are different from what they used to be. Few managers in charge of large corporations would argue, these days, that corporations should be concerned with making money and nothing else.

What is a 'proper' rate of profit? Attempts are made, from time to time, to come up with an answer to that question. They are invariably linked to efforts to determine a 'fair' price. 'A fair price,' say cynics, 'is 10 per cent more.' A fair price, say others, is 'the same price that everybody else charges' or 'a price which has stayed in line with other prices'. In Britain, the Prices and Incomes Board established by the Wilson Government in 1965 debated the subject at considerable length and eventually concluded that it was, in the words of its chairman, 'impossible to determine what is a proper rate of profit'.* The nearest it got to an objective measurement was through a comparison of the prospective return on an investment with the cost of the needed capital. In America, where a similar body was created in 1971, it was decided to concentrate on profit margins – that is, the ratio of profit to sales. Prices could be increased to reflect certain cost increases after taking into account improvements in productivity, but not to the point where they raised a firm's overall profit margin before tax above that earned in the best two of the three previous financial years. The same approach was later adopted in Britain and incorporated in a new Price Code. Predictably, it has caused bitter argument. Much of the discussion has tended to get lost in a mass of technical detail, but industry's case against the system is, basically, that it diminishes the normal incentives to improve efficiency, removes any reward for cost-saving investment, continually reduces profit margins, and leaves no chance of generating cash to finance inflation, let alone expansion. In other words, it does more harm than good. Let the market decide: if buyers and sellers generally have free access to the market you will get a fair price. It is not, of course, an attitude which commends itself to socialist politicians and it goes against the constant public insistence that 'something must be done' about inflation. But the free-market men do have a telling point: despite active Government intervention the annual rate of inflation in Britain reached an astonishing 27 per cent in 1975.

* Aubrey Jones, *The New Inflation*, André Deutsch, 1973.

Chapter Eleven
Easy Money?

With money in your pocket, you are wise and you
are handsome and you sing well too.
YIDDISH PROVERB

Establishing a 'fair rate' of profit is, inevitably, even harder in
the case of deals. Socialists tend to argue that any profit made
from 'financial manipulation' is immoral and, therefore, impossible to justify on *any* grounds. Make and sell things, and
you can just about be forgiven for doing well. Engage in
'financial manipulation' and you are condemned without a
hearing.

The most abused figure in capitalism is the speculator. In
communist countries, he has always been the officially desig-
nated villain. He loyally served Marx, Lenin, and Mao Tse
Tung – indeed it is no exaggeration to say that, without him,
the communist system might never have come into being. He
was, and still is, the man everyone loves to hate – the devil in
a top hat. The Soviets have never thanked the speculator, or
at least acknowledged their debt to him. Nor, for that matter,
have the Chinese. If there is one thing which unites this vast,
mysterious country it is a Peking-inspired-and-approved contempt for speculation. Next to the war-lords of the Pentagon,
the speculator is the one figure still clearly identifiable as the
arch enemy.

What really hurts, however, is that the speculator has, over
the years, found himself increasingly condemned by his own
side. The London Stock Exchange disowned him some time
ago. Needled by phrases like 'gambling casino' and 'speculators' paradise', the gentlemen who run this august institution
insisted that they had never really approved of him. The Stock

Exchange, we were told, existed to serve *investors* – worthy citizens prepared to back Britain by putting their life savings into a damned fine blue-chip. It did not, repeat not, exist to make money for idle, unscrupulous rascals who had no interest beyond buying and selling. I have never quite understood why the Stock Exchange should be so anxious to reject the profit motive. Backing Britain is all very well, but making a few thousand overnight is even better. Any member of the Stock Exchange who says otherwise is a hypocrite, or an idealist who should seek a different profession.

It was easier to accept the Macmillan Government's decision to punish speculators by introducing a new tax on capital gains. The Chancellor of the day was trying to get trade union co-operation on wages and, like all those who have followed him, he thought it could be won by attacking their traditional foe. It didn't work. The tax, however, stayed. So did Ministerial dislike of the speculator. Harold Wilson used to get terribly angry about 'the manœuvring of odious speculators'; the 'successive waves of speculation'; the 'speculation at home and abroad'. In speech after speech he conjured up visions of a sinister, tightly knit group of politically motivated men hell-bent on 'selling Britain short'. The speculator, it appeared, spent his day swigging brandy and communicating absurd gossip to Paris and Zurich. His sole interest was in bringing Labour – and, therefore, the country – to its ruin. Even profit, it seemed, took second place. When sterling was devalued in 1967, Harold naturally blamed the speculators. And guess who cost him the 1970 General Election? Right first time.

In 1971, President Nixon joined the game. Richard Nixon! The speculator, he claimed, had been 'waging all-out war on the American dollar', forcing the administration to take steps against those 'who thrive on crises'. In short, if you don't like what the administration has done, you know whom to blame. Nixon has gone, but the same convenient ploy has since been used by other politicians. I am glad that I'm not an American father, trying to explain it to my children. I mean, it does rather cut the ground from under one's feet, doesn't it? If speculation is sinful, what is Daddy doing reading the *Wall Street Journal?* If speculators are awful people, what should Daddy do about the cheque he has just had from his broker? If making a fast buck is wrong, what else is left for a good American to believe in? The only answer, I suppose, is to go on the offensive. One could start by hinting that, even for the capitalist world's politicians, the speculator is a convenient – nay, indispensable – figure. His existence ensures that Prime Ministers and Presidents have someone who can be held responsible if anything goes wrong. He is less likely to answer back than, say, a foreign power. And he makes it possible for leaders to become national heroes by 'saving' the currency from his 'manipulations'. One could point out, too, that the late John F. Kennedy's Daddy made much of his money through speculation and that the ranks of speculators do nowadays include some very respectable gentlemen. Indeed, our villain is much more likely to be a responsible gent than a rascal: most of the currency speculation, certainly, is done by bankers paid to make the best use of their clients' money, or by the finance directors of big corporations who have entered into extensive commitments abroad, and decide to buy their foreign currency in advance. They don't like the word 'speculation'; in their book, it is called 'money management'. Businessmen, they say, do not have a patriotic duty to risk losses or forgo a possible profit: it's the job of governments to maintain confidence in money.

Incomes policies have, inevitably, increased resentment of people who appear to be making easy money from deals. Much of this is purely emotional and, more often than not, contradictory. People don't mind winning £300,000 on the pools, or making £1,000 from backing some horse, but they profess to be outraged when a property developer brings off a successful coup. They hope for – indeed, they expect – some capital gain when they sell their house, but write angry letters to *The Times* when they read that a banker has made money from a takeover deal. They buy shares, paintings, property bonds, and antiques because they expect prices to go up, but complain when some millionaire is seen to be doing the same thing on a larger scale. In Britain, where this sort of complaint is much more widespread than in the United States, public hostility has been fed not only by the politicians but also by the incessant publicity given, over the years, to self-made property tycoons like Max Rayne and Joe Hyams, and to a group of clever young men who, in the sixties, became famous as 'asset strippers'. At first their activities were viewed with fascination. Their successes drew admiring comments from financial editors. They were typical products of the 'go-go years': brash, high-spirited, unconventional. But success attracts resentment as well as admiration, and as Britain's economic crisis worsened they increasingly came under attack. How *dare* they do well when others were being asked to economize!

The guru of the group was an entrepreneur called Jim Slater – and his downfall, in 1975, delighted both socialists and envious Conservatives. Slater came from a comfortable, but certainly not rich, suburban background. His father ran a small building business in North London and Jim went to grammar school until he was 16. He recalls that he used to come about tenth in the form, 'although I was always pretty good at mathematics'. And he spent a fairly orthodox post-school period articled to a firm of accountants. At 29 he caught the eye of Donald Stokes, who made him deputy sales director of Leyland Motors. Two years later, while recovering in Bournemouth from a virus he had picked up in Spain, Slater decided that he should 'play the market'. He sent out for the financial papers and began studying form on the Stock Exchange. He bought all the back numbers of the *Investors Chronicle and Stock Exchange Gazette* for the previous two years and read every word. And because his savings amounted to barely £2,000 he went to his bank manager to borrow another £8,000. In short, he was a typical small-time speculator. Fourteen years later he had built up a banking group valued at £300 million and Slater himself was a millionaire. At his company's annual meeting in 1974 adoring old ladies in flowery hats hissed as one long-haired critic got up to speak, and a *Times* reader called him 'the Billy Graham of the financial world'. Slater himself found such tributes embarrassing and recognized the danger of exposure. The publicity was useful in the early days, but by 1974 he wanted, above all, to be regarded as a solid member of the banking establishment. It was already too late: clever financial deals had become distinctly unfashionable.

To his critics Slater has always been part of what Ted Heath, as Tory Prime Minister, called 'the ugly and unacceptable face of capitalism'. He has little time or understanding for the actual business of manufacturing and selling; people who devote their lives to such mundane activities are 'thing makers'. What made him different from so many other hopeful young men of the sixties was a self-taught ability to spot potentially profitable deals, and backing his words with swift, bold action. He moved into a metal window firm called Crittall-Hope, sold off surplus and money-losing assets, and was left with £5 million of 'liberated' cash, plus a business making half its old turnover. In the process Slater's personal vehicle, Slater Walker, was transformed from a fringe operator to a promising conglomerate. One deal followed another and, as he went along, he built up a whole team of mini-Slaters – men like John Bentley, Malcolm Horsman, and Chris Selmes. He taught them how to make a fortune and they went off and did it. Whatever the Labour party and the City establishment thought of his views and tactics, here was a group of disciples who had reason to be grateful. And Slater claimed, with some justification, that they were helping Britain in the process. Their raids forced things out into the open and stirred lazy managers into action, just as people like Charles Clore had done a decade earlier. Company boards were made uncomfortably aware that incompetence and inefficiency were likely to attract the unwelcome attention of Slater and his friends. They took steps to put their house in order.

Gossip columnists found Slater disappointing: he didn't live as they thought a young millionaire should. He didn't smoke, liked plain food, drank little, didn't have a yacht, and disliked travel. He played an occasional game of table tennis and enjoyed backgammon, but so did countless ordinary people.

When he resigned from the board of Slater Walker in 1976, after strong criticism of a major Far East deal, there were few public expressions of sympathy. The super speculator (a label which Slater himself, of course, rejected) had speculated once too often and lost.

Do we need people like Slater? Well, they perform a useful maverick function. Should we allow them to indulge in 'financial manipulation'? Yes, as long as they do so within the framework of the law. A capitalist system should always have room for able people who are willing to take risks. The law can and does put an effective curb on excesses. Controls have been tightened considerably in recent years, and financial institutions like the Bank of England and New York's Securities and Exchange Commission nowadays exercise strict supervision. Profits from deals, moreover, are subject to heavy taxation – which means the public shares in the success of the Slaters.

Every businessman is, to some extent, a speculator. The manufacturer who introduces a new product speculates on the response from consumers. The company which puts up a new factory takes a chance on the level of demand four or five years hence. Builders who construct a new apartment block take a risk on the future level of prices. Finance houses who lend an inventor money speculate on the success, or failure, of his invention. Pension funds which buy shares for the benefit of their members speculate on the future of the companies concerned. Oil and mining firms which spend millions on exploration take the very real risk that nothing of value will be found. Even governments are not above speculation: the most costly gamble of recent years is the £1,000 million expended on Concorde. So the flat condemnation of speculation is clearly absurd.

Critics are on firmer ground when they attack stock market manipulation and complex financial schemes whose main purpose is to avoid taxation, and one could argue that legislation ought to be firmer still. There is scope for argument, too, about the level of profits from transactions which directly involve the public interest, such as land deals. But there is nothing immoral about deals as such.

Next to making money from a financial deal, the worst sin in the socialist book is to have unearned income. The term itself arouses instant hostility, implying as it does that the recipient is making totally undeserved profits from other people's toil. People with unearned income are the idle rich, lolling about on their yachts in Cannes or shooting grouse in Scotland.

There are people like that, of course, and it isn't hard to find examples to back one's argument. But such blanket condemnation is both foolish and unjust. Millions of ordinary people have unearned income – from savings, from pensions, from small shareholdings bought with money earned during their working lives. Even those who claim to be bitterly opposed to the whole principle may share, directly or indirectly, in some form of unearned income. The trade unions invest their money in Government stocks, ordinary shares, and property. So do company pension funds. Insurance companies rely on interest and dividends to finance policies and pensions. The benefits go to a very wide range of people who would otherwise be entirely dependent on the State.

To condemn unearned income is also to condemn the whole concept of savings. People who put money on deposit with a bank or a building society are, or will be, in receipt of interest. Does that make them part of the 'idle rich'? Or how about the shopkeeper who saves a little every year for thirty years and, in his retirement, gets a modest income from property or shares? Should it be taken from him? Then there is the founder of a small manufacturing company who retires at 65 but still gets dividend from his shares. He has worked hard, built up a prosperous business from nothing, and wants to spend his remaining years in comfort. Would you deny him the right to do so? And the owner of a seaside boarding house who sells out to a young family and agrees to take part of the purchase price in

177

the form of payments from future earnings. Would you stop him?

It is, as noted earlier, one of the most unappealing features of socialism that so many of its passionate advocates are fiercely opposed to the idea of self-reliance. No one should covet more than the State is willing or able to grant him. Anyone who steps out of line must be punished, either by the highest possible taxation or outright confiscation. This is very different from the view, which I can share, that the better off have some obligation to help the needy. It is a moral judgment, and as such an intolerable threat to freedom.

It is also bad economics. The money put into savings or investments helps the Government and is needed to help finance industrial expansion. A Chancellor who boosts savings needs to raise less by way of taxation. How do you think deficit spending (that most desirable of socialist devices) is financed? By raising taxes or by borrowing. Borrowing from whom? The saver. Who, of course, gets unearned income. Imagine that, instead, he decided to withdraw the money from his savings account and spend it in the shops instead. What do you think would happen? Right, first time. We would have runaway inflation. It is another one of those little lessons every new Labour Chancellor learns while in office. It does not, of course, prevent them from having a go at people who have had the temerity to accumulate capital – the temptation to score political points is too strong. 'I intend to go a great deal further before I have finished,' Denis Healey told the Labour Party, apologetically, after he had raised the top rate on investment income to a staggering 98 per cent early in 1974.

Industry's need for savings is no less obvious. Take this simple illustration. A manufacturer wants to build a new factory, but hasn't been able to plough back enough profit to meet the cost. He goes to his bank to ask for a loan. The bank looks at his case and agrees to lend him £100,000. That £100,000 comes out of deposits and earns interest; the bank, in turn, pays interest to the depositor. The manufacturer is happy, the depositor is happy. The money could, of course, have come from the

State – but why should the taxpayer be called upon to take the risk? Assume the bank says no, or the manufacturer wants more permanent finance. If his company is quoted on the Stock Exchange, he may well decide to offer new stock to existing holders. No one forces them to buy it and, if they do, the money is their own, not the taxpayers'. So is the risk. If he succeeds they gain; if he fails, they share in his failure. Does *that* strike you as immoral?

The risk is real enough, both with governments and private industry. The money lent to governments, by putting it into national savings banks or buying gilt-edged stocks, has consistently lost value. The term 'gilt-edged', especially, has become a joke and, in the case of undated stocks like War Loan $3\frac{1}{2}$ per cent, a fraud. Far from being dependable, War Loan has lost more money for trusting people than some of the City's worst bucket-shop operations. It is 'safe' only in the sense that governments can't go bust – though they have a damned good try. There is no obligation to repay at any particular date and there is certainly no guarantee against loss. Ordinary shares – supposedly the best hedge against inflation – have also proved deceptive. Laymen usually take up share-buying because they are led to believe that it's an easy way to make money (see page 80). The City columns tend to encourage people in this view: tips are far more popular (and therefore more common) than advice to sell. But even the bluest of 'blue-chips' can let you down. The company may go bust – as in the case of Rolls-Royce – or it may simply be that you bought it at the wrong time. A company does not necessarily do well just because it is big. Timing is of paramount importance. Contrary to socialist myth, success in the stock market is far from guaranteed.

I have always had a good deal of sympathy for small investors. Perhaps it's all those letters I answered in my years as a City Editor: they made me very much aware that I wasn't just writing for the privileged few. I tried to put myself in their place. There were the old ladies living in Bournemouth, or Hove, and relying on a 'portfolio' acquired in more active years. It wasn't a matter of greed, but of sheer survival. They were naturally anxious about the fate of their investments and I tried to help as much as I could. It never occurred to me to sneer at their concern with unearned income, even when I became financial editor of the *Guardian* (a paper which Tory die-hards regard as a socialist propaganda sheet) because I accepted and, I hope, understood their position. They could not, with the best will in the world, have secured a reasonable job. They were too old to work and, in many cases, too ill. They needed someone to take care of them, and that cost money. I dare say it could have been squeezed out of the State but they were much too independent to go through the process. They, or their husbands, had worked for the assets they possessed. Now, in their old age, they were relying on the comforts it could bring. They could, of course, have sold their shares and used up the capital. But for how long could they have done so? And how do you allow for inflation? What if they lived to eighty, ninety or even a hundred? So they bought stocks and shares and hoped for the best. Should I have written back and accused them of selfishness and greed?

Then there were the small businessmen who had left for sunnier shores – and a more relaxed way of life – because their doctors had urged them to do so. It could, they had been told, lengthen their lifespan by ten years or more. Again, it had to be paid for. They were sitting in Malta, or Gibraltar, or one of the many resorts in Spain anxiously watching the ups and downs of the *Financial Times* index. They wrote to me, at the *Guardian*, asking for advice. Should I have told them that they were parasites, feeding on the honest efforts of people in their twenties and thirties? No. I might, one day, be in the same position. We have no law – yet – which says that one has to live out one's life, like a prison sentence, in an inhospitable climate. Many people have no choice, to be sure. But it is not for me, or anyone else, to deny those who can escape the opportunity to do so.

Socialists would no doubt reply that it is not their intention either. 'If you put it like that,' one socialist MP once said to me, 'I'd have to agree.' Well, I *am* putting it like that. I am more than willing to accept that they mean well – but this is one of the practical effects of their blanket condemnation which seldom gets any publicity. Let there be no mistake: I am not basing my case solely on the plight of widows in Bournemouth or retired greengrocers in Malta. I firmly believe that we should *all* have the right to order our affairs to the best of our ability. I have no moral objection to a young man making a fortune, investing the proceeds, and spending the rest of his youth in Florida or the south of France. Good luck to him. I have no moral objection, for that matter, to parents doing the best they can for their children. It is entirely natural that they should want them to make the most of what life has to offer. Let them spend two or three carefree years roaming around the world, or longer if they have a mind to. It may produce all kinds of problems which neither they nor their parents have bargained for – but that's their business, not yours or mine.

Socialists take a different view, or at least appear to. The spectacle of prosperous young people having a good time fills them with righteous anger. It doesn't matter that they are doing so at private, not public, expense and that they usually settle down, after a while, to a demanding job. It's enough that they should be 'getting away' with pleasures denied to those considered less fortunate. Since we are, once again, in the area of moral judgment this may be as good a point as any to take a closer look at this particular argument. It is, of course, closely connected not only with unearned income but also with socialist attitudes to wealth, leisure and what is contemptuously dismissed as 'conspicuous consumption'. The notion that only the rich can afford to enjoy life is one of those myths which are kept alive only for the sake of convenience. Intelligent socialists know perfectly well that countless young working-class men and women, throughout the so-called capitalist world, manage to do just as well. Enjoyment doesn't have to be measured in terms of caviar and champagne. Go to any holiday resort, in the summer months, and talk to the young Britons, Germans, Americans, or Scandinavians there. You will find that most of them come from working-class or middle-class homes, and that they don't spend all their time cursing the rich. On the contrary, they will probably express pity for hard-working millionaires who are held captive by the machines they have created – middle-aged men who insist that they can't take holidays because they are 'too busy'. But it suits socialist would-be reformers to pretend that leisure is the exclusive preserve of those they regard as the privileged few. It permits the conclusion that wealth is bad and must be confiscated. Some would like to 'seize' all assets over and above a certain figure which they, and they alone, feel competent to fix. Others want to see much higher taxes and an even tougher attitude to inherited cash, shares, and property than we have at the moment.

Labour Ministers have, so far, shown themselves reluctant to go along with the first part of that formula. Seizing assets may sound marvellously simple, but it is fraught with political and economic consequences which may well backfire. Using the tax 'weapon' has always seemed a good deal easier.

Chapter Twelve
Nothing Certain but Tax

It is the part of a good shepherd to shear
his flock, not to flay it.
TIBERIUS

Most of us nowadays accept without protest that taxation is
a necessary evil. We thinks ourselves lucky if the Government
manages to 'give us a little more' – a phrase invented by politicians to disguise the fact that, in reality, they are simply allowing us to *keep* a little more of our income. But we do not dispute
its right to levy taxes and we leave it to Ministers to decide
where the axe should fall. We do not even challenge their right
to pry into our personal financial affairs, and to haul us up in
Court to answer whatever charge the Commissioners decide to
make against us. We not only agree that the Government can
do all this, but share its indignation that some people should
try to slip through the net by moving to Switzerland or to the
Bahamas. In short, successive Governments have brainwashed
us into accepting that the tax burden as a whole is not only
inevitably, but also morally correct.

It was not always so. Earlier generations put up a long and
valiant struggle against taxation. If they had not done so, we
might never have had a Parliament, and America might not
have won its independence. The history of taxation is full of
cunning tricks played upon a gullible electorate. A favourite
device, for example, has been to use national emergencies as
a pretext for introducing temporary taxes which, somehow,
turned out to be permanent. This is how Britain first got income
tax in 1799. The younger Pitt needed money to finance his war
with revolutionary France, and called his new tax a strictly temporary measure. It stayed around, on and off, for seventeen

years. Gladstone introduced an income tax in his 1853 budget, and promised to repeal it within seven years. Some hope. In 1854 the Crimean War broke out, Government expenditure rose sharply, and Gladstone declared that he couldn't keep his promise. Purchase tax is another wartime innovation which was not supposed to last, but did. It came in during the Second World War, and was simply intended to boost wartime revenue. Chancellors have long since forgotten its original purpose – and so have we.

Economists and politicians alike have never found it difficult to invent new taxes. The introduction of the Excise, during the English Civil War, opened the way for an extraordinary range of devices, including a hearth tax and a window tax. The Puritans invented it, but the Excise stayed on when the monarchy was restored in 1660 – and, of course, remains with us today. So does a wide range of other taxes – on death, on capital gain, on gifts, on dogs, and on just about everything we buy. Far from protesting, many people keep writing to the Government with suggestions of still further imposts – all, needless to say, designed to hit other people. It isn't difficult, therefore, for Ministers to push through legislation, especially if it is aimed at the minority known as the rich.

British socialists have always assumed that taxation could not only be used to impose their own concept of 'justice', but that it could also be made to finance all their pet schemes. Money could never be a problem; all one had to do was to take a little more from the 'better off'. Periods in opposition have been devoted to thinking up new taxes rather than devising ways of creating wealth. Party leaders, eager to please the electorate, have cast themselves as modern Robin Hoods. Indeed, this is how they have presented themselves to the public. 'Robin Hood,' the party's deputy leader declared just before the 1974 General Election, 'will be back in business.' It is, you may feel, an odd but appropriate choice as a hero figure. There are various versions of the legend, but all agree on at least one point: Robin was a thief. We know he took from 'abbeys and houses of rich earles' but there is no proof that he ever gave a penny to the poor. Stow tells us that he was an outlaw who 'entertained one hundred tall men, all good archers, with the spoil he took'. So, by all accounts, did Bernard Cornfeld. But let's not quibble. The point is that 'soaking the rich' has always looked like the easiest of all political gambits. But the idea has taken some rather uncomfortable knocks in the past year or two. First, an independent parliamentary investigation into the feasibility of a wealth tax came up with no less than five reports, none of which was acceptable to a majority. There was a great deal of talk about 'horizontal equity' and 'vertical equality' but only one point met with general agreement: the yield from a wealth tax would be remarkably modest. Then the Chancellor made an even more uncomfortable discovery: inflation had pushed many Labour supporters into the tax brackets hitherto reserved for 'the rich'. They were beginning to notice the weight of taxation more than the handouts and they didn't like it at all. As long as the Welfare State appeared to be 'free' there were few complaints about the cost. The rich could pay. But now the millions so effortlessly tossed around by the Government were beginning to look unpleasantly real. Mr Healey, reading the danger signals, warned his Cabinet colleagues that if public spending wasn't checked the State would soon be taking a minimum of 50p in tax and social security contributions from every pound earned. A week or two later, the Prime Minister told the National Council for Social Services that the average wage-earner was 'paying about as much as he can stand'. He went on: 'We are therefore reaching a situation where we must consider very carefully to what extent we can reasonably ask the ordinary taxpayer to reach still further into his pocket.' Mr Healey chipped in again with the comment that he'd like to cut income tax for people on £4,000 to £8,000 a year. They had, he said, 'taken quite a caning' and he wanted to help them. It's rare enough to hear a Labour Chancellor talk about reducing taxes, but the range was even more illuminating: two years earlier he would not have hesitated to describe an £8,000-a-year man as rich, one of the privileged class he was determined to make 'howl with anguish'. He added, naturally, that it might mean raising the tax on unearned income. But the basic point was clear enough. Here, for the first time, was a Labour Government admitting that taxation *did* have limits.

Complaining about taxes is a national sport in many countries: few other subjects inspire so much bitterness, and tax collectors (who are, for the most part, overworked and underpaid) are subject to a never-ending stream of abuse. Ask a Japanese business executive what he thinks of taxation and he will give you the same answer as a French or American businessman. But few have quite as much genuine cause for complaint as the men who run British industry. The British chief executive of a large company is the worst paid, pays the highest rate of marginal tax, and stands second lowest to the Swede, in his differential of earnings compared with his workers, of Western company bosses. He earns only half as much as his opposite number of France and Germany, let alone America, and that is before tax. After tax the comparison becomes even more depressing. The take-home pay of a senior British manager is unlikely to be more than about a third of the money enjoyed by the European managers with whom he may have to do business and compete. Management consultants have calculated that average after-tax lifetime earnings of a managing director who is looking after a fair-sized company is only about $2\frac{1}{2}$ times that of an unskilled manual worker; for a middle manager the ratio is about $1\frac{1}{2}$ times. In Germany and France the margin between a managing director's earnings and those of an unskilled worker is about seven times. In Latin countries it is higher still.

Not surprisingly, international companies find it increasingly difficult to persuade executives who have been working abroad to accept promotion which would mean coming back to Britain. There is a well-developed system of 'perks', with company cars and subsidized lunches high on the list, but the Government frowns even on those and they no longer make up for the difference in taxation. (Besides, perks are not exactly unknown in other countries either.) It is simply not possible in Britain to reward people adequately for working much harder and accepting more responsibility, achieving more than other people. There are, of course, other incentives which cannot be measured in numbers – power, status, job satisfaction – but they are just as readily available elsewhere.

Recruiting agencies regard Britain as a happy hunting ground. Of the 'workers of merit and ability' (including managers) emigrating to the United States in 1973, one in five was British, compared with one in ten of all emigrants. Overall, nearly half a million people are leaving for various destinations every year. With Britain such an overcrowded island – arguably the main reason for so many of our economic problems – this may not strike you as such a bad thing. But the people who are leaving are, for the most part, those we can least afford to lose. I am not referring to sports celebrities and showbiz stars, whose well-publicized departure to America and sundry tax havens has been dubbed the 'fame drain'. It is, to be sure, the kind of publicity Britain could well do without but it is certainly not the most important loss. My concern is with the innovators, the decision-makers, the future Lew Grades and Charles Fortes. Recruiting agencies are not interested in labourers or even pop stars. They want the best men in business, the academic world and the professions. We have all heard of the flight of the medical profession, and although the problem has probably been exaggerated (there is plenty of new talent coming up) the unnecessary loss of able people must always be a matter for regret. They are the young, the energetic, the ambitious. And they usually leave without their parents or other elderly relatives. Britain is already burdened, in economic terms, with an ageing population. The number of retired people who have to be supported by the rest is steadily increasing. To say this is not to criticize the old or to begrudge them their pension: I merely want to underline the importance of looking after – and hopefully retaining – those who are creating wealth.

No less regrettable, in many ways, is the fact that high taxation has turned us into a nation excessively concerned with 'getting round' the system. I have already drawn attention to the difference between tax avoidance, which is legal, and tax evasion, which is not. I am all in favour of people making the most of whatever legal loopholes are still open. But I very much regret the vast amount of time, effort, and money which is nowadays devoted to the whole business.

In countries like Italy, tax evasion has long been part of everyday life. People will tell you, with pride, about their latest ploy. Anyone who admits to paying his taxes in full is regarded as a fool, even by tax collectors themselves. (The usual strategy was to declare half your actual income: the taxman would automatically assume that you had done so, and double his assessment. The trick now is to declare a quarter, or less, and to keep him arguing for the next ten years.) In France, too, people have always looked upon taxes as a challenge to one's imagination, and battles with tax collectors as one of the things which make life interesting. We used to look upon all this with detached amusement: the British did not have to indulge in such childish games. But attitudes have changed. We do not, as yet, march on Government offices as the French are apt to do, but we do increasingly engage in paper warfare. And we have managed to persuade a considerable number of tax inspectors to switch sides; they are, after all, taxpayers too.

The Government has countered with all sorts of threats and, as in Italy and France, tries to make 'examples' of the more blatant transgressors. But the plain fact is that the Inland Revenue, like the police, depends on public goodwill to make the system work. It simply cannot cope with the tornado of paper that is now whirling through its corridors. The head of its staff federation admitted, early in 1976, that there were three million letters and four million forms which had not been answered. It is one thing for politicians to think up taxes and all sorts of penalties; it is another for the administrative machinery to deal with the everyday implications. If it fails, the whole system ceases to command respect. This is the lesson taught by the Italian experience and, like many people, I am deeply sorry to see us going the same way. I am also disturbed by the increasing scope for blackmail which accompanies it. It is a sad business, for any country, when people start denouncing each other for petty personal reasons. It is happening in Britain today and, to me, it is very much part of a trend I want to have nothing to do with. There is already a tax dossier for every taxpayer and the day will come – if it has not done so already – when it is not only easy for me to make trouble for you but when Government departments will all exchange their information and the life and times of every citizen will be open to inspection.

The row over the Chancellor's plans announced in the 1976 budget, to extend the right of tax inspectors to enter people's homes to search for evidence against them, underlined what has long been an unpleasant fact: an Englishman's home is no longer his castle. A series of Finance Bills have over the years given the Customs and Excise power to do almost anything they please. And no less than 250 different Acts of Parliament nowadays bestow Government agents with the right of entry to private premises – including factory and health inspectors, social security, environment, rating and waterboard men, VAT collectors, inspectors from the Inland Revenue, Treasury investigators and social workers. Some of the tactics used by VAT collectors, in particular, show an appalling lack of respect for personal freedom. It is of little consolation that the situation is even worse in countries like Sweden, where the revenue authorities seized writer-director Ingmar Bergman during a rehearsal at Stockholm's Royal Dramatic Theatre – a move which, for him, was the last straw. The British have always assumed that Orwell's *1984* could never happen in their own country. Alas, it is closer than most people think.

Chapter Thirteen
Small is Difficult

The loftiest towers rise from the ground.
CHINESE PROVERB

Let us now turn to a group of people who are widely believed to be in imminent danger of extinction: small businessmen. Caught between state capitalism and the giant corporation, it is said, they have no chance of survival. If socialist governments don't get them, big business most certainly will.

Walk down any shopping street in America or Europe and this broad statement will strike you as a vast exaggeration. There are countless small businessmen who are obviously managing to survive – hotel owners, restaurateurs, grocers, publishers, bookshops, boutiques, radio and television retailers, florists and many, many more. A look at the businesses listed in the Yellow Pages of any big city's telephone directory will further strengthen the impression that the small firm is far from finished. But, of course, appearances can be deceptive. Many of those businesses belong to a larger group or chain; often two shops which seem to be keen rivals, proud of their tradition and well-established names, will in fact be part of the same umbrella organizations. The merger boom of recent years has mopped up countless small companies, especially in countries like Britain. And there is, without doubt, a growing sense of disquiet, disenchantment and, in many cases, distress among the owners of small enterprises.

Since the war both major political parties in Britain have pursued the cult of bigness. The Labour party, especially, has actively encouraged the move towards fewer and larger companies. Public finance has been made available for mergers and acquisitions, and legislation has been used to make the small businessman's life as hard as possible. Officially, the reasoning has been that, in today's tough international trading conditions, we must have industrial giants big enough to compete. There has been a great deal of talk about the 'economies of scale'. Unofficially, socialist planners have admitted another motive: the eventual state take-over of the resulting concerns. Mr Wilson used to boast that he was 'dragging Britain kicking and screaming into the twentieth century'; it was his theme in both the 1964 and 1970 election campaigns. We haven't heard that phrase for quite some time, and I am not surprised. The kicking has frequently produced unexpected and unwelcome results – from the closing of factories, with politically embarrassing effects on employment, to the ruthless exercise of monopoly power in the market place. The 'economies of scale' talked about glibly by economists have often proved short-lived or completely illusory. Not least, we have seen that size is no guarantee of survival (Rolls-Royce!) or greater efficiency. If size is the prime objective (as I pointed out in my book, *Merger Mania*, published in 1970) a company can topple under its own weight.

On a personal level, studies have shown that big companies tend to offer less scope for creative intuition: there is a perhaps natural inclination to avoid risks. They also make at least some of their employees feel that they are nothing more than a tiny cog in a vast machine to which they owe no loyalty. Labour relations are frequently much better in small companies than in large ones because people feel more involved – and because, more often than not, the founder/owner works hardest of all. One of the most dramatic factors revealed by the Bolton Committee, which reported in 1971 on firms with 200 employees or less, was that small firms hardly ever had strikes. The Committee looked at firms in the two years to 1969. It found that less than 8 per cent had been affected by strikes at all. Of these only $1\frac{1}{2}$ per cent – yes, $1\frac{1}{2}$ per cent – had experienced strikes in their own firm. The remaining $6\frac{1}{2}$ per cent were affected by strikes in other firms. Experience also shows that small firms are frequently the source of new products and techniques. In Tokyo, a few years ago, the head of Sony told me how he – as a young technician without money – first came across transistors on a visit to the US. The big American company which had the rights was unenthusiastic: the idea was amusing, and no doubt a small firm could make it work, but it would never make the kind of profits they were after. He said nothing, went back to Japan, saw four different banks (the first three refused to help) and set up in business. There is, today, a growing feeling on both sides of the Atlantic that big is often bad. Many industrialists are trying to achieve smallness *within* large organizations, by splitting them up into semi-autonomous units, and some bankers nowadays spend more time undoing mergers than they do in arranging new ones. Others have publicly stated their determination to stay small. The Stay-Small strategy is simple. As a small company grows, its problems multiply and it becomes progressively more difficult to run. Eventually a point is reached – many people put it at around 300 employees – where the company reaches a critical mass and the severity of its problems then begins to increase explosively. One clear warning signal comes when the proprietor or founder no longer knows how many children each of his employees has. When he does not know everyone's name the threshold may already have been passed – and if any of them do not know who he is then it certainly has. Result: they may cease to trust him. Once that happens the company is wide open to infection from militants and has lost, for good, a small firm's most valuable asset.

Stay-Small enthusiasts have another telling point: they are more likely to be left in peace by governments. *Some* companies can still escape monopolies commissions, nationalization, supervisory boards, closed shops, equal pay, planning agreements and price restraints. Who are these lucky firms? Small ones.

Politicians have lately taken to praising small businessmen and promising them help. But words are a poor substitute for action. The sad truth is that Governments do little of real value to ensure the survival of small firms. As one British Treasury

Minister put it in private conversation not long ago: 'The idea of small businessmen building up their organisations to pass on to the next generation is *passé* ... the new pattern should be "clogs to clogs in one generation".' Cosmetics like Small Business Bureaux can never have the same effect as, say, tax policies designed to encourage the energetic and enthusiastic entrepreneur. Recessions such as we have seen in the past few years are particularly hard on small businessmen; they have so little to fall back on. The money may not be there to keep the enterprise afloat until trade improves. Many owners, as noted earlier in this book, make tiny incomes and the risk of failure is high. They may stay in business largely for love and the psychological reason of liking to do things their own way, to experiment and hope for that breakthrough.

I have particular sympathy for small businessmen because, to me, this has never been an abstract subject: throughout my working life I have played with the idea of starting a business of my own. As a very young man I used to dream of opening a bar or small hotel in my favourite Sicilian island, Lipari. I would hire buxom girls from Norway to cook fish on a handsome charcoal grill, make my own wine, and run profitable boat services on the side. At other times, I have wanted to launch a magazine or newspaper of my own. I never aimed to make millions; it would be enough, I felt, to be independent and to enjoy life. As one gets older, of course, one sees all the drawbacks and, increasingly, one is tempted to settle for second best: running a small business within a large organization. That is what I have been doing for the last seven years – a magazine publishing group is a business like everything else – and I have enjoyed it more than I can say. There is enormous personal satisfaction in building up something you really care about, and making life-long friends in the process. Journalism couldn't really work any other way but I would feel the same about any other activity which suited my particular character and inclinations. The one thing I couldn't take is boredom and regimentation; no amount of profit could ever be adequate compensation for what I would have to give up. Most small businessmen, I know, feel the same: it is the one factor which makes them go on despite all the awful frustration.

Do they have a future? Or are the days of the enterprising, independent-minded individual numbered, as so many people claim? The answer to the first question must be an unequivocal 'yes'. This certainly goes for the United States, a vast market which still offers sizeable rewards for originality and enterprise. But it is also true of countries like Germany, France, and even Britain. Unless and until we turn into a Soviet-type society, which I for one regard as highly improbable, there will always be room for the maverick. But a great deal clearly depends on several key factors. First and most obvious is the particular industry or trade in which each businessman operates. It would be very difficult these days to build up a business in heavy chemicals or heavy engineering – or, for that matter, to make a fortune by launching a new daily newspaper. These things require a vast capital outlay, without any guarantee that it will pay off. To survive in industries dominated by giants one has to specialize. In engineering, many survivors have concentrated on sub-contracting. They perform jobs which are too modest for the large organizations to handle. In other industries, small businessmen have flourished through franchising arrangements. They have, in effect, rented another company's good name and product, and made money from it. In agriculture, the grocery retail trade, and elsewhere, there are also arrangements under which small firms can join a co-operative buying or marketing organization.

Sometimes profitable ideas are picked up on trips abroad. Just as Sony's founder stumbled on the transistor in America (and Walter Raleigh discovered the delights of tobacco) so others have made fortunes from the inventiveness of foreigners. The Japanese are, of course, the outstanding example: much of their early success was due to their talent for finding better ways to make and design the same products. But they are certainly not alone. Sometimes the ideas have been simple and easy to adapt: the supermarket crossed the Atlantic with ease and there was no problem about copying other marketing techniques, such as mail order and discount stores. At other times the traveller has managed to secure the rights to sell some product exclusively in his country. Or he has come across a simple, commercially unexploited formula which could be acquired for the price of a drink. In the last century a British Governor of Bengal, Sir Marcus Sandys, returned to England with a recipe for a rare sauce. He had tasted exotic Hindu dishes whose marvellous flavour and piquant tang were based on it, and he immediately sought out the small shop of two chemists, John W. Lea and William Perrins, in his home town of Worcester. He entrusted his recipe to them with orders to make up a small amount for his own use, and for presentation from time to time to fellow-members of the nobility. He entertained frequently and lavishly and word soon got around. The two chemists secured permission to sell the sauce to some of their other customers, and soon its production took up their entire time. Eventually they acquired the recipe for good and today Worcester Sauce (known in America as Worcestershire Sauce) is famous all over the world and there are several Lea & Perrins factories.

There are countless other stories, many of comparatively recent origin. And, of course, it hasn't been all one way: many ideas have been sparked off by visitors. One of the most remarkable – and absolutely true – tales concerns the invention of chewing gum. The person held responsible for starting the chewing gum industry is none other than General Antonio Lopez de Santa Anna, the famous Mexican commander. Taken prisoner by the Americans, he entered the United States and came to New York. He brought with him a large chunk of chicle, the dried sap of a Mexican jungle tree (sapodilla) which the Aztec Indians used for chewing. He met an inventor and induced him to experiment with the chicle as a rubber substitute. It didn't work, but in the course of his conversation with Santa Anna the inventor noted that the General occasionally took a small pinch of chicle from his pocket and chewed it with great gusto. His own son had also enjoyed chewing the stuff. So he went to work, mixing the chicle with hot water until it was about the consistency of putty. He rubbed, kneaded, and finally rolled it into a couple of hundred little balls, and persuaded a local drugstore to put them on sale. They sold so well that he bought more chicle, rented a factory loft, and put his gum (which then was still tasteless) into boxes with the legend: *Adams' New York Gum – Snapping and Stretching*. The rest, as they say, is history.

Inventions have built so many personal fortunes that a lot of people still see them as the key – a way of getting past or even beating State industries and large corporations. It didn't take heavy capital outlay, after all, to invent the can opener or the zip fastener. The hair clip with the double bend made for several years more money in the United States than any other invention. Flat hair clips often fall out; bent ones stay in – that's all. And wouldn't you *love* to have been the first man to think of the alarm clock, the mousetrap, cat's eyes, or the ball-point pen? Cat's eyes brought a farthing to their inventor for every cat's eye put down on the roads anywhere and made him a very rich man. (It also brought him personal satisfaction: it's nice to know that one's idea has saved thousands of lives.)

The great thing about so many stunning inventions is that they seem both obvious and simple. 'I've got this piece of wood; I'm going to call it a coat-hanger.' Or: 'you bend this bit of wire like this and, Eureka, you have a paperclip.' Unilever, one of the world's largest industrial empires, began with an equally modest ploy – cutting soap into tablets and wrapping them individually in gaudy paper. No wonder that inventors still queue up at the Patent Office. In Britain alone there are around 40,000 patent applications a *week* – and that must be a fraction of the inventions in the United States and the rest of the so-called capitalist world. A lot of them, of course, don't make it. They may be obvious and simple, but that doesn't necessarily make them commercial. The Patent Office has a fascinating record of ideas that got away. There was, for example, the 'apparatus for the prevention of snoring' which, like the dual-spouted teapot, made its début in 1931 and was never heard of again. The same fate befell the musical toilet-paper holder, patented in 1912, and William Mumford's reversible trousers, invented in 1907. An engineer called Arthur Pedrick, once an Examiner at the Patent Office himself, invented golf balls with wings and, as we have not enough arable land to feed humanity, he suggested the building of farms, rather like giants' saucers, in the middle of the oceans. He also offered a practical solution to another dream: making the Sahara and other deserts bloom. The ice of the Arctic is to be melted and taken through pipelines to the deserts, and this irrigation on a grandiose scale will turn the deserts into vegetable gardens and endless fields of colourful flowers. Mr Pedrick is still waiting for someone to take him seriously, but I dare say they laughed at the inventor of the horseless carriage too.

Even if you have a commercial idea, there is always a risk that someone else will steal it or, more likely, talk you into parting with it for a trifling sum. This has been the fate of many dreamers. Inventors, alas, seldom make good businessmen. They are preoccupied with the idea itself, and they lack the money and marketing techniques needed to make the most of it. (Often, of course, they make their discovery while working for a firm – in which case the employer understandably claims the right to develop it.) Here again, though, there are plenty of exceptions. Take the case of Dr Edwin Land. Land's preoccupation with the polarizing of light was meant to lead to a breakthrough in car headlights; instead he made a fortune out of non-glare sunglasses and, eventually, developed the Polaroid camera. There were bad years, to be sure, but he persisted and saw the stock market value of his family's shares climb to a staggering $700 million. The point is that it *can* be done. The end result, as mentioned earlier, doesn't necessarily have to be a million: many people are satisfied with much less.

We have already mentioned certain fields in which the individual, so contemptuously dismissed by Marx and his disciples as 'intermediary class', still manages to do well. One could add many others. There are, and will continue to be, areas where flair counts for more than mass production and marketing skill – fashion, publishing, real estate, catering, antiques, advertising and others. Film-makers can still make huge sums with one good idea. So can writers and the people who back them. Hugh Hefner's discovery that people were interested in sex (a fact which, apparently, had escaped the notice of established multi-million firms) led to one of the most remarkable post-war successes in the publishing business. Pierre Cardin, Mary Quant, André Courrège and many more have proved that you don't have to be a giant corporation to sell clothes. France and Italy are full of wine-growers who sell precisely because they are *not* giant corporations. And everywhere you go in the free world there are individuals who provide what nationalized industries and big corporations find increasingly difficult to come up with: service. The hotelier, restaurateur, or shopkeeper who has his own business will invariably try harder than his big rival. He *has* to. Contrast the attitude of, say, the *patron* of a restaurant in Paris or London with that of the manager of a similar establishment in Moscow, Budapest, or East Berlin and you have, at a stroke, the best possible reason for supporting private enterprise. Ask him if he thinks the small businessman has a future and you will get an even heartier 'yes' than mine. Whatever his misgivings he is, on balance, an optimist because he wants to succeed and is willing to work towards that end. And he makes life more pleasant for others in the process.

There really is no better way to illustrate the point – as opposed to airing theories – than to look at a few case histories. Take, first, Bill Lacy and his wife Margaret Costa. They run their own restaurant in London and, as he says, 'You've got to love to do it.' Bill Lacy has an impeccable gastronomic background; he worked for Eugene Herbodeau, a star pupil of the formidable Escoffier. At the age of 23 he commanded one of the finest kitchen brigades in London. Margaret Costa, one of the leading wine and food writers in the country, worked with Raymond Postgate on *The Good Food Guide* for fifteen years. When they decided to open up on their own they both knew exactly what they wanted. Now five years later Lacy's has won accolades, stars, and rosettes, but it has cost a great deal physically and emotionally. For Bill the day begins at 8.00 a.m. For the next eighteen hours he walks the tightrope of the perfectionist. 'It's like being in the theatre, I suppose. The only difference is that we have *two* performances every day we're open. And when you do finally get home your mind is running over the day's successes – and failures.' In the last four years, apart from Sundays and the three-week annual closing, Bill has only had four days off. 'Nothing goes down to the restaurant without my seeing it. The kitchen is the heart of the operation and when things go well you get a marvellous feeling.' Maragaret works in Lacy's almost every evening, often at lunchtime. She has a considerable following in the States as a result of her restaurant articles in *Gourmet*; Americans have been known to walk into the Connaught and order the identical meal with the identical wines 'that Miss Costa had!' Her ideas for new dishes are taken by Bill and translated. There are easier ways of making money, but neither of them has any regrets. 'I suppose I live on my nerves,' says Bill. 'But I'd never work for anyone else again.'

His story is typical of successful operators in what is still a business dominated by independent individuals. You'd hear much the same from countless other small businessmen whose life is dedicated to their trade – butchers, bakers, grocers, fishmongers, jewellers, boatbuilders, hoteliers. The misgivings, as I have said, have grown considerably in recent years. There has always been a certain harsh reality behind the glamorous front: loans have to be repaid, holidays are difficult if not impossible, and sickness can be catastrophic. Today one must add not only high taxes and official indifference but also sharply rising costs of raw materials, rental and rates, help, maintenance, and credit. The Business for Sale columns in the newspapers are always long, and so are the lists of small businessmen in the Bankruptcy Court. It takes courage to start out on one's own. But people will clearly go on doing so, no matter what.

Some even take on the formidable challenge of starting up abroad. Take a young Englishman called Steven Spurrier who bought a wine shop in Paris in 1970, when he was only 29. 'I'd been in the London wine trade before,' he says, 'but I had no idea how to run a business like this. So at first I worked as a delivery boy for the other proprietor. It taught me a lot, and of course it gave the customers a chance to get used to my face. If I'd just walked in there, a brash new owner, I might have been in trouble.' Finance? 'Well, I didn't have any cash, so I went to my bank in England. They turned me down flat. So I went to the Paris branch of another bank, Barclays. I had some money elsewhere but it was tied up; they willingly accepted that as security.' Spurrier says the main lesson he has learned is that it costs more than you think to get going, that buying an existing business makes more sense than launching one, and that you need a very understanding bank manager.

One could add a few other rules, guidelines which apply whether one starts a restaurant, a wine shop, or a small engineering business. The first thing is to consider, as honestly as possible, whether you are going to be happy in your own business. People who want their future to be mapped out and to coast home to a pensioned retirement are unlikely to be happy out on their own, however good their ideas are and however hard they work. The key to success is enjoyment; you can never succeed in a job you find consistently disagreeable. If you think you can make it, don't decide on a particular business solely because it seems like a surefire way to making money. Select a business because it will involve doing the kind of work you like to do, in the kind of environment you prefer, among the sort of people you enjoy being with. You also need to assess the character of your partners (if any) in the venture. The easiest way of ensuring disaster is by falling out with associates; working closely with other people in a small-business environment is very different from being fellow-employees in a large company. Having got over the temperament hurdle, it is also necessary to examine whether there is a good balance of talents. Most small organizations need a salesman, an administrator, and a backroom boy. These qualities are seldom found rolled into one person, but they ought to be present in the company. For example, two academics in the driving seat are unlikely to make much progress, unless one is more of a businessman than an academic and the other lets him have his way.

The best ideas for start-up situations tend to come from the previous experience of the entrepreneurs, not from thin air. It is dangerous to depart from existing areas of expertise. Timing is also a crucial factor, for a mediocre idea stands far more chance in boom conditions than a good idea in the middle of a recession. And it obviously helps to discuss one's project with as many people as possible, especially those who are already in the same line of business. Finance, inevitably, tends to be more of a problem for the newcomer than for an established business and, as a rule, you will be expected to put yourself at risk. This usually means a second or third mortgage and a lot of personal guarantees. You will also be expected to present your case with skill and conviction. Many loan applicants are turned down simply because they don't appear to have done their homework. It is the man who fully understands his business and his requirements whose request for finance will fall on the sympathetic ear. Financial expertise, alas, is seldom the small company's strong suit. Typically, its growth has revolved around a few personalities with either commercial or engineering expertise, and concern over the purely financial end of things has been restricted to the occasional consultation with the company's bank manager. A balance sheet is often regarded as something that has to be compiled for the benefit of the Inland Revenue or the bank manager – a compulsory discipline, in other words – and not something that should be studied, understood, and used as a management tool. As for financial planning, and such terms as cash flow, these usually remain a mystery. Quite often the owner or manager of a small business will be vaguely aware that he is running short of capital for, say, stock or for tiding him over until a customer pays his debts. But more frequently he will not know exactly how much he needs, in what form he needs it, and for which part of the business. This is where the smaller man really fails, and it is for this that he is often penalized.

The attitude of banks, of course, varies a good deal. Some are more favourably disposed towards small businessmen than others, and even within one large bank people may take very different views. In some countries the Government has encouraged certain banks to specialize in lending to small and medium-sized companies. In Holland, for example, the Nederladsche Middenstandsbank, third largest of the Dutch commercial banks, provides special Government-trade loans to this kind of applicant. In Italy, the Istituto Mobiliare Italiano fulfils a similar function and in France – where small firms still account for three-fifths of output and manpower – a whole range of devices is available. In Britain, finance houses and organizations like the Industrial and Commercial Finance Corporation may take a bolder view than clearing banks.

John Jessop is a clever young man in the north-east of England who persuaded his bank to back him in a highly competitive field – electronics. His training and expertise in electronics and marketing made him well qualified to identify a market opportunity and then devise the best method of exploiting it. Like many other small businessmen, he is a firm believer in the advantages of specialization. The selection of thick film circuits as an advanced product has wide applications, from guided missile systems and computers to cars and TV sets, and a number of advantages in size, cost, and weight over other types of circuit. It is a growth market of considerable potential. 'Yet no one,' he says, 'has been making a good job of developing this advanced type of circuit. Large companies make the mistake of trying to set up thick film units under the umbrella of existing management structure. The sales approach is indistinct and development loses momentum.' Divisionalization is one answer but total specialization is better. Hence J.J. Electronic Components Ltd – John Jessop's own business idea. Having identified the potential, Jessop had the option of trying to persuade a company to employ him, or to set up a separate division. The advantages would have been the easy availability of cash, equipment, and personnel as opposed to his alternative of finding finance, spreading it thin, running on minimal help initially and turning himself into a one-man band of managing director, accountant, sales force, general manager and cleaner. At this point he heard about a 'Build Your Own Business' competition sponsored jointly by Barclays Bank and the North-East Development Council, with £10,000 as the prize, and decided to enter. The competition attracted 1,000 initial applicants of whom 304 sent in projects for a manufacturing or service industry based in, but trading beyond, the north-east. Jessop's scheme was judged the best of an excellent field, and J.J. Electronics was on its way. 'Starting up in a shack,' says Jessop, 'would have been going too far. But on the other hand, spending all available capital on premises and equipment would have been wrong.' So the company was established in a new 5,000 square-foot, two-year rent-free factory from the Northumberland County Council in South Nelson Industrial Estate, and the expensive electronic equipment needed to make and check thick film circuits to infinitesimal perfection was leased through the bank's leasing company. The advantage of the leasing scheme is that it enables the manufacturer to start with new equipment and tailor rental payments to the demands of the cash flow forecast. It still left the problem of finding lucrative contracts, but Jessop's positive approach made a good impression on potential clients as well as the bank and local authority.

Once a small businessman is established, of course, his options grow. Some businessmen have only one ultimate ambition: to build up their company to the point where it can be sold for a large enough amount to enable them to spend the rest of their lives in the sun. Others want to create a bigger empire, to emulate people like Charles Forte and Hugh Fraser. It is the great merit of private enterprise, as I have stressed throughout this book, that it allows individuals to make the choice.

Chapter Fourteen
Keynes and After

O that we now had here
But one ten thousand of those men in England
That do no work today!
KING HENRY V, 4, III

One of the chief aims of people who have tried running their own business is, of course, job security. No discussion of trade unions – or, indeed of private enterprise – could possibly be complete without a look at this increasingly complex subject. Economists tend to see it as a theoretical problem, an abstract issue, a factor which in economic management has nothing to do with moral rights and wrongs. I have never been able to share that view, and my many friends in industry do not do so either. A belief in private enterprise does not, and certainly should not, imply a callous indifference to people who lose their jobs, often through no fault of their own. This *is* a moral issue: I have no time for people who argue, smugly, that 'a bit of unemployment never hurts anybody'. (The same people, needless to say, are the first to plead for sympathy when they find themselves involved in rationalization programmes and other measures which, by their very nature, lead to redundancies.) Unemployment may not be the financial hardship it once was – especially in countries like Britain – but it is still a loathsome business. Have you ever lost a job? I have. Many years ago, a newspaper I was working for suddenly went out of business. It wasn't my fault – I had worked as hard as anyone could – but it caught me nonetheless. I well remember the atmosphere in the office: the first rumours on the editorial floor, bewilderment when they turned out to be true, the panic among some members of the staff when we discovered that there was little hope of compensation. I was in my twenties, unattached, and confident that I would manage to squeeze in somewhere else, but the experience taught me never to make supercilious remarks about the supposed delights of unemployment.

I am glad that, by accident of birth, I missed the Great Depression. To see unemployment rise from 10 per cent in 1929 to 16 per cent in 1930 and a staggering 21 per cent in 1931 must have been a traumatic experience. To be part of that 21 per cent, without much hope of improvement, must have been devastating. In Germany it led to the rise of Hitler. The British had more sense, but it is not surprising that the experience turned many people permanently against capitalism. Some of my friends will not vote Conservative, regardless of how much the party's policies may have changed, simply because of what their parents went through in the early 1930s. It is a purely emotional response, easily countered by pointing out that post-war unemployment in Britain has reached its highest level under a *Socialist* government. As a nation heavily dependent on exports we cannot, with the best will in the world, hope to isolate ourselves from what is happening elsewhere. But the emotion is understandable; it is shared by many people who support the Tory party.

Adam Smith had little to say about unemployment because, in his day, agriculture was still by far the most important activity and in agricultural society the line between being employed and being unemployed tends to be blurred: the whole family works but may be underemployed. The man who, by common consent, has made the greatest contribution to the subject (and, many people would argue, saved capitalism in the process) is John Maynard Keynes. We have already referred to him at various points in this book and his name will come up again.

Keynes was born in Cambridge in 1883 (the year that Marx died), the son of a don who was himself a lecturer in economics and logic. He won a scholarship to Eton, where he distinguished himself both in studies and in the notorious Eton Wall Game, and went up to King's College, Cambridge, in 1902. He did just enough mathematics to end up with a First, but his main interests lay elsewhere. He studied philosophy for his own pleasure, became President of the Union, joined various discussion societies, and took up economics. A year after taking his degree he sat the Civil Services examination. He got a relatively low mark in the economics paper and had his own characteristic explanation: 'I probably knew more about economics than my examiners.' Nonetheless he passed second into the Civil Service and was assigned to the India Office. He soon grew bored and, after two years of office hours spent mainly on private work, he resigned, claiming that his only official achievement had been to get one pedigree bull shipped to Bombay. He returned to Cambridge, first as a lecturer in economics and later as a fellow of King's, a post he retained for the rest of his life.

Keynes was, by all accounts, an entertaining as well as clever companion. Nicholas Davenport, who knew him well, says in his *Memoirs of a City Radical* that he has 'never met anyone so gay, so brilliant, and so witty in conversation'. The wit, of course, could hurt as well as entertain. Keynes never learned to suffer fools gladly. He also had a healthy disrespect for the views of bankers, politicians, and fellow economists. It didn't exactly endear him to the Establishment and his own theories, challenging financial orthodoxy, certainly did not meet with universal acceptance. His advice was frequently ignored or rejected, and he once described his contribution to the debates of the twenties as 'the croakings of a Cassandra who could never influence the course of events in time'. But he was not merely a brilliant theorist; his policy suggestions were practical enough – as well as correctly timed – to appeal to politicians in desperate search of solutions. (Keynes proved his understanding of the way things work in other ways: he was a highly successful stock market speculator who made money both for himself and for his college. Davenport thinks that at one time he was worth £1 million.) He published a number of pamphlets and books, but the work which really put him on the economic map was his *General Theory of Employment, Interest and Money*. The reaction to the book, and the subsequent professional debate about its contents, is a vast subject and there is no point in going into all the details. The controversy continues to this day.

Keynes adopted basic premises a little closer to reality than those of his predecessors. He argued against *laissez-faire*, and made a strong case for Government intervention to compensate for the uncontrollable vagaries of capitalism, even if it meant governmental deficits. He advocated a permanent policy of keeping interest rates low, and put heavy emphasis on the need to maintain full employment. It is a measure of his success that the basic ideas he was trying to convey now sound remarkably simple. But it was in the United States, not Britain, that the first attempt was made to alleviate unemployment through public works. Under Roosevelt's 'New Deal' the administration started to spend large sums of money over and above what it received in tax revenue on roads, dams, harbours, irrigation and land reclamation works, public buildings, housing estates and projects of many other kinds. Keynes' detractors maintain that he had very little to do with this; it would have happened anyway. But his ideas were well known in the United States and he had acquired a considerable following. There is certainly no doubt about his warm approval of Roosevelt's experiment. 'You have,' Keynes wrote in a famous open letter to the President late in 1933, 'made yourself the trustee for those in every country who seek to mend the evils of our condition by reasoned experiment, within the framework of the existing social system. If you fail, rational change will be gravely prejudiced throughout the world, leaving orthodoxy and revolution to fight it out. But if you succeed, new and bolder methods will be tried everywhere, and we may date the first chapter of a new economic era from your accession to office.' In Britain, at this time, the emphasis was still on 'good housekeeping': expenditure was cut and taxes increased in an attempt to get the budget into surplus, even though it involved the doubling of unemployment. By the time his ideas gained acceptance in official circles we were at war again. In 1944, however, looking forward to the end of hostilities and determined to avoid the economic disasters which had followed the First World War, the British Government published a White Paper committing itself for the first time to securing 'a high and stable level of employment'.

Some economists argue that his role has been overrated – that the post-war economy would have performed differently even if he had never existed. Large-scale Government spending on defence and social services, the liberalization of international trade, and a rapid rate of technological progress, all combined to stimulate activity and keep up employment. They have a point, of course. But Keynes did have a very considerable influence not only on Ministers and his contemporaries at the Treasury but also on the next generation of politicians and economists. What is questionable is whether his techniques have all that much relevance to the more complex problems of the 1970s. The limitations of this kind of demand management have become all too apparent and, as noted earlier, there is another, less welcome side to massive Government spending – namely, runaway inflation.

The trend in recent years has been to concentrate on specific rather than general measures. There has been more emphasis on special aid to particularly depressed regions, re-training programmes, and subsidies to enable firms to retain workers who would otherwise become redundant. Subsidizing people at work, it is argued, is cheaper for the taxpayer than keeping them on the dole. There have also been various attempts at 'job creation' – the kind of thing which Roosevelt went in for for under his New Deal and which, before him, enabled Egypt's Pharaohs to build the pyramids. And of course the effects of unemployment are nowadays cushioned by all kinds of welfare benefits. Some people, as noted earlier, are actually better off out of work than they were when they had a full-time job. The fear that a 3 per cent plus unemployment rate would lead to anarchy, so widely expressed in the fifties and sixties, has proved to be unjustified. The fact is, nevertheless, that unemployment remains a considerable problem.

In Britain, as in most other countries, the official statistics include a large number of so-called 'unemployables' – people who, because they are disabled and sick, cannot take on jobs and are therefore supported by the rest. There are others who happen to be between jobs and, during some months of the year, several hundred thousand students who sign on in order to collect supplementary benefits. But even allowing for all this the number of people out of work during recessions such as we have experienced in the last few years is disturbing. It is of little consolation, to those without a job, that the percentage is higher in countries like the United States and Germany – and higher still in most developing nations, including those who have chosen to adopt a socialist system. Statistics don't mean much to men and women who want to work but cannot do so.

To some extent, the relatively high unemployment totals seen in 1975–6 must be reckoned to reflect that old bogey, the trade cycle, which Keynes sought to banish. This *should* be a temporary phenomenon; as industrial countries pull out of their recession, unemployment should begin to fall. But there is more to it than that. In Britain, at least, there are also certain basic defects. One is the reluctance of industry to invest in new capacity (which could create new jobs) against a constantly changing background. Another is that, for some years past, trade unions have put higher money wages before expanded job opportunities. One doesn't have to be an economist to see that, in a country heavily dependent on exports, a comparatively sharp rise in costs is bound to produce a fall in orders and, eventually, a decline in the number of people who can be usefully employed. Governments have propped up 'lame ducks' – failing companies and sometimes whole industries – in a well-meant but often futile endeavour to evade unpalatable facts, and trade unions have used their power to maintain bizarre and antique restrictions on work and output. One can understand why they should want to do so; no one likes unemployment. But such a policy, along with all the subsidies and job creation schemes, represents a viewpoint which is essentially short-term. It puts the accent on preserving jobs rather than pursuing prosperity. Unfortunately the job security which the Government so eagerly seeks is likely to prove largely illusory.

It would be pointless to pretend that there are simple answers – that a 'new Keynes' will emerge with an Instant Miracle. Unemployment is a world-wide problem which results from many factors – rising populations, diminishing resources, technological changes, slower growth. Various efforts are being made to find solutions at an international level. The Common Market is one of the relatively new institutions which permit, if not actively encourage, greater labour mobility. The multinational companies, so fiercely attacked by socialists, also maintain that their activities offer workers a wider choice than they have had in the past. The International Labour Organisation, among others, is trying to take all this a great deal further, and may well come up with worthwhile suggestions. But for Britain, the practical issues have become increasingly clear. The end result of trying to cure unemployment by an *excessive* reliance on Keynesian techniques is bound to be rapid inflation. You can't keep on printing jobs. Over the years successive Ministers have tried to persuade American, German and Japanese companies to invest in Britain. Many have done so. But many more have turned elsewhere – for one very good, understandable reason. They had no guarantees that the unions would take a positive view, or that the Government would be able to resist the temptation to interfere at every stage, now and in the future. Today's industrialists are very different from the heartless men portrayed in countless novels and plays about the Victorian era; they have to be. But one can hardly expect them to ignore reality.

Chapter Fifteen
Can Capitalism Survive?

Nothing is permanent but change.
HERACLITUS

The last few chapters have been largely concerned with adaptation – the willingness, already demonstrated in many ways, of private enterprise to come to terms with a changing world while, at the same time, retaining the freedoms which most people in the West regard as so vitally important in terms of personal happiness. It is a subject which has exercised a great many minds in many different countries and will continue to do so. Some people feel, with Alexander Solzhenitsyn, that it is already too late: that capitalism is doomed and Western civilization with it. Robert Heilbroner, an economist, and author of *An Inquiry into the Human Prospect* argues that 'a high degree of political authority will be inescapable in the period of extreme exigency we can expect a hundred years hence'. This, he says, 'augurs for the cultivation of nationalist, authoritarian attitudes, perhaps today foreshadowed by the kind of religious politicism we find in China. The deification of the State, whatever we may think of it from the standpoint of our still-cherished individualist philosophies, seems therefore the most likely replacement for the deification of materialism that is the unacknowledged religion of our business culture ...'

This view is now so widely shared that it seems almost foolhardy to challenge it. State control is obviously growing everywhere – including countries like the United States and Germany, where free enterprise has maintained its hold more firmly than in Britain. One very good reason is, simply, the growth in population. Another is that people expect more, in terms of material prosperity, than they have done in the past and think that the State can meet those expectations. These are, indeed, formidable issues and I do not for one moment doubt that we will move further towards totalitarianism. I would not have troubled to write this book if I thought otherwise. The danger is real enough. But I take comfort in a number of facts.

First, and perhaps rather frivolously, there is the fact that events rarely turn out to be as grim as the forecasts. Experts said that the *Titanic* was unsinkable, that the Maginot line was impregnable, that the tank wouldn't replace the horse, that the aeroplane would never be a weapon of war, and that the Americans would win in Vietnam. They said that thalidomide was harmless, that Picasso had no future as an artist, and that Edison's telephone system would blow up the streets of New York. They also said that the earth was flat and that it rested on the backs of four white elephants. Then there was the Bomb – remember how we worried ourselves sick about it twenty years ago? We were convinced the world would come to an end tomorrow, or at the very latest the day after. Futurology is a booming profession because governments, companies, trusts, foundations, and plain, simple, ordinary millionaires cannot and will not accept uncertainties. They will pay for, and commission, almost anything providing it is stated with enough assurance. This is why Think Tanks have become so enormously popular. One of the best-known is the Hudson Institute, whose portly chief, Herman Kahn, likes to use words like 'wargasm' and 'surprise-free projection', and who spends much of his time developing 'outbreak scenarios'. He recently came up with the world-shattering finding, after months of costly study, that 'it is incredibly hard to get a major war started' – which, if nothing else, is a reassuring thought. 'We are,' says one of the other Institute members with disarming frankness, 'the product of affluence. People with money come to us as an oracle because they can afford an oracle and, who knows, they may get something out of it.'

Kahn has a number of rivals, notably the Rand Corporation,

whose soothsayers talk grandly about 'opinion technology'. They have developed a process called Delphi, which is based on the simple premise that in making a forecast 'X' heads are better than one. Its method of forecasting is to ask twenty or thirty experts to make a prediction. The first estimates are tallied and the resulting opinions fed back to the experts, who then respond again after reflecting on the first-round thoughts of the other experts. Eventually there is some sort of consensus; Delphi has, for example, told the White House that it would take 225 A-Bombs to wipe out the American arms industry. There is also the so-called 'relevance tree'. Relevance trees are, as the term suggests, graphic representations of the future that, when drawn, look like trees. They are, says the inventor, 'created as coherent outlines identifying all the potential events, discoveries, threats, opportunities, short cuts, and alternative routes along the trails leading to a major objective'. The director of one of America's leading research centres has a tree, made of clear plastic, which represents the country from 1960 to the year 2000. A solid trunk extends from 1960 to 1970, at which the tree develops three major branches that continue to sprout new branches through to the 70s, 80s and 90s. At the top of the tree, which represents the year 2000, there are eleven major branches each representing alternatives for the US. Each of the branches has a name representing the state of society at that point. They are: Collapse, '1984' Theocracy, Authoritarian Recession, Pollution Stalemate, Welfare Stultification, Garrison State, Philistine Comfort, Socialist Success, Satisfied Plenty, Exuberant Democracy, and Manifest Destiny.

Some tanks have concentrated on population trends and their conclusions are truly awful. If people go on having babies at the present rate, by the year 3700 the weight of all the human beings on earth will equal the weight of the earth. Some 1,700 years later, in the year 5400, if everyone on earth were put into a hollow ball, its radius would have to be 20,000 times that of the earth and the ball would have to expand at an alarming rate to keep up with the constantly increasing number of babies. An American professor, G. K. O'Neill of Princeton, has come

213

up with a solution: he wants and expects to see cylinders containing you, clouds, lakes, fish, ski-slopes, electric cars, food, and other amenities rotating beyond the earth.

Kahn and more serious forecasters argue that, by producing grim predictions of this kind, they persuade us to take action which will avoid it. They obviously have a valid point. Concern with the environment, for example, only took off in any meaningful way with the publication of all those doomsday books a few years ago. And I am sure that Solzhenitsyn and Heilbroner would readily agree with their basic objective. If it takes forecasts of real disaster to make people sit up and take notice, then a little exaggeration is well worthwhile.

Can capitalism survive? Yes, if one means private enterprise and all that goes with it – though obviously not in the same form as in the nineteenth century or even thirty years ago. There is no reason why the mixed economy cannot be made to work, as indeed it has been made to work successfully during most of our lifetime. There will, inevitably, be recurring crises of some kind or another, reflecting the more complex kind of society we live in. But, as we have seen, communist countries have crises too. They are evolving and, as they do so, they will put more emphasis on 'individualist philosophies' than they do today. We already see evidence of this in the Soviet Union and other iron curtain countries, whose attitudes and methods differ increasingly from those of countries in a lower stage of development, like China. Freedom may not mean much to a coolie but it certainly has meaning for a teacher, a farmer, or an engineer. Materialism alone may be inadequate as the 'unacknowledged religion of our business culture', but the liberties and opportunities which go with it matter far more to people than is generally acknowledged. This goes as much for developing countries which, for the time being, have adopted a more or less totalitarian régime as it does for countries like Britain and the United States.

In Africa, every individual is expected to drop on his knees at least once a day and thank his leaders for delivering him from the clutches of his former masters. In Uganda, of course, this is a sick joke. But even in countries like Tanzania gratitude is wearing a bit thin. *Uhuru* has proved to be a mixed blessing: for many people it merely means freedom to do as the Government likes. Wearing Mao-style jackets (a gift from Peking along with railway tracks and 'plum blossom' toilet paper), Tanzania's leaders insist that personal freedom is a luxury which a poor country like theirs cannot afford. Yes, the heads of African Governments did draw up a charter of Unity, back in 1963, which grandly pledged that 'it is the inalienable right of all people to control their own destiny' and that 'freedom, equality, justice, and dignity are essential objectives'. But no, that doesn't mean Tanzanians can buy their own land, decide where they would like to live, travel abroad, have a free press, or vote for an opposition party. Nor does it mean that students can choose how and where they would like to study: 'Their education must be dictated not by their own wishes but the need of the masses.' In Arusha, the state-owned press is used chiefly as a vehicle for Ministerial threats. When I was there, early in 1975, the Minister of Labour announced that 'people who cannot read or write by the end of next year will be sacked', and President Nyerere warned that his Government would 'detain people whose main preoccupation is to empty bottles of beer'. People who refused to leave their homes for Government-designated villages, Nyerere's own distinctive form of collective farming, would be 'treated as enemies of the State' and anyone who spent foreign exchange on, for example, sending children to study abroad would be considered guilty of 'an act of high treason'. Nyerere says he is building a socialist state; revolutionaries, he insist, have to be ruthless. Tanzania's problems certainly make ours look insignificant, and his methods may be right for Africa – though, by common consent, the economy is getting worse rather than better. But Nyerere would have been the first to bellow '*Uhuru*' if a British administration had shown such ruthlessness. Exiles in London console themselves with the thought that such autocratic – and impulsive – behaviour can't last forever, and they may be right. African countries *have* been known to change régimes.

It has been all too easy, in recent years, for politicians to blame capitalism for all the world's economic ills. People are always ready to believe that their problems can be solved by confiscating the property of the rich – and, of course, capitalism has a lot to answer for. But disappointment invariably follows. You can abolish private wealth but it won't necessarily cure poverty: indeed, sometimes the poverty grows worse. You can throw out the alleged 'oppressor' but a new one invariably takes his place. There are belated protests and attempts to change the system – Dubcek tried it in Czechoslovakia, and the Hungarians might have succeeded some years before if it had not been for all those Russian tanks – but totalitarian states are expert at the art of self-protection. No communist or socialist country has ever returned to a truly capitalist system, nor is it likely that people will want them to. But the values associated with free enterprise have a basic appeal which should not be underrated and certainly not be ignored. The assumption that communism must triumph everywhere – and, once established, could not be exorcised or even moderated – is, I believe, totally mistaken.

Capitalism – or, rather, free enterprise – will continue to change and adapt because that is what the market system is all about and because more and more businessmen are willing to make the effort. This is fact Number Two. The businessman today has to compete with several *élites* – notably administrators and trade unionists – and to take account of all kinds of factors which would have been ignored fifty or even thirty years ago. His ability to inspire imperialistic wars (a pet subject for so many historians) has gone, along with the power to shape national policy. Consumers, environmentalists, academics, politicians, journalists, trade union leaders, and many others nowadays influence his thinking – and, if he is sensible, at least some of his actions. Intelligent business leaders acknowledge, and in varying degrees accept, that they have new and wider responsibilities. As one of America's leading industrialists put it not long ago: 'As long as it serves as an instrument to help elevate the quality of life for all Americans, the private corporation has a reason for existence beyond profits. If it should ever again restrict its responsibilities within the narrow perimeters of the past, its right to exist could be seriously challenged.' There are, to be sure, companies which dismiss all this as fanciful talk: they don't mind paying lip service to the 'quality of life' but are reluctant to do anything about it. Recessions such as we have had in the past few years encourage them in the short-sighted view that, say, concern with pollution is something of a luxury. But the climate has changed for good and, by and large, industrialists throughout the Western world have shown themselves more willing to adjust to the needs of the 1970s and beyond than their predecessors would have thought possible.

Quality of Life

Concern with the environment is, as I have said, of comparatively recent origin. For centuries businessmen felt no need to concern themselves with some of the by-products of their endeavours: there were always more forests to demolish, more rivers to take industrial waste-products, more lands to cover with factories and office buildings. Industrialization was a means to a desirable end. It wasn't until the late 1960s that academics and others disturbed by pollution were able to make any sort of impact on public opinion. For me, one of the most memorable – and illuminating – episodes was the electoral battle over 'Proposition Nine' in California during 1972. Memorable because I was there; illuminating because I was able to see both sides of the coin. In California, as you know, they have a system of state propositions on which voters are asked to give their verdict. We in Britain pride ourselves on our love of democracy, but make an awful fuss when someone suggests that we should have a referendum on major issues like entry into the Common Market. In Los Angeles and San Francisco I have listened to people arguing about the height of buildings and pension increases for police and firemen. There's even been a proposition to 'eliminate unnecessary wordage in the

217

Constitution, making it more understandable without changing its original meaning'. But Nine, known as the 'environment initiative', created more than usual fervour. It was the brainchild of a flamboyant one-time used-car dealer named Edwin Koupal and his wife Joyce. Originally, back in 1968, they set out only to fight the notorious Los Angeles smog, but later decided to broaden the campaign. Using volunteer workers recruited mainly from college campuses with a scattering of housewives, democratic political candidates, Hollywood entertainers, and a few of the smaller ecology groups, they drafted a bill, collected more than half a million signatures from registered voters, and got in on the ballot. The legislature, they argued, was so dominated by special interest lobbies that only a radical mandate would impress lawmakers.

Proposition Nine turned out to be the toughest anti-pollution law ever submitted to a State-wide vote, and it needed a simple majority for adoption. The twenty-three-part measure aimed to ban new coastal drilling, impose a five-year ban on the construction of nuclear powerplants, forbid use of DDT and related insecticides, impose stiff fines on air polluters, sharply restrict the amount of sulphur allowable in diesel fuels, and require that lead be removed from gasoline by 1976. Thoroughly alarmed, more than 200 of the State's biggest corporations got together to shoot it down. The giant Standard Oil Company hired a public relations firm to run a counter-campaign which they decided to call 'Californians against the Pollution Initiative'. Equipped with more than a million dollars, the PR firm decided on a two-part strategy. One was to attack Koupal and his supporters as 'eco-freaks'. The other was to terrify potential supporters. Passage of the measure, they suggested, would mean unemployment and starvation. 'If Proposition Nine is adopted,' said one of their newspaper ads, 'you will not be able to provide yourself and your family with the basic necessities of life. You can lose your job. You may have to go back to the scrub board and laundry tub for washing clothes.' Each night, watching television, people were told of other dire consequences that would befall them unless the proposition was defeated – statewide economic paralysis and bankruptcies, higher taxes, food shortages, pestilences, and diseases. Customers of the San Diego Gas and Electric Company were informed, by post, that crippling electric power blackout could be expected if the bill went through. Echoed by newspaper, radio, bill-boards, bus cards, a deluge of pamphlets and flying squads of speakers, the warnings became almost hysterical. I saw an advertisement headed 'the Sacred Mosquitoes of California'. It showed a giant mosquito and asked: 'Who wants to bring back typhoid? Malaria? Or encephalitis? Only the people who love mosquitoes. The sponsors of Proposition Nine make illegal the use or possession of a long list of chemicals, including the only effective pesticides for controlling various pests.'

Koupal dismissed the charges as 'terror tactics' and 'preposterous doomsday cries' – and promptly did some crying of his own. 'During smog alerts,' he announced in full-page ads, 'our children are kept off the playgrounds while industry is allowed to continue emitting poisonous gases into our air. . . . A nuclear accident from one nuclear power plant would release radiation equal to 100 Hiroshima-type atomic bombs. . . . Smog costs the average American family an additional $268 a year: unnecessary doctor bills, extra car repairs, lost property values, and higher food prices. . . . He claimed that responsible Californians supporting Proposition Nine included Dr Paul Ehrlich, Jack Lemmon, Walter Matthau, and 'Friends of the Earth'.

The PR firm, undaunted, produced an even longer list of 'responsible Californians' who, it said, were determined to say 'no'. They included several professors and organizations such as the 'California State Council of Carpenters' and the 'Sportsmen's Council of the Redwood Empire'. Art Seidenbaum, a columnist for the *Los Angeles Times*, summed up the general feeling on polling day. 'The main reason I've been quiet,' he wrote, 'is that I've been confused and still am. I've heard the pro-9 forces jab at my confusion with selected facts from serious scientists. I've even received a piece of payola called "Poisoned Power", a paperback of almost 400 pages on the perils of nuclear plants. I've talked to university scientists around town, many of whom don't have axes to grind or grants to get with major industry.... I expect to go into the polling place about as torn up as I am right now. How I vote will be an emotional decision. If I'm feeling optimistic and responsible, I may vote no, on grounds that there are better ways to serve survival. But if I'm feeling righteous spite, thinking we must take our lives in our own hands, I'll vote yes. Even the weather will matter.'

The weather turned out to be fine, with hardly a whiff of smog, and Proposition Nine was defeated by a ratio of two to one. Koupal said he had been beaten by big money, and the manager of the winning side credited the intelligence of the electorate. My own view, having watched the affair with growing interest, was that Koupal's 'People lobby' defeated itself by going too far. But it certainly made an impact: both politicians and businessmen were forced to take notice.

Could a similar campaign have been mounted in the Soviet Union, where industrial pollution has become just as much of a problem? No prizes for the correct answer.

Since then, of course, we have had other campaigns linked to the environment, including several concerned with the need to conserve resources. The oil crisis, in particular, has made people very much aware that the earth's resources are limited. The crisis, as such, was sparked off by purely financial considerations: the Arab world suddenly discovered they had more power than they realized. But the effect on public opinion (and, in turn, on politicians and businessmen) has been much more profound. There is, today, a much greater awareness of the need to avoid waste than there has been at any time in the world's industrial history. And it is only partly due to political pressure: at least as important, in practical terms, is the fact that private enterprise, with profits as the driving force, always does its best to cope with increased costs. There is more emphasis on saving fuel – for example – because economic realities dictate that it should be so.

There is, without doubt, a great deal more that can be done

and no reason to suppose that it won't be. Inevitably, too, it has raised a question mark over the basic issue of economic growth. Until people like Koupal began to make a fuss, and the oil crisis underlined the need for conservation, few people had seriously questioned the long-established view that growth was the key to universal happiness. Communist countries like China and the Soviet Union, much further behind in terms of industrial development, saw even less reason to challenge it than old-established industrial societies like Britain, the US and Germany. Only growth could pay for the material progress everyone needed and desired. The Gross National Product was synonymous with the Quality of Life.

I don't know who invented that splendid phrase, the Quality of Life; but I do know that the GNP is no longer the God it used to be – at least not in the West. People want material progress, of course, but they also want clean rivers and beaches, fresh air, and cities one can live in. It is a feeling which, in America, has been summed up in another phrase: 'life-style depression'. Americans, so the argument runs, have been spoiled by prosperity. What the country needs is 'a policy of de-growthing society'.

Two university professors, putting the case in a letter to the *New York Times*, said: 'A decline in our standard of living need not be too discomforting. In one short year we learned that we could keep our temperatures down in the winter and up in the summer. We have cut down on highway speeds. A compact with no air-conditioning became acceptable. The birth rate tapered off. Thus we have in a real sense already engaged in a de-growth process, and we lived through it without severe dislocations. Too often we have cultivated growth indulgence for the new, for the slightly improved and for the superfluous. It is time to introduce managed de-growthing. Less this, less that. . . . There are many of us who can remember that once life was not unbearable without two cars, without a backyard pool, without . . . without. . . . Riding a streetcar was once fun and not a symbol of some sort of impoverishment.'

I don't much care for the jargon, and I think the (no doubt) comfortably placed academics might have acknowledged that many Americans still have to reach first base. It is a lot easier to mock the Gross National Product from a four-bedroomed house in the better suburbs of Washington (or, for that matter, London and Frankfurt) than it is from a Baltimore slum. But one can see why their argument should have appeal. Most of the environmental literature published in the last few years takes much the same approach. One could add, as the environmentalist does, that there is ample scope for self-help.

Be willing to pick up other people's litter. Buy a bicycle. Don't use paper towels when a sponge will do. Don't throw away clothing that someone else can use. If you want more children, adopt them. Plant trees; 'a tree makes a marvellous gift for a wedding anniversary'. Call the Salvation Army to see if you can get rid of your junk. Re-use envelopes. Build a compost heap. Ask yourself whether you really need a pre-soak cycle in a washing-machine, or an automatic ice cube-maker for the refrigerator. Try a non-powered form of boating – learn to row instead. Share your vacuum cleaner with the next door neighbour. Politely decline to have purchases put in a bag, and explain why. Don't buy TV dinners that come with a disposable metal cooking dish. Buy your ice cream in a cone.

One suspects that most of the people who write this kind of thing don't take their own advice. But again, one can see why it should appeal. Is it compatible with capitalism – or rather, free enterprise? I don't see why not. The market system has always forced companies to adjust themselves to changes in public moods and habits. No one compels *consumers* to buy their products. Companies which no longer have a market simply go to the wall. A 'lifestyle depression' may mean fewer companies competing for the favours of the public, and force those who survive to become more efficient, but the system itself can certainly cope. What matters is that people should be able to *choose* whatever life-style they feel suits them best. Under capitalism that choice is theirs; under communism and most forms of socialism the choice is largely in the hands of planners.

Planning Mania

There are, of course, economists who think that planners know best – that it is impossible to cope with the demands of modern society unless we put our future into the hands of people who are trained to draw up blueprints for Utopia. We have touched on this before, at various points in the book, but the argument is worth another look. Superficially, the case for planning is impressive. No businessman today conducts his organization without some element of forward planning, based on the best knowledge available about his business operations and his market. And not even the most ardent advocate of *laissez-faire* (which I am not) would deny the obligation of governments to maintain the level of total demand and to plan fiscal and financial politics sufficiently flexible to achieve this end. What these policies should be is debatable; that they should exist is fairly common ground. But there are many people who would certainly deny the obligation or right of governments to plan every detail of economic behaviour. It isn't just that, sooner or later, Government by bureaucracy becomes an intolerable burden. No less important is the proven fact that the planners so often get things desperately wrong. The Soviet Union is one of the most planned economies in the world yet, as we have seen, it still gets into the most awful economic troubles. The usual response is to sack the chief planner, but that doesn't solve the basic problem – namely, that excessive planning generally does more harm than good.

A Soviet economist once estimated that more than 10 million citizens were engaged in collecting and processing data. More recently, Academician Glushkov has estimated that if the planners in the Soviet Union were really to get down to the ultimate and plan every activity in the economy several quintillion relationships would have to be examined and appraised. He added that it would take a million computers processing 30,000 operations a second, several years to appraise all of them. By that time the answers would not matter since the original imput data would be out of date anyway. In Britain we have not quite reached that stage but we are well on our way. A large and still growing number of people are devoting their working lives to gathering all kinds of information and an equally large number of experts are busy using it to produce an endless stream of detailed instructions. Most of them are rubber-stamped by Ministers – if they see them at all. The process has spread to town halls all over the country. Everywhere hard-working and determined officials are throwing up table after table of fascinating information on employment structures, historical mobility, population growth and past planning trends. Everywhere planners are telling the rest of us what to do. If only all that energy could be used to benefit the economy!

The most publicized – and futile – exercise in central planning ever carried out by a British Government took place in 1965. Mr Wilson, the Prime Minister, called it 'one of the biggest revolutions in the machinery of government which Britain has ever seen in peacetime'. Central to this revolution had been the creation of the Department of Economic Affairs, 'charged with preparing a national plan aimed at maintaining a steady expansion in industrial production year by year and, in particular, of strengthening those sectors of the economy which are essential both for increasing exports and for avoiding internal strain'. The National Plan emerged soon afterwards and was launched with another Wilsonian fanfare. It was, he declared, 'a breakthrough in the whole history of economic government by consent and consensus'. Alas, the 'breakthrough' was short-lived: Mr Wilson's National Plan was formally buried after less than a year, and the DEA followed not long afterwards.

What ditched them was a sudden sterling crisis; it forced Ministers to introduce hurried measures which ran counter to all their careful planning. But that was not the whole story. Even before that crisis many people had developed doubts about the wisdom of such elaborate projects. The uncertainties seemed far too large for that. For one thing Britain was likely to join the Common Market before long and, if it did, a lot of the assumptions made by the planners would become invalid.

For another, the promulgation of a plan for 4 per cent annual growth not only seemed wildly optimistic but, inevitably, encouraged wage and salary earners to expect and demand a roughly corresponding increase in incomes. Since the 4 per cent proved to be too high, the plan constituted a built-in inflationary pressure. There has been no National Plan since.

Sir Frank McFadzean, former head of Shell and now chairman of British Airways, is one of many prominent industrialists who have spoken out against 'the science of targetology'. In a lecture at the University of Strathclyde some years ago he denounced what he called 'the intervention of the amateur planner with his assumptions of knowledge about the future which he simply does not possess'. The whole weight of evidence, he thought, was to the contrary. In view of the record it was 'strange how little modesty there is among planners. . . . It is difficult to know whether the assumption of superiority is based on intellectual arrogance or ignorance. It is probably a combination of both; they are usually found together.' McFadzean went on to argue that the market economy performed more speedily and kept up to date the vast range of education that, in the case of the Soviet Union, Academician Glushkov stated would take a million computers several years to appraise and then the exercise would be useless. 'Under the administered price system in the Soviet Union the planners were approaching a stage of knowing the prices of everything and the value of nothing. This is why we are seeing the reintroduction of market pricing, profit, and capital charges over an increasing range of the Soviet economy, and even more speedily in some of the satellites. At a time when the Soviet Union is appreciating the merits of the price system, its constant undermining in the free world by people who fail to understand its role has been one of the main reasons for the popularity of planning. Bewildered and confused by the intricacies and enormous range of market adjustments, they come to believe that the economy is a jungle which somehow must be tamed by the planner. It would be silly for anyone to maintain that the price system in a free economy is a flawless mechanism. It is not. Prices can be manipulated; anti-monopoly legislation is necessary. Reactions can be sluggish. But no one has yet devised a better system for co-ordinating the economic activities of large groups of people at both a national and international level; for changing production in response to changes in consumer demand or failure of production, as during the Suez crisis, in one locality or another; for enabling the consumer to spend his income according to his own wishes; for enabling people to follow the occupations chosen by themselves instead of dictated by politicians with their false claims of knowing what is better for the individual than the individual himself.'

Sir Frank insisted that he was 'not delivering a polemic against the Labour party'. The guilty were not restricted to any particular persuasion: the Conservatives had been as gullible.

They were to be just as gullible again. Under Heath, the party not only took on more planners but went further than any previous Labour Government in controlling the economy, curbing profits, and limiting dividends. Free enterprise became 'the law of the jungle' and any attempt to challenge the assumption that the State always knows best was met with the angry cry, 'Who governs Britain?' In the end the electorate declined to give him backing for a policy which the Tories themselves had heatedly rejected just a few years earlier. It was Mr Heath's weakness, as a leader, that he himself had no deep ideological commitments and certainly no passionate attachments to free enterprise. He was a decent man who wanted to do well – for himself, for his party, and for the country. He asked to be judged simply on managerial competence. Forget the idealism – are we better than the other lot? The trouble with that sort of approach is that governments have less power than they like to pretend: there is a limit to the amount of planning one can do in a mixed economy.

His successor as Tory leader, Margaret Thatcher, has tried to restore an ideological base. 'We lost,' she said after the 1974 Election, 'because we did not appear to stand firmly for anything distinctive and positive.' The new formula, developed by

Sir Keith Joseph's Centre for Policy Studies, is a 'social market economy' – as opposed to what Sir Keith calls a 'command economy'. The expression is borrowed from the Germans, who developed a social market economy in the immediate post-war years and, as a result, were said to have performed an economic miracle. Let me quote from a pamphlet produced by the Centre in 1975: 'A market economy may be defined as an economic system in which the mechanism of variable prices functions freely to signal consumer preferences and, through its effect on profitability, to encourage the allocation of resources – man-power, capital and raw materials – so as to satisfy those preferences. The consumer exercises choice by voting with his purse. It is an impersonal system which permits decentralized initiative in the use of resources; this in turn promotes competition and efficiency while maximizing the range of consumer choice. A market economy can be contrasted with a command economy – such as exists in the USSR and Eastern Europe – in which consumer preferences are registered primarily by the appearance of shortages, and resources are allocated by administrative discretion, that is to say, by bureaucratic direction. It should be emphasized that, in a market economy, employees are free to develop and offer their skills to the company which will pay the most for them. The alternative to such a system is the collectivized one of communist countries where the direction of labour to specific functions by the bureaucracy has been the natural consequence of the direction of capital. Free trade unions can only operate in a free economy; in a command economy they inevitably become the tools of the state.'

And a *social* market economy?

'The notion it conveys is that of a socially responsible market economy, for a market economy is perfectly compatible with the promotion of a more compassionate society. Indeed, by encouraging the energies and initiative of the creative and sturdier members of our society, the resources available for helping the aged, the sick and the disabled are substantially enlarged.'

Support for the market system, the pamphlet goes on, does

not imply advocacy of *laissez-faire* in the sense of wishing to outlaw government from economic affairs.

'Historically the market economy is neither a right-wing nor a left-wing concept. And it can in principle embrace all of a multiplicity of forms of ownership – large private and public companies, state-owned corporations, one-man firms, partnerships, producer and consumer co-operatives, and so on. Its principal characteristic is the ubiquity of choice for consumer, employee and investor – which demands a multiplicity of production units competing vigorously for the consumer's approval, the employee's services, and the investor's savings. Experience has demonstrated conclusively that these conditions can be more assuredly satisfied the larger is the privately-owned and managed sector of industry and the greater are the number of competing firms within that sector. There is now abundant evidence that State enterprises in the UK have not served well either their customers, or their employees, or the taxpayer. For when the State owns, nobody owns; and when nobody owns, nobody cares.'

The need for some Government intervention – and planning – is acknowledged. But the basic point is clear enough:

'Since the war politicians have been trying to do too much; they are taking decisions which should be taken by individuals as parents, consumers, managers, and responsible citizens. Having set out to provide a safety net for the minority who cannot cope for themselves, the state has proceeded to put a cage around everybody.'

As a declaration of faith, all this has the merit of at least being clearly distinguishable from socialist policies. But there is still the problem of getting the message across to the electorate in language that laymen can understand. Perhaps Mrs Thatcher ought to try quoting the words of Dr Ludwig Erhard, the man who presided over Germany's achievements under the system. 'What took place in Germany,' he wrote in his book *Prosperity through Competition* 'is anything but a miracle. It is the result of the honest efforts of a whole people who, in keeping with the principles of liberty, were given the opportunity of using personal initiative and human energy. If this German example has any value beyond the frontiers of the country it can only be that of proving to the world at large the blessings of both personal and economic freedom.'

Law givers or revolutionaries who promise equality
and liberty at the same time are either Utopian
dreamers or charlatans
GOETHE

Outside the Communist bloc, planning mania is at its most
advanced in the bureaucratic paradise of the EEC head-
quarters in Brussels. But governments are close behind. Actively
encouraged by politicians, the planners (few of whom have any
practical business experience) are extending their efforts to all
kinds of areas they know little or nothing about.

One of the more absurd and dangerous examples is the
attempt to impose equality (the thing itself as distinct from
equality of opportunity) by central and local government de-
cree. Absurd because it involves bureaucrats in all kinds of
value judgments which they are not qualified to make – such
as the relative worth of dustmen and physicists, nurses and airline pilots – and which get both them and us entangled in a mass
of often contradictory rules and regulations. Dangerous because
it inevitably involves some loss of liberty. For British reformers
equality has always meant equality of treatment, of respect for
the individual, equality in the sense of an equal chance to develop one's personality and to live a full and free life. Legislation
in areas like race and sex discrimination is very much in line
with this approach, and no one could reasonably object to it.
But to strive for equality by limiting a citizen's freedom of
choice is something else.

Methods or models for achieving equality have historically
been collectivist; they have invariably been based on the
assumption that all resources belong equally to all people, and
that public ownership will bring about equality. But when all

the people own everything, they really do not own anything, enabling the officials who govern in the name of the people to make themselves more-than-equal and to restrict political liberties. One sees this at work in the Soviet Union and other communist societies. 'Socialism,' says Alexander Solzhenitsyn, 'begins by making all men equal in material matters only (this, of course, requires compulsion; the advocates of all brands of socialism agree on this point). However, the logical progression towards so-called 'ideal' equality inevitably implies the use of force. Furthermore, it means that the basic elements of personality – those elements which display too much variety in terms of education, ability, thought and feeling – must themselves be levelled out. The English saying "My home is my castle" stands in the way of socialism.'

In recent years the Labour Government has sought to reduce or eliminate choice in all kinds of areas. The trade union closed shop has been given the full backing of the law; the effect is to deny access to outsiders and, in many cases, locking a worker into one narrow job classification for life. In education parental choice has been restricted by an emotional attack on fee-paying schools. If entry to Britain's educational establishment were determined by class this might make sense. But this is no longer so. Merit matters more today than background, and the ability and willingness to pay for education is certainly not confined to the upper classes. It is natural for parents to want to do the best they can for their children, and if they believe that their talents are more likely to be fully developed in a private school (which is not always so) they should be permitted to follow their own judgment. In the name of equality we have destroyed many excellent schools and, as Dr Bryan Wilson has pointed out, surrendered all kinds of values. 'People have stopped thinking of education as a personal concern in which the individual's inner resources are cultivated, his mind furnished and his competences developed both for the enrichment of his own life and for his livelihood. Instead, older children often see it as a type of compulsory national service, in which one should do as little *for them* as possible. For some parents its best function is the provision of free custodial care of children. While politicians increasingly talk of education only in relation to the planned economy, as a way of providing so-and-so-many labour units. . . .'

In medicine, the left-wing attacks on private treatment have, at times, become almost hysterical. Yet Ministers have shown themselves ready enough to accept accommodation in private wards at the first sign of illness: it is remarkable (though hardly surprising) how attitudes change when socialists are concerned with themselves rather than other people.

Much of the antagonism, as noted in Chapter Nine, comes from a touchy preoccupation with class. The Britain of today is nothing like the portrait usually presented on American and European television: an 'Upstairs, Downstairs' land divided neatly into aristocratic swells lolling elegantly about at Henley and grim-faced proletarians toiling and striking in about equal proportions. The distribution of income is closer to equality than that in Communist Yugoslavia and the rate of social mobility is higher than anywhere else in Western Europe; two people in every five end up in a social class different from that occupied by their parents. But a certain amount of class consciousness undeniably exists even now, especially among older people, and it suits politicians and trade union leaders to keep it going. A politically stimulated working-class consciousness is Labour's power base. And it is the trade unions, rather than Britain's employers, who insist on maintaining the emotional division between Them and Us.

An upper class does still exist, but it is too small in numbers, too diffuse, and too ready to disclaim its status to be of much political account. The rich (or, rather, the very rich) have surrendered their dominating hold over the bulk of Britain's personal wealth; by conventional measurements, the share of wealth owned by the richest 1 per cent has fallen from more than two-thirds at the beginning of the century to less than one quarter today. Dukes and earls have increasingly become figures of fun; even in the City of London a title now tends to be a handicap rather than an advantage. The Prime Minister of the day is the son of a petty officer and went to an elementary school. The Conservative front bench is made up of commoners from widely different backgrounds. Even the civil service has become much more concerned with ability than the possession of old school ties. In short, we no longer have a clearly definable 'ruling class'.

Even the so-called middle class has changed dramatically. In social terms there is not one middle class but a multitude of middle classes, extending economically from rich to poor, and occupationally from lawyers and business executives to small shopkeepers and clerks – or, for that matter, aspiring trade union representatives. This diversity largely explains why the middle class, or classes, appear so defenceless. They do not recognize themselves as a class, have no inclination towards class solidarity, and therefore are no match for organized and determined groups of trade unionists and socialist politicians. They put up with State intervention in every aspect of their lives because they have a deep-rooted regard for democratically elected authority and because they want to do the 'right thing' by their country. Protest has always seemed uncivilized. In Italy, professional people do not hesitate to organize public protest marches and in France shopkeepers and farmers have, from time to time, resorted to violence. In Britain, though, such behaviour has always been regarded as rather undignified. In recent years some people have joined white collar trade unions and there have been occasional attempts to defy local councils and tax collectors, but by and large the middle classes have shown remarkable restraint.

They may not do so for much longer – or at least one hopes they won't. The key lies not so much in the older generation's resentment of a changed social order as in the attitudes of educated and intelligent young individuals. If there is one thing which can be said to represent middle-class attitudes it is the belief that one's achievements in life depend on one's own efforts and *not* on the whims of some bureaucrat. That achievement need not necessarily be measured in financial terms; it may very well be judged by one's contribution to the community, the welfare and happiness of one's family, and the fulfilment to be had from performing tasks which, though not 'commercial', afford great personal satisfaction. The notion that ceilings should be set on this and that – so basic to the whole concept of absolute equality – should fill any young man or woman with dismay.

It certainly has that effect on me. I came to Britain, from Hanover, early in 1949. I was fifteen and had left school a year earlier. My father had been, in turn, a waiter, a policeman, and a civil servant. He and my mother parted during the Second World War and in 1948 my mother married an English soldier, a sergeant. They went to London and took my young brother with them; I joined them later. When I arrived I had ten shillings in my pocket and barely spoke English. I had no idea what I was going to do with my life. My new stepfather got me a job as a messenger boy in the City of London, the citadel of British capitalism. I worked for a firm of stockbrokers and I suppose I ought to have become a socialist revolutionary, clamouring for equality with the rich men who walked in and out of the office. But I hadn't heard of the British class system and it never occurred to me to feel resentful: the war and its aftermath, spent on the wrong side, had taught me the value of self-reliance and I thought of Britain as a country where anyone could make good if he tried hard enough.

It is, of course, a familiar story. Britain has, over the years, found room for many thousands of immigrants – refugees from Hitler's Germany, Hungarians, Poles, Pakistanis, and others. Some have abused the hospitality but many, many more have become useful members of the community – without any help from planners and angry politicians. If you have had a rough past you do your best to make something of the future. And you are grateful that you have been allowed into a country which allows you to do so. When I applied for a job, in my schoolboy English, no one asked where I had been educated or what my father did. It was enough that I was eager to do well. There was no closed shop and, although the old-boy network certainly existed, I was given no reason to feel that I could not succeed because I had been to the wrong school or mixed with the wrong sort of people. A few years later I answered an advertisement in the *Daily Telegraph* and got my first job in journalism, with a paper called the *Stock Exchange Gazette*. The editor was S. T. Ryder, who was later to become a highly successful business executive, a peer and head of the powerful National Enterprise Board. He didn't ask me about my schooling either. I went to evening classes to study economics and, at 21, became deputy city editor of a newly launched daily newspaper called the *Recorder*. It was a shoe-string venture and it didn't last long. When it ceased publication I went to work for the *Financial Times* and after a few years caught the eye of another immigrant who was to have a tremendous influence on me – Lord Beaverbrook. Beaverbrook was, in many ways, a difficult man. But he had great vitality, even in his eighties, and he didn't give a damn whether you were an aristocrat or a pauper. He made his own judgment. I was 24 when I first met him and he taught me, among other things, the importance of enthusiasm. He wanted to launch a weekly news sheet for investors, and none of his elderly City editors wanted to do it. I was ushered into his presence and, of course, agreed to have a go. Eighteen months later, at the age of 26, he made me City Editor of the London *Evening Standard*, at a generous salary.

I tell this story only to show why I believe in equality of *opportunity* but not in some state-imposed, state-regulated, egalitarian system. There must be room for upward mobility. Set artificial ceilings and you deny people the chance to improve their lives through their own efforts. The lowest common denominator becomes all-important. The speed of the convoy becomes the speed of the slowest ship. We have not reached that point yet and, I hope, never will. But it is already more difficult to enter Fleet Street (union rules make it difficult, if not impossible, to come in from the outside, as I did) and if the planners have their way the scope for self-improvement will be restricted even more.

The concept of a completely egalitarian society is so fanciful – even under communism – that it is difficult to take it seriously.

Who, under absolute equality, would do the dirty work? Who, if anyone, would take decisions? How would one prevent new inequalities from arising? I have yet to meet anyone who wants equality; what most people are concerned with is equity, fairness. Set ceilings and they will simply look for new ways of adding to their income. 'Moonlighting' will become the order of the day and people will, wherever possible, exchange their services for someone else's. Carpenters will make furniture for garage mechanics who, in turn, will repair their cars. This is the reality – not some utopian vision on a drawing board.

Which really brings me back to the question of incentives. Socialists reject 'appeals to materialism'; they prefer to think that people will happily perform whatever task they are allocated without bothering too much about financial reward. There are, they say, other rewards: job satisfaction and the glow that comes, or is supposed to come, when one is helping others. I have no doubt that some people fit the bill, but try telling a miner or a dustman to 'reject materialism'. The truth is that, with few exceptions, people go to work to earn money. They have to keep their families, and they are naturally keen to improve their standard of living. From this, inevitably, arises pressure for bigger rewards – and for taxation policies that allow a man to retain a bigger slice of them. The working man is, as a rule, interested in equality only if others tend to be more equal than he is. He does not want to work overtime so that the Government can be more generous to others. If a large chunk of the extra earnings is taken away from him in the form of taxation he does not bother to go on exerting himself. 'Working for nothing' is, for him, a mug's game. Much the same applies to middle-class executives and small businessmen, though here job satisfaction and other intangibles tend to have greater importance. There is no law compelling them to make extra efforts if they consider the net reward to be insufficiently worthwhile. There is no law, either, which says they have to stay. They can and do secure jobs in countries where the approach to Mammon is more realistic.

Successive governments have made the error of trying to sell incomes policies as a crusade. If an incomes policy is to work at all – and Britain's experience suggests that it can do so only if it is a voluntary exercise – then it must be based on practical considerations. Wage restraint has to be shown as a workable alternative to runaway inflation and high unemployment. Unless one can do that – in language people can understand – and accompany it with sensible tax policies, incomes policies will never turn out to be more than a short-term palliative.

Much of the demand for greater equality is really a protest against the injustices that a capitalist society could perfectly well remedy, while remaining capitalist. A key factor, clearly, is the future rate of economic growth, and it is encouraging to note that many thoughtful economists now reject the doomsday views of the anti-growth lobby. Professor Wilfred Beckerman, in particular, has put up a persuasive case* against the argument that, unless growth is brought to a halt at once, rising pollution and declining raw material supplies will lead to disaster. And early in 1976 the Club of Rome, which aroused intense controversy in 1972 with its report on 'the limits to growth', announced that it had reversed its position. Growth had to be selective, but it was after all possible to combine it with improvement in the quality of life.

* *In Defence of Economic Growth*, Jonathan Cape, 1974.

Chapter Seventeen
The Rich in Future

The larger a man's roof, the more snow it collects.
PERSIAN PROVERB

Can the *rich* survive? I dare say they'll manage somehow. They always have. Family fortunes have come and gone throughout the centuries, millions have been won and lost, political upheavals have produced countless riches-to-rags stories. Russian aristocrats, white farmers in Angola and Tanzania, European kings and Indian princes, stately owners of stately British homes, financiers who grew too ambitious – the list of casualties is long and formidable. But the rich, like the poor, are still with us. Inevitably, they are less welcome in some places than in others. Drive around Palm Springs in Florida, or Cannes in the south of France, and the question of survival sounds absurd: the rich seem to be both more numerous and more prosperous than ever. The very idea that America might one day seek to do away with them seems so far-fetched that it is hardly worth serious consideration. Yet the rich in St Petersburg felt equally secure a mere sixty years ago. So, in an earlier era, did the proud French aristocrats who laughed at the idea that one day France might see a revolution. The climate has grown increasingly hostile, even in famous playgrounds like the Caribbean. In Jamaica the rich huddle together in well-protected ghettos like Round Hill because life outside is no longer safe. In sunny Italy they surround themselves with bodyguards, and try to keep out of the public eye, because they are terrified of being robbed or kidnapped. The great *palazzi* stand empty or are occupied by embassies from the Iron Curtain countries, including the Soviet Union, whose officials now live the Good Life once reserved for Rome's great families. Communism is making head-way everywhere and the risk of confiscation grows each year. The number of really safe countries has dwindled steadily and is likely to go on doing so. There are few places, nowadays, to match dull but cosy Switzerland.

The life style of Europe's rich reflects their decline. They still dress up for fashionable events like Ascot and sip champagne at Annabels, but no one today builds great country houses like Goodwood, Woburn, and Blenheim. The grandeur of even a hundred years ago has gone. Private patronage of the arts – still the best chance for the truly original, the completely unortho-dox – has been overtaken by State sponsorship. Committee men have replaced the individual (and often delightfully eccentric) patron. Even fortune hunters have become a 'vanishing breed', according to one of Europe's richest young women, Isabel de Rosnay. 'Fortune hunters,' she told the London *Daily Express* recently, 'are the most entertaining men around. But it's a con-tracting industry, too risky for most of them, I think, these days.'

And yet the rich survive. Indeed, their ranks are constantly augmented by newcomers: as one drops out another takes his place. What has changed – to a far greater extent than is gener-ally realized – is both the nature of their wealth and their atti-tude to it. Not great fortunes, but great corporations are nowa-days the important units of wealth, to which individuals of property are variously attached. This is particularly true of America, where the very rich are no longer dominantly an idle rich – if they ever have been. There *are* still people who devote themselves almost exclusively to the art of living, but they are vastly outnumbered by those who are economically active.

While writing this book, I spent some time with a man whose name is a household word – Henry Ford II. Grandson of the Henry who founded what is now, in terms of sales revenue, the fourth largest corporation in the world, he isn't short of a hundred million or two. Yet no one could ever accuse him of living a lazy and wasteful life. On the contrary, most people find it puzzling that he should work as hard as he does. He has been at the head of his empire for three decades and works long hours; nothing essential is ever done in the whole corporation unless it has been approved by him. He used to talk of retiring at 40, but never got around to it. Now 58, he has a mild heart condition and doctors have advised him to slow down. 'I am trying to relax a bit more,' he says, 'but it's not easy.' Why doesn't he just spend the rest of his days on some beach in the Bahamas? 'I have,' he says, 'a responsibility to the company. I wouldn't be happy with myself if I didn't fulfil that responsibility.' It is the kind of remark one feels compelled to take with a large pinch of salt, but Ford's record suggests that he is absolutely sincere.

By everyday standards, of course, Ford has a luxurious life. He owns several houses, including a country house in Oxfordshire and a lodge in Canada which he uses as a base for duck shooting. But he doesn't have a private jet or yacht (he hires one occasionally for a Mediterranean holiday) and although he has given away large sums to his ex-wife and two grown-up daughters he insists that he doesn't believe in throwing his money around. During our long conversation I pressed him to tell me whether he had bought anything really extravagant over the past year – the sort of thing critics would say was typical of the foolishness of the rich. He thought for a while and then said: 'A Honda motor cycle.' Anything else? 'A horse. But I sold it again; it was too wild.'

Like David Rockefeller, Ford enjoys an easy relationship with Prime Ministers and Heads of State, including those of Communist countries. He argues that global corporations like this have an important and useful role to play, not only in terms of the efficient use of resources but also as a force for a world people. The idea of a 'world without frontiers' appeals to him as much as it does to every other head of a multi-national enterprise. But he strenuously denies that he has ever tried to dictate to governments. 'You might be able to do it in parts of the third world,' he says, 'but you certainly couldn't do it in the industrialised countries.' He is, nevertheless, very conscious of the fact that multi-nationals are widely disliked and mistrusted, and agrees that they have only themselves to blame. 'We've got to behave properly if we want people to understand us,' he says. 'You can't do business by handing out bribes and telling ministers what to do. The powers of the multi-national corporation have been much exaggerated, but things do go on that shouldn't be going on.' He thinks that attitudes are changing, and welcomes the fact: big business, he maintains, has become more 'socially responsible' than it was ten years ago. Does that include attitudes to the environment? 'Oh yes. The problem is more clearly understood and something is being done about it. But the cost involved is enormous and it simply isn't possible to go too far too fast. Industry has been polluting the environment for a very long time. We've had dirty water and air for more than a hundred years, and you can't clean it up in five. The law now compels corporations to conform to certain standards and it is right that it should be so: it can't all be done voluntarily. But one mustn't get too impatient.'

The Ford Foundation – like so many other foundations set up by the very rich – sponsors all kinds of research. But Ford himself has a healthily sceptical approach to the work of so-called Think Tanks. 'So much of what they do,' he says, 'is imaginative guesswork. In our experience you can't make any reliable predictions for more than the next five years, and even then you may have to revise them every year.'

One prediction which does, however, seem fairly safe is that his son, Edsel Bryant Ford II, will eventually find himself on the Board. Now in his late twenties, he works in the company's California sales office and is being trained for top management – though, his father insists, with absolutely no privileges. If and when he does get to the Boardroom there is bound to be criticism, just as there was criticism when Henry II was elevated all those years ago. But Henry isn't fussed; son or not, Edsel will be expected to do his very best.

People like Ford apart, the richest men today are generally first generation tycoons, untouched by death duties, who have hit on some particular money-making scheme. With Getty dead, the world's wealthiest millionaire is probably the almost completely unknown Daniel K. Ludwig. 'Ludwig,' one newspaper wrote not long ago, 'is so secretive that he makes Howard Hughes look gregarious.' He has given only one press interview in his life, travels incognito, and the only personal information gleaned about him during the past seventy-eight years is hardly sensational: he doesn't smoke or drink and is determinedly anti-social. The son of a Michigan estate agent, he showed early promise at the age of nine, salvaging a sunken barge and renting it out to friends. He bought another barge for $5,000 when he left school, and moved in this modest way into the bulk transport business. He bought his first oil tanker in 1921. Fifty-five years later he owns, among other things, a huge fleet of tankers, a shipyard in Japan, a chain of hotels, a large share in the National Mortgage Bank in America, a million acres in Venezuela, three million acres of Brazil, and large chunks of Australia and the United States.

A million dollars is not what it used to be (only $156,000 in turn-of-century dollars) but a millionaire is. An economist at Pennsylvania State University, who has made the study of wealth his life's work, recently estimated that America now has six times as many millionaires under the age of 35 as there were in the early 1960s. They are, for the most part, hard-working and ambitious and you will find the same kind of people in Germany, France, Greece, Britain and other countries. But there are also rich young men and women who use inherited money to finance projects which have little chance of commercial success – such as underground magazines – or who support charitable work which the community at large chooses to neglect.

The new, new rich are, of course, the Arabs and it's easy to make fun of them. There they were, a hundred years ago, eating sheep's eyeballs, selling camels, and generally indulging in all sorts of unspeakable pastimes. Then came the motor car – and, whoopee, here they are, having the time of their lives. The cash keeps piling up at an incredible rate and no amount of spending can possibly soak it up. If things continue at the present pace the states will by 1980 have an income greater than the combined earnings of all the major US industrial corporations. Saudi Arabia alone will have greater monetary reserves than the US and Japan combined, to be shared among a population smaller than London's. The sheikhs themselves have already stocked up on everything one could possibly want – Cadillacs and gleaming Rolls-Royces, luxuriously fitted jets, yachts moored in Cannes and other playgrounds, gold door-handles, Swedish blondes, French chateaux, and English country mansions. Hotels in every oil-rich state are filled with western businessmen intent on helping them to spend their money. Real estate agents have set up offices throughout the Gulf, and castles and mansions are regularly advertised in the Arab press.

Travelling through the Middle East, as I have done, one is inevitably struck by the contrast between those millions and the lives of ordinary people. Despite all their wealth, most of the Arab oil-producing states are still far behind other countries in terms of ordinary development. Some have gone mad about modernizing their capitals, putting up vast concrete blocks and, in some cases, indulging in decidedly fanciful schemes (I have a recollection of Abu Dhabi, with a splendid new motorway soaring majestically twenty miles out of town, to where it stops abruptly in the middle of the desert). Vast sums have also been spent on tanks and other hardware – making fortunes, in the process, for middlemen like Adnan Khashoggi, a well-connected Arab who jets around the world in a blue-and-white Boeing 727. The fittings alone cost him £1 million, but he can afford it. In a little over ten years he has put together a $400 million business empire which straddles eight countries and controls some fifty companies, nearly all of them private. Among his interests are an insurance company in London, property in Germany and France, meat-packing in Brazil, furniture in the Lebanon, and ranching in Arizona. He also owns two banks in California, a trucking firm in Washington State, a truck trailer concern in Mexico, and a large stake of the construction material and electric power business in Saudi Arabia itself. One of his latest and more extraordinary projects is the building of a glass-covered pyramid on the desert sands near Cairo as the centre-piece of a $600 million tourist resort.

But for most of the Gulf states all the expenditure on Cadillacs, arms and buildings takes care only of the small change. With the rulers growing more aware of the needs of their people, an increasing amount is now spent on more useful amenities. For example, Kuwaiti citizens pay no income tax, get free medical care, and have their children educated at Government expense. Ironically, this largesse has tended, in some ways, to be counter-productive. It has produced a high rate of inflation and, worse, the envy of an army of 'guest workers' (mostly Palestinians and fellow Arabs) who resent their privileges. But these are problems which money can solve, given time. Meanwhile I don't blame the sheikhs for hedging their bets with outside investments: recent events in Beirut, which a few years ago was boasting that it was just as attractive a financial centre as Zurich, have again underlined the unpredictability of life in the turbulent Middle East.

Visitors apart, the oil millions have naturally attracted a good many Western fortune-hunters prepared to put up, for a few years, with the stifling heat and puritanical attitudes towards drink and *Playboy* in return for a chance to join the rich. They are there for the cash (including a percentage known locally as ('boredom money') and they accept that one can't just arrive with an empty suitcase and expect the sheikhs – or the Shah of Iran – to stuff it full of dollars. I met some of them in the exclusive Teheran Club not long ago. Making a fortune, they all agreed, was rather more difficult than they had bargained for. They were irritated and mused by go-go head office visitors who look at the newspapers back home and get their secretaries to book a seat on the next jumbo. 'You take them for a drink and the questions start. This place is booming. *The Times* says so. Why aren't you doing better? We tell them about the red tape, the inefficiency, the frustrations, the competition. But they think we're just making excuses,' Even so, most expatriates seem willing enough to stay. 'Anything,' one told me, 'is better than the constant talk of economic doom at home.'

For many other young Europeans, eager to do well, the Promised Land is not Teheran or Kuwait, or even Australia, but Canada and the United States. Yes, even now. My American friends, accustomed to headlines like 'the Dying Dollar' and 'City Diseases that can kill you', invariably express astonishment that this should be so. But America has always attracted ambitious Europeans – partly because of the sheer size of the market and partly because Americans seem so much more receptive to new ideas. This still holds good today. The vitality of cities like New York and Chicago can be rough and exhausting; American Big Business has no time for failure. But success is rewarded in a way which is simply not feasible in smaller countries. Ask Mary Quant and David Ogilvy. Ask David Frost, Tom Jones, Richard Burton, and Rex Harrison. Ask Henry Kissinger. Much has been written about the 'American invasion' of Europe, but European business is also well established in the US – from Volkswagen, Shell, and British Petroleum to Nestlé, Gordon's Gin, Wilkinson's, and Schweppes. Parke Bernet, New York's leading auction rooms, are a subsidiary of Sotheby's, and Capitol, one of the biggest names in records, is owned by EMI. The list is long and impressive. Some firms use America as a huge test market for new products; others are there simply to pick up new techniques and developments. Rupert Murdoch, who owns newspapers in Australia and Britain, now spends much of his time in New York because he thinks that the US newspaper business still offers more scope than any other in the West. Authors, actors, designers, teachers, pop singers and – yes! – economists have all done well in America and will, no doubt, continue to do so. The same goes for young men who prefer to marry into fortunes rather than go through the tiresome business of making them.

Forty or fifty years ago this was an overcrowded field. Second and third sons of good families were expected either to go into the army or marry an heiress. Much time and effort was devoted to learning the trade. One practised riding, dancing, driving, dressing, and talking. One found out about wines and horses, music and books, poetry and politics. Some young people still do just that, but one can see why fortune hunting should be, in Miss Isabel de Rosnay's words, 'a contracting industry'. It requires an investment of both time and capital, without guarantee of success. Spoiled young ladies are notoriously fickle, and spoiled old ladies even more so. They are also a good deal less interested in marriage than they used to be. She may take your time and capital, and then turn to the next investor. And even if you do succeed in getting her to the altar there may be some rather nasty surprises.

Fortunes always look better on paper than they do in reality. They are frequently locked up in trust funds, or in shares which cannot be sold without wrecking Daddy's business. Either way, you cannot get at them. And when Daddy has finally departed to that great Boardroom in the sky, the Government will step in and claim the major share. Meantime, there is a very real risk that he will see you not as an entertaining companion for his daughter, born to practise the art of living, but as the son he never had. Before the honeymoon is over you will be installed in the executive suite and asked to work as hard as he does – which means that you might, at best, get two or three days off every year. The huntress is on somewhat firmer ground. Providing, that is, she tries to ensnare an older man who has already made his millions rather than a young buck who may, or may not, get his share of the family loot at some future date. To a rich old man, a young and glamorous wife is as much of a status symbol as a mansion or a private jet. And he accepts that such symbols are expensive. He doesn't demand much in return, because his business absorbs whatever time and energy he may have. And he can generally be relied upon to remember his wife, or wives, when he draws up his will.

If you want to try your luck at fortune hunting, Florida and California probably offer the best chances for both sexes. If you have a title, so much the better. If you haven't, you can always make one up: that's what the Italians do. In Europe, the south of France is still the place to be during the summer months. Never – but never – go on a package tour to Benidorm.

But you may well be one of the many people who want to make a modest fortune the hard way. Here again America still looks the best bet. If I were 25, I should probably be on a plane to New York or San Francisco. But even Europe still offers ample opportunities – and, of course, a citizen of one EEC member country can take employment, or set up in business, in another. It all depends on how much effort one is willing to make. Many people have no desire to become rich, *ever*, and I wouldn't dream of condemning them. By the same token, I strongly believe that able, hard-working people should be allowed to make a fortune if they wish – and if they enrich others in the process, so much the better. My own son left school at 15 and has been trained in the hotel business; his ambition is to emulate Charles Forte. What matters to me – and I hope to you – is that the system should leave him free to do so.

Young people on the so-called Left have always been more militant than those who are said to belong to the Right. This is particularly true of universities and, as a result, students come to be regarded as a single class – a rebellious movement presenting a united front against the establishment. But there never has been a 'united front'. The left has made louder noises than the rest and therefore has attracted bigger headlines. So-called 'right-wing' students (i.e., students who don't reject the system) have been getting on with their studies. One would like to think that they will be more inclined to speak up in future, and if this book helps I shall be delighted. I do not wish to exaggerate the 'Red Menace' and I certainly do not suggest, as some politicians have done, that societies like Britain are already communist states in all but name. This clearly is far from the truth. But I do suggest that the threat to freedom of choice and freedom to supplement the other liberties – of thought, of speech, of association and so on – is real enough and likely to grow stronger. No man or woman can hope to behave exactly as he or she likes towards fellow members of the community. I do not seek to be free to burgle your home or sell you LSD. But I do want to be free to decide how to live my life, with a minimum of bureaucratic interference. And I believe, with Lord Keynes, that 'it is better that a man should tyrannise over his bank balance than over his fellow citizen'.

Don't you?

Index

Also available in Sphere Books:

WHAT'S WRONG WITH BRITAIN?

EDITED BY PATRICK HUTBER

The state of the nation . . .
Inflation, apathy, pessimism, political corruption, erosion of
individual freedom – these are just some of the present-day
problems that add up to 'the English sickness'. And
although there has been a great deal of argument as to the
cause, very few people would deny that Britain is in a state
of decline.

Patrick Hutber, City Editor of the *Sunday Telegraph*, freely
admits that he doesn't have a magic formula for putting
Britain back on its feet. But in this book he has asked some
highly distinguished commentators to give their views of
'the state of the nation'. The result is a thoughtful, informed,
sometimes wry and occasionally alarming picture of Britain
as it is, and as it could be in the future.

Foreword by Lord Home

0 7221 4832 1

WORLD AFFAIRS/POLITICS

All Sphere Books are available at your bookshop or newsagent, or can be ordered from the following address: Sphere Books, Cash Sales Department,
P.O. Box 11, Falmouth, Cornwall.

Please send cheque or postal order (no currency), and allow 19p for postage and packing for the first book plus 9p per copy for each additional book ordered up to a maximum charge of 73p in U.K.

Customers in Eire and B.F.P.O. please allow 19p for postage and packing for the first book plus 9p per copy for the next 6 books, thereafter 3p per book.

Overseas customers please allow 20p for postage and packing for the first book and 10p per copy for each additional book.